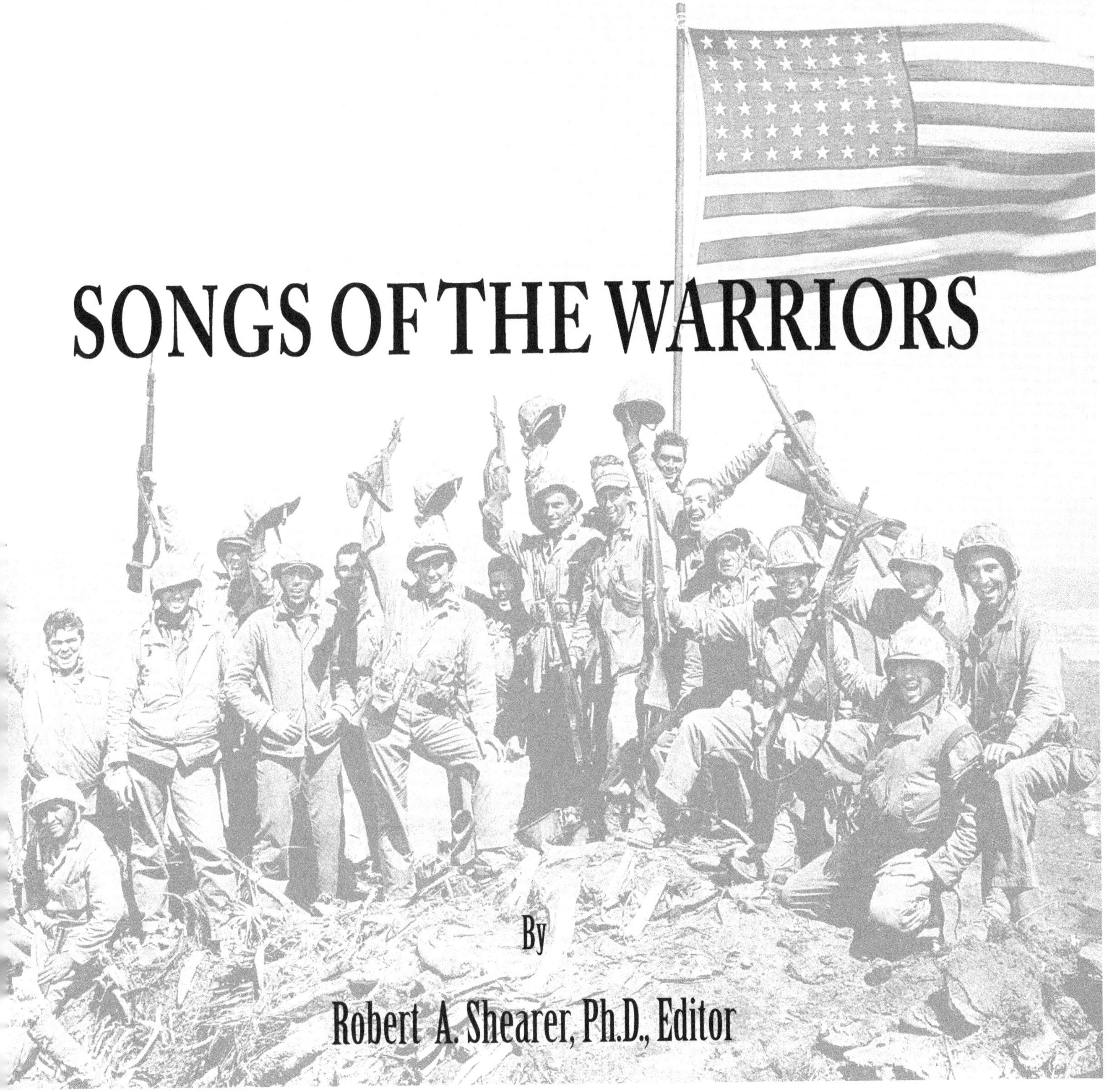

SONGS OF THE WARRIORS

By

Robert A. Shearer, Ph.D., Editor

STEPHEN F. AUSTIN STATE UNIVERSITY PRESS
2017

Copyright ©2017 by Robert A. Shearer

All rights reserved. Printed in the United States of America.

For more information:
Stephen F. Austin State University Press
P.O. Box 13007 SFA Station
Nacogdoches, Texas 75962
sfapress@sfasu.edu
www.sfasu.edu/sfapress

Book design: Jonathan Grant and Thomas Sims
Cover design: Thomas Sims
Distributed by Texas A&M Consortium
www.tamupress.com

LIBRARY OF CONGRESS CATALOGING-IN-PUBLICATION DATA
Robert A. Shearer
Songs of the Warriors/Robert A Shearer

ISBN:978-1-62288-173-4

Dedicated to the warrior poets,
especially those who didn't return

Contents

Introduction 7

The Poets 7

The Publication 9

War Poems 11

Section one: Couplet Poems 13

Section two: Quatrain Poems 15

Section three: Poems about Love and Romance 21

Section four: Humorous Poems 45

Section five: Poems about Military life 79

Section six: Poems about War 117

Section seven: Poems about Death 143

Section eight: Philosophical Poems 159

Section nine: Featured Poets 165

    Carlyle A. Oberle 165
    Keith Campbell 167
    John Readey 169
    Irving Caress 172
    Elizabeth Itzen 175
    Harold Applebaum 177
    Richard Armour 180
    Josephine Pagliai 182
    Margaret Jane Taggs 183
    Bob Stuart McKnight 186
    A. L. Crouch 190
    John Behm 194

Section ten: Featured Poem **199**

Section eleven: Reflections **199**

       Documentation 200
       Transition 200
       Orientation 200
       Chain of Command 200
       Cross Communication 201
       International 201
       Women 201
       Mortification 201
       Contribution 201
       Alienation 202
       Racism 202
       Origination 202
       Progression 203

Introduction

Between the years 1942 and 1945, hundreds of American men and women in the military wrote, submitted, and published poems during the war. They were the "War Poets." They were stationed at military bases and camps around the world, and their literary contributions have nearly been lost over the ensuing seventy years. Certainly, they are not readily accessible. The **War Poems Project** was an attempt to recover, compile, rediscover, re- appreciate, and re-enjoy these national literary treasures. So, the project is literary archeology. The poems represent the war poets' expressions of love, joy, death, loneliness, boredom, depression, humor, and frustration while they were on active duty in violent combat zones or remote bases around the world.

The poets succeeded in making a literary contribution, but their writings also provided a glimpse of the history, geography, military, and home front during World War II. The **War Poems Project** was not an attempt to analyze, interpret, or deconstruct the poems. The poems are presented as they were written by their authors.

The result of the project, "Songs of the Warriors," is an anthology of the poems organized into sections with a variety of thematic elements. The result is a historical, non-fiction book of poems written by military personnel during World War II and re- presented in the Twenty-First Century. The war poets, in most cases, poured their hearts and souls into these literary works. Specifically, the poems reflect their feelings, perceptions, thoughts, and dreams. This book is the reslult of a project to recover these poems. "Songs of the Warriors" is an anthology of the poems.

The poets deserve to be recognized for not only their service to their country, but also for their literary talents and contributions. The primary guiding ethic in the re- publication of these poems was: *The poems constitute not only a national historical military treasure, but also a national literary treasure.* The poems should never be hidden or lost again.

The Poets

The poems in this anthology were written by soldiers, seamen, airmen, marines, and nurses. Most were enlisted men with the rank of private, corporal, or sergeant who had not previously or formally been recognized as poets. The magazine where the poems appeared boasted that the stories, pictures, poems, and other material were written by enlisted men of the United States Army, which included the Army Air Corps. Several poems written by officers were also published,

Fortunately, the name of each author of the poem appeared with the poem and the location where the soldier was stationed. But, the location of the soldier was usually quite general, especially for soldiers stationed outside the United States. In several cases, the magazine published poems written by Army Nurses, one who was an officer. These poems are included in this anthology.

"One week in 'Poet's Cornered' we gave one writer all our space. What's more the writer was an officer and officers are not usually allowed to contribute to this paper. But this officer is a girl, an army nurse. We feel the exception is justified. Her name is 2nd Lt. Elizabeth Itzen, and she comes from Wyckoff, N.J."

Compared to the millions of men and women who served in World War II, the war poets were probably very similar to their fellow service men and women. What stands out about the war poets is their motivation and talent to write and submit poetry for publication. Furthermore, they likely submitted literary works to other publications. One poem written by Corporal Lester Asheim, "Complaint to An Empty Purse," even suggests this possibility. What is clear is that the war poets were different from the millions of service men and women in World War II, because they created a legacy of enduring literary treasures.

Any information about the poets, beyond their writings, has largely been lost to history in the seventy years since they shared their creative talents. It is entirely possible that some of them could have been killed in the war after their poems were published. Hopefully, all of them returned home and continued their literary pursuits.

Caution needs to be exercised in drawing conclusions based on the poems that have survived since 1945. First, the poems we read today could have been altered or edited by military censors. The publication clearly states, "Contents reviewed by U.S. military censors." Though it seems remote to us today, in the case of poetry, what the war poets submitted for publication may not have been the same as what was subsequently published. The country was at war, so censorship was vital for national defense.

Second, the poems that we read may not represent the entirety of the poet's work, because other poems could have been rejected or censored. In other words, the poet could have submitted ten poems, nine of which were of poor quality, and only one was accepted. Vise versa, a poet could have submitted ten high quality poems, but only one was accepted. We don't know the selection process, so the war poet could have been more talented than a single work revealed.

Third, the war poet could have submitted poems to other civilian publications so that the war poems are not a true sample of the author's work. Finally we don't know what the competition was for space in the weekly publication or the rejection rate for submitted work. What has survived is poems that are intensely personal, realistic, historical, and passionate literary expressions. Because there was so little information available about the war, the poems were probably enjoyed by many military personnel and civilians near the camps and bases.

What is certain is that the poets were likely to share a cluster of similar personal characteristics and traits that differentiated them from the millions of military personnel who didn't publish poems between 1942 and 1945. At the risk of wild speculation, it would seem that the war poets shared some, if not all, of the following characteristics:

First, the war poets were literate. They could write legibly and spell correctly. They likely had access to a typewriter, especially in rear echelon areas; Second, they were expressive individuals and deft raconteurs; Third, they were obviously clever and creative writers; Fourth, they were reflective, because the poems indicate they thought about what was happening around them, to them, and to other soldiers; Fifth, they were perceptive and keen observers of the physical world around them. They could see beyond themselves and see a greater reality and absurdity beyond their circumstances; Sixth, their poems reflect a high level of emotional sensitivity or emotional IQ. They were comfortable with strong emotions of sadness, loneliness, fear, boredom, and meaningless, for example. They saw in the pictures in the magazine the pain and suffering of other soldiers and wrote poems about what they saw and read; Seventh, they were introspective. They seemed to express how they felt internally about what was happening in a world that didn't make sense to most people. They tried to make some sense of it to themselves; Eighth, by publishing a poem they could communicate and validate their existence in a world war in which there was very little communication between themselves and family back home; Ninth, they surely were aware that a poem published in a magazine that was distributed around the world would establish a legacy, both personal and literary, of their creativity, whether they survived the war or didn't survive. In this case, the poems were small personal memorials, living or dead. At an even higher level of awareness, the poems sent a personal existential message from the author to a reader that communicated, "I'm here and I'm still human in an inhuman, savage, and macabre world."

Finally, most of the poems were not written by soldiers in front line combat positions. Frontline soldiers were preoccupied with day to day survival, so they would have had few opportunities to write poems. In many front line campaigns, the casualties were high, so the poem, if it was written, wouldn't have survived for us to enjoy. In a way, the poems written that have survived serve as a literary memorial for the soldiers who didn't survive the war. Over four hundred poets who wrote over seven-hundred poems contributed to this anthology.

The Publication

All of the poems in this anthology were published in *Yank, the Army Weekly* between June 17, 1942 and December, 1945. The magazine was published in four volumes by the United States Military, written by enlisted men in the armed forces, and distributed around the world. It was made available to soldiers, sailors, airmen, and nurses serving overseas and at home. It was published at facilities around the world, including British, Mediterranean, Continental, and Western Pacific editions. Each issue was edited in New York City and then shipped for printing around the world. Staff editors added local stories in the various locations. Noticeably absent from the magazine were political commentaries, news reports, editorials, or commercial advertising. Furthermore, the magazine, understandably, didn't contain any information about specific troop locations, movements, or strengths or any other information that could jeopardize the safety of the troops. Contributors were obviously aware that censors screened the contributions.

Several humorous poems, "Censor's Woes," by 1st Lt. George A. Gillespie in Australia, "Ballad for Beating the Censors," by Pvt. Burt Harris in Italy, "Lines to a Censor," by Sgt. John Percussia, in India, and "To a Censor," by Pvt. Herb Kraus in Hawaii, illustrate this awareness.

The poems appeared in four sections in the magazine, "Poets Cornered," "War Poets," "PX," or "Post Exchange," in almost every edition. Along with the poems, the publication regularly included feature stories, puzzles, book reviews, cross-word puzzles, short stories, cartoons, art work, pictures of pin-up girls, messages, mail call, radio guide, sports features, and war photos. In the September 30, 1942, issue (Volume 1, Number 16), the following notice appeared: "Ed. Note: We want all of the poetry you're inspire to send in, but try to hold yourself down to three or four stanzas!"

Two of the enduring features that were remembered for years after the war were the cartoons, "Sad Sack" and "GI Joe." Many famous subsequent movies stars appeared as pin-up girls in full page photos: Lucille Ball, Ingrid Bergman, Esther Williams, Lena Horne, Betty Grable, Rita Hayworth, Jane Russell, and Gale Storm.

The publication was printed in black, white, and red with an occasional different background color. All of the photos, cartoons, and drawings were in black and white, i.e. there were not any color photographs in the publication, although the December, 1943 issue had some coloration. The publication was printed on very thin, poor quality paper and most original copies existing today are very fragile and tattered.

The magazine was delivered to combat zones around the world and to bases or post exchanges. The magazine actively solicited subscriptions. In Volume 1, Number 1, June 17, 1942, an ad appeared:

"Your copy of Yank is available at the nearest post exchange. However, if you prefer to have YANK mailed to you, send this coupon and 75 cents to YANK, The Army Newspaper, 205 East 42nd St., New York City. Your subscription will entitle you to 26 issues of YANK---one every week for six months."

In the same issue, the magazine featured the following solicitation:

"Are you a frustrated poet? YANK wants your poetry, even if your best pal won't read it. Long or short, funny or serious, mail it to us from wherever you are and we'll print all we can." The magazine emphasized that "Only men in uniform can receive subscriptions to YANK." The result of this policy was that civilian libraries rarely obtained the magazine and complete collections, outside the Library of Congress, are quite rare. Most of the magazines were discarded far from the United States or thrown away when bases closed after the war. They were distributed to camps and bases in the United States and around the world, but many of the camps were located in remote areas or near small towns that did not have public libraries where donated issues could be saved. Furthermore, no one was responsible for collecting and saving the magazines. These historical variables make retrieval of the poems difficult and incomplete.

Perhaps, the rarest and most unusual edition was the Caribbean Edition that was published in Puerto Rico, HQ Antilles Dept., and Port of Spain, Trinidad. On the cover, it stated the magazine cost five cents "Or the local equivalent." The Caribbean Edition contained the same poems found in a variety of other editions distributed around the world. Due to limited distribution and the hot and humid climate of the region, very few copies survived.

The following notice appeared in the November 2, 1945 issue: "YANK TO DISCONTINUE PUBLICATION. The issue of YANK published in the last week of December 1945 will be the final issue of YANK as a magazine of this war. The War Department has directed that YANK discontinue publication, both overseas and in the U.S., by the end of this year. The original mission of the magazine, to spread news of the global war to enlisted men all over the world, has been officially completed. Command newspapers and camp publications will continue to take care of news in their local theaters, and YANK, as a publication, will accept its discharge from armed services. YANK subscribers who are caught short with unexpired subscriptions by this closing date will be repaid according to the number issues they miss. Checks will be mailed to cover all such unexpired subscriptions, both domestic and overseas. Naturally, no new subscriptions will be accepted."

The poems became less frequent by the end of July, 1945. There were no poems in the last issue of December 28, 1945.

War Poems

The poems in this anthology appear in several sections that reflect a number of thematic areas: War, Death, Love and Romance, Humor, and Military Life. In addition, sections present the works of featured poets who submitted several poems to the magazine over the years of publication. Next, a section is reserved for the featured poem in the anthology. Finally, the anthology concludes with a presentation of reflections about some of the trends that emerged in the content of the poems during the four years they appeared in the magazine.

In most cases, each poem is accompanied by the name of the poet and where the poet was stationed in the world. In all cases an attempt was made to faithfully present the poems as they were written, including grammar and spelling: No poems were corrected, censored, or altered.

Thematic areas were rationally determined at the risk of being overly simplistic designations. Many of the themes in the poems overlap. For example, a humorous poem may have serious undertones, a war poem may have serious death undertones, and a poem about day-to-day Army life may have several serious undertones and subtle themes.

In addition, the assignment of poems to thematic areas was subject to editorial interpretation. This interpretation may have led to errors in the assignment of poems. It is entirely possible that several readers may interpret the poems differently. Hopefully, the value of the entire collection of poems overshadows any glaring mistakes in assignment of the poems.

The poems in this anthology were retrieved from copies of *Yank* magazine in the Texas A & M University, Evans and Cushing libraries, the University of Michigan Library, and the editor's private collection of the magazine. An attempt was made to include all of the poems published in the magazine, but some poems were not included for the following reasons: First, because the magazine was so widely distributed in several editions, it is possible that poems were not recovered. Second, poems that did not include an author were not included. Third, poems published in the magazine written by well-known civilian poets and previously published elsewhere, were notincluded.

Finally, some poems were lost due to damage or deterioration of the magazine. Nevertheless, the poems in this anthology represent the vast majority, easily ninety-nine percent, of the poems that appeared in the magazine.

The "Songs of the Warriors" appear on the following pages. Reading the sonnets, lyrics, odes, limericks, jingles, and songs was a profound and diverse emotional experience ranging from feelings of joy to angst to sadness. The unique and rich collection of poems in the anthology offers a window into the hopes, fears, pain, prayers, and observations of the poets during World War II. It was an honor to recover, compile, and rediscover the poems. Hopefully, the reader will have a similar experience reading the poems.

Section One
Couplet Poems

THOUGHT ON STAGGERING BACK TO THE BARRACKS AFTER A PLEASANT EVENING AT THE NCO CLUB

Military frolic
Is mostly alcoholic
—*Wright Field, OH, Cpl. Scott Feldman*

TO FUTURE INDUCTEES

Do not with your noncoms try to reason,
For in the Army they call that treason.
—*Jefferson Barracks, MO, Pvt. William Carpenter Good*

RE: YOUR LETTER

V-mail is quicker
Air mail is thicker.
Southwest Pacific, Pvt. Raymond Carlson

SAD THOUGHT FROM A COLORFUL — THOUGH REMOTE---PACIFIC ISLE

I admit this is an amazing world
But I'd prefer a place more liberally girled.
—*Cpl. Scott Feldman*

CAMOUFLAGE

Even the trees
Are in ODs.
—*Dale Mabry Field, FL, Cpl. Richard E. Bodtke*

CODE OF THE LATRINE ORDERLY

When eating oranges, remember our code:
No peeling's in the commode!
—*AAFBU, Inglewood, CA, Sgt. Shelby Friedman*

DIRECTIVE

From *femmes fatales* should soldiers refrain?
Depends, of course, upon the terrain.
—*Camp Claiborne, LA, Cpl. Robert N. Myers*

NERVES

The longest war of nerves, I guess,
Is sweating out shipment to OCS.
    —*Sheppard Field, TX, Pfc. Marv Lore*

NEWS ITEM

----and if a single bomb falls on Berlin, you can call me Meyer—in a speech to the German people.

Herman, Herman, Berlin is burnin'.
You big fat liar, Your name is Meyer.
    —*Fort Hamilton, NY, Irving Rockmore*

CULINARY NOTES

The sorriest sound ever heard in a mess
Are the sibilant syllables SOS.
    —*AAFSAT, Orlando, FL, Cpls. Eisengerg and Cooley*

SPLIT AFFINITY

I wish I were a schizophrenic:
Just one of me would calisthenic.
    —*AAFSAT, Orlando, FL, Cpls. Eisenberg and Cogley*

A COUPLET

If you want to get skinny
Go to New Guinea.
    —*New Guinea, Sgt. Charles D. Pearson*

ADVICE LONG AFTER HERRICK

To tips on popularity let's call this song.
Women who are really chaste are rarely chased long.
    —*Selman Field, LA, A/C M J Flanagan, Jr.*

AFTER DORTHY PARKER

A service dance is not much fun
With dancing ratio ten to one.
    —*Camp Rucker, AL, Pvt. Gene Wierbach*

ANOTHER COUPLET

In my present mood
I'd prefer you nood.
    —*Olmstead Field, PA, Pfc. Norman Rubinstein*

AND ANOTHER

Soldiers shun lasses
Allergic to passes.
    —*Camp Crowder, MO, Pvt. Louis Fisher*

A MAJOR DETAIL

Of all the words of soldier men,
The saddest are these: KP again.
    —*Lowry Field, CO, Pvt. Charles Lehman*

THE VOICE OF IRE

The howitzer's wrath is tender and muted
Compared to a louey who has not been saluted.
    —*AAF, Hyde Park, NY, S/Sgt. Henry Lefer*

Section Two
Quatrain Poems

WORLD WAR ONE

World War One has started a reign
Of world wars, that is plain;
Or is it just that previous wars
Were given provincial monikers?
—*Camp Crowder, MS, Pvt. Louis Fisher*

THE BUGLER

The bugler wakes us up each day;
I wish to heck that he would play
Over the hills
and far away.
—*Headquarters Company 722nd Military Police
Battalion (Z1) Corporal Arden L. Melott*

BURIAL ON THE SPOT

An earthen mound, a cross of wood,
A dog tag to tell whose work is done.
But we can't salute him as we should,
For taps must wait till the island's won.
—*Camp Murphy, FL, Pvt. Robert J. Kirkwood*

BOOMERANG

Now that food's to be rationed
Among America's millions,
Soldiers'll soon be sending
Packages home to civilians.
—*AAFTTC, Miami Beach, FL Pfc. Samuel P. Grapman*

BARRACKS BAGS

A necessary nuisance:
Everybody's got 'em.
Everything you look for
Will be found at the bottom.
—*Miami Beach, FL, Cpl. Samuel P. Grapman*

A YARDBIRD'S PRAYER

Dear Lord---
All I ask Of thee,
Please let me die
A P.F.C.
—*Seattle, WA, Pfc., Allen Robertson*

A THOUGHT FOR HITLER

On the granite face of cliffs
Pharaoh carved hieroglyphs.
He is dust; his words are stone
Read by heedless winds alone.
   —*Camp Shelby, MS, Sgt. Grant A. Sanders*

TOBACCO THROWED

I flipped a cigarette into the air;
It fell to earth, I know not where.
The CO saw the scene depicted---
That is why I'm now restricted!
   —*Inglewood AAF, CA, Sgt. Shelby Friedman*

GEOGRAPHY LESSON

Via letter and wire and by word of mouth,
 Send the endless protest forth;
It is simply that the "Hospitable South"
 Is located here up North.
   —*Shenango Replacement Center, PA, Cpl. M.B. Schoen*

CHEMICAL WAR-FAIR

I named her Chloropieric
Because she made me weep,
And was so darned persistent
She lingered for a week.
   —*Fort Hancock, NY, S/Sgt. Mark R. Curilovic*

DISCHARGES

There's a Section VIII and a CDD
For the sick and the mentally poor.
If I had my way there's be one
For the guys with a GI snore.
   —*Fort Ord, CA, T/5 Ralph Allen*

HAPPY SOLDIERS

It's easy to pick California soldiers;
They are not in the least downhearted.
They're smiling because they're right at home
Now that the Autumn rains have started.
   —*Italy, Cpl. Harry P. Volk*

ACQUIREMENT

I've acquired something quite useful in the Army
That a genteel person despises:
The ability to dispense all kinds of profanity
Whenever the occasion arises.
   —*Camp Crowder, MO, Pfc. Louis Fisher*

PUZZLE

Though I've known her all my life
I think that I shall never
Understand what she means
When she signs "as ever."
   —*North Africa, Sgt. E. Blackwell*

BLUES IN THE NIGHT

The camp they left was always bliss
For those GIs who reminisce;
But oh the agony and hell in
The post or station they now dwell in.
   —*AAB, Charleston, SC, Cpl. Carl Fenichel*

STRIPES

I can't get any stripes,
 My hopes are forsaken;
There's more hand-shakers here
 Than hands to be shaken.
   —*Dow Field, ME, Pvt. Samyel J. Profeta*

JINGLE

I cannot stand my middle name,
 I even hate to spell it.
If I had (NMI) for mine
 You'd surely hear me yell it.
   —*Africa, Sgt. E. Blackwell*

QUERY?

The purity of Army names
Brings forth this pond'rous question:
 Will Gen. Patton then be called
"Aged Plasma and Intestine"?
   —*Fort Benning, GA, Pfc. Robert Nicolai*

NO WORMS TODAY

The early bird can catch the worm;
I never faced foods that squirm.
Ho-hum, I'll languish late abed
And catch a little sleep instead.
—*Dale Mabry Field, FL, Pfc. Sidney Mason*

NOTES ON GUARD DUTY

There's a time 'twixt the day and darkness
That all clock-watching soldiers revile;
When you can't read your watch by the daylight,
Yet you can't read your luminous dial.
—*Beloit College, WI, Pvt. John W. Sullivan*

MORAL LESSON

The leopard cannot change his spots
The Ethiopian his skin.
But NCO's can lose the stripes
They buck so hard to win.
—*Pvt. Joe Sims*

MEMORY AID

To kiss and tell is bad, but dear,
Gossip isn't fatal yet;
I'd rather have the whole world hear
Than have you kiss and just forget.
—*Los Angeles, CA, Pvt. Bob Downer*

GRIPE

The chicken roast is crisp and brown,
The portions large, its fragrance balmy;
The guy before me gets the last---
And I get franks and cold salami.
—*Kirtland Field, NM, S. Sgt. Morton Brooks*

G. I. WHO'S ZOO

I'm just a little zebra,
Sitting down to bawl.
I've got more stripes than anyone,
But I don't rate at all.
—*Esprit De Corps*

GI MUFFETT

Little Miss Muffett sat on her tuffet
Eating her curds and whey;
A German came by her and sat down beside her---
Period. (She was a booby trap.)
—*Fort Taylor, Key West, FL, 1st Sgt. Luman S. Nutter*

FALL GUY

Autumn's filled with sadness,
How my poor heart grieves---
They had me out this morning
Picking up the leaves.
—*Alexandria AAF, LA, Cpl. Jason Marks*

ENCIRCLEMENT

It will take no great diplomacy
And very little tact
To draw up an armistice
 Between the AEF and WAAC.
—*Army Flying School, Greenville, Miss Sgt. Walter Stewart*

DOUGH GIRLS?

Buck private is the name for me,
But this I'd like to know:
Are dainty privates in the WAAC
 Yet classified as Doe?
—*Williams Field, AZ, Pvt. John B. James*

DATE FOR A UNIFORM

They run the race of female gender
From sweatered chick, for week-end bender,
To Junior Leaguer, strictly class,
Who only plays the higher brass.
—*Camp Campbell, KY, Pvt. Gene Wierbach*

LETTER

There's nothing better
Than a letter
Unless it's some remittance
To help along the monthly pittance.
—*Fort Houston, TX, Cpl. Jack B. Hughes*

LAMENT

I might have been a commando,
I might have driven a tank.
But here I sit at the USO,
Writing this junk for Yank.
—*San Diego, CA, Cpl. Raymond Kass*

PROFILE

Pvt. Jones my patience taxes
Though I'm the most patient of men
He thinks that a prophylaxis
Is a side view of Adolph and Ben.
—*TCAB, Charleston, SC, S/Sgt. Louis Fox*

PUZZLER

All kinds of names have Army men---
Names without wherefore or why,
But the middle monicker I don't ken
Is brief mysterious "NMI."
—*Greenland, S/Sgt. Ed O'Meara*

QUERY

Breathes a GI
On the face of the earth
Who possesses the rating
He thinks he is worth?
—*Pvt. Julian S. Weil*

QUESTION

Will WAACs and WAVES,
In civil lives,
Enlist again
As humble WIVES?
—*Camp Wolters, TX, Sgt. W.C. Allison*

REQUIEM

Old and tattered, stooped and bent,
Dazed by a thousand storms he went.
I saw him pass and how he reeled,
The last man leaving Sheppard Field!
—*Sheppard Field, TX, Cpl. Marv Lore*

SUBTLE DIFFERENCES

The sergeant flays his cringing brood,
 With curses lurid, crisp and crude.
The colonel's equally emphatic,
But uses swear words more grammatic.
—*Armored Castle, Ft. Benning*

INCIDENT

Earth will outlive her pockmarked face.
On some dim midnight, far from now,
All that troubled our angry race
Will wrinkle a history student's brow.
—*Alexandria AAF, LA, S. Sgt. Russell Speirs*

JEEP

What is a jeep?
A functional flivver,
Which ridden too wildly
Plays hell with your liver.
—*Camp Gordon Johnston, FL, Cpl. William H. Cole*

JINGLE

Gather ye brass bars while ye may
 And live your life in clover;
For he who the war makes a shavetail today
 Will be a soda jerk again when it's over.
—*Davis-Monthan Field, AZ, Pfc. Ralph D. Powell*

JOTLING

Here's a beer to and a cheer to
The guy who doesn't state
When GI Willy does something silly:
"He's buckin' for Section Eight!"
—*Camp Davis, N.C.T-4, T.J. Luneburg*

THE WAAC

She cannot lie in bed till ten,
Nor mess around with gentlemen.
For now her bed is lined up neat,
Where no dame can be indiscreet.
—*603rd C.A. (AA) Burbank, CA T/5, John Owens*

TO "BABY" (A JEEP)

Philosophy ruins my slumber,
For war is a hell of a game
When every man has a number
 And every truck has a name.
—*Camp Roberts, CA, Pvt. Bob Downer*

TODAY'S LADY

In Armentieres, the mademoiselle
Was quite adept at raising hell,
 But she'd place second to the filly
This lad met in Piccadilly.
—*England, T/S Peter Alfano*

T-O-J-O

T is for tearing your hair out I'll bet.
O stands for odor, yours lingers yet
J is for justice, we'll deal out that.
O means it's over, you're finished, you rat.
—*Hawaii, Sgt. Alfred Nunn*

TO THE SERGENTS AND GENERALS

Feel not your oats too much,
Proud wheel horses of Mars;
A zebra has more stripes than you,
The sky has still more stars.
—*Australia, Cpl. Clyde Kenneth Hyder*

PIN-UP PROBLEM

The pin-up pretties, I am quite sure, were meant
For men in barracks and men in the tent.
But how can a tent-dweller keep his chin up
When there's no dam place to pin up a pin-up?
—*New Guinea, T-4 Arthur M. Zipser*

Section Three
Poems about Love and Romance

SANCTUARY

My mind is a quiet place in the forest,
A clearing where many men come and go,
And you remain there.
Music I hear with you is more than sound,
Poems we read are more than words.
I dare not even breathe the air.

Often we talk, and you are the cool hand on the brow
That untangles the nervous tendrils of despair.
What part of my soul I am free to give
Has been in your care.

My mind is a quiet place in the forest.
I meet you there.
—*Marianas, T-4 Stan Flink*

BUT GENTLEMEN PREFER. . . .

Oh, Sailor Jack
He just leaned back
And roared and jibed,
"Yer WAACy";
He chortled loud
When the Army bowed
And grabbed the gals in khaki.

The Leatherneck
He snarled, by heck,
That a schoolmarm or chorine
Would never be
An auxiliary
To a rolling stone Marine.

It wasn't long
Jack changed his song; The Navy stilled his raves;
He's got no jokes 'Bout Army blokes
And WAACS; He's got his WAVES.

Now if some kind And pow'rful mind
In Washington would listen, He'd sign brunettes
As Marine-ettes
And stop THEIR doggone Hissin'!
—*Fort Niagara, NY, Pvt. John L. Dougherty*

BIRTH OF A JOURNEY

I'm daffy-down-dilly, Outrageously silly,
My writings refuse to make sense. I jot will-nilly
And romp like a filly,

All aimlessly, hither and whence.

I make no excuses to him who peruses
Inanities that I may jot. I'm up for probation...
I'm down on rotation...
The Army's forgotten me not! Farewell to all sorrow,
I'm leaving tomorrow,
The dying man's got a reprieve; Hey, civilization.
It's time for elation;
My wife is about to conceive.
—*Philippines, Cpl. Dan H. Laurence*

A WALK WITH YOU

The lonely stars that stay awake
And keep a vigil all night through
Invite a stroll along the lake
Beside the woodland tipped with dew;
And yet, I do not care to take
A walk with you.

This solitary room can make
A cozy, quiet place for two;
And why, my dear, should I forsake
My haven for a sky of blue?
Ah no, I do not wish to take A walk with you.
—*Fort Benning, GA, Sgt. Leonard Summers*

A WAAC, A WAVE AND A WOLF

For centuries a uniform
Has played a major part
Both upon the battlefield
And to win a woman's heart.

Since Galahad and Lancelot
We've moved at rapid pace;
Women now wear uniforms
Instead of yards of lace.

But chivalry is not yet dead
And to me it does behoove
To announce the formation of
A manly branch of WOLVES.

We men in uniform and out
Are bound by sacred oath
To maintain chivalry and love,
We'll forever cherish both.

You've seen us in each cocktail lounge
From Orleans to Duluth;
Wherever there's a WAAC or WAVE
There will always be a WOLF.

So if your femme has joined the ranks
Do not worry for her part;
Remember that we'll do our best
To console her lonely heart.
—*Morrison Field. FL, Pvt. Robert Jame Vergeront*

AMBUSCADE ON FURLOUGH

The staunch little boat with the celluloid sail,
Forlorn in the sand box with shovel and pail;
The red bike on the porch with its saddle askew
'Mid the trains and the planes and the picture books new;
Here the trowel and hoe in the plum tree's shade
By the little boy's garden where lately he played---
Seems odd that son isn't waiting for me.
Ah, the double-barreled popgun is missing, I see.

As I turn to continue my search in the rear,
The faint jingle of juvenile laughter I hear;
Sharp from hedgerow and hill, from
the trees and the brush,
Like ten bellwethers' bleating assaulting the hush,
Rants the vocalized din of machine-gun fire
Trilling out in falsetto democracy's ire,
And enveloping me in a two-pronged attack
The commandos advance with their strident ack-ack!

Like the Saxon confronted with Roderick's clan
I stand firm and resolved to go down like a man!
But these warriors are fair and I haven't a gun,
They surround me with glee while the littlest one
Twines his arms round my neck as a conqueror's yoke;
Boy of mine, I am lost! What avails heart of oak?
Your objective is taken at cost of a smile,
Though the secret I'll keep: it was yours all the while.
—*Britain, Pvt. Charles A. Werner, Jr.*

ALWAYS, LOVE

Were there some transcendental tongue
That could soar beyond the
Limitations of a language that anchors us
To an expression which at best
Wears a 10-cent lipstick
And a hand-me-down dress.
Were there some winged speech
Scented with my heart's perfume

And sprinkled with my heart's alchemy;
Were the poem unsung, the tear unshed,
Had the sigh been bridled, the lash not drooped;
But mortal tongue speaks mortal word.
With banal phrase, with deification crafted
In time beyond memory,
"I love thee."
—*Ft. Benning, GA, Pfc. Sidney Schneider*

ANGELA

So demure you look, Angela,
As you sit upon the red-and-silver stool,
One elbow poised delicately on the bar's edge
To let your red-nailed hand support the softly cleft chin,
The other fingers lightly tapping the ashes into the red and guilt tray.

So refined, so politely reserved every line of your graceful body.
Perhaps you droop your shoulders a bit more than necessary
To accentuate those tempting full breasts;
Perhaps the black dress hem is a trifle too high,
To certify, rather than suggest, the grace of those sun-tan legs.
Perhaps, but no one could assert it.

The band of red felt just calls notice to the glowing
crown of dark hair Drawn up above those pink translucent
ears, So soft, so appealing and yet not inviting
The occasional accidental glance that one catches.
You wouldn't mind, would you, Angela, really if that young
lieutenant came over and spoke to you? That faint blush upon
the firm, tingling cheeks---Were you embarrassed when the
sergeant misunderstood?

So speculative, so faintly mysterious, so sedately aloof
your whole manner, Angela. Are you gazing on the human
scene and reflecting on man's variety? Are you analyzing the
characters of all these people at the noisy bar?
Do your eyes reflect a mild interest in human motives,
human hopes? In other words, does your pose and manner
indicate philosophic meditation, Angela?

It might seem so, but I'm afraid I doubt it.
I'm more inclined to think that you know the lieutenant is
paid more than sergeant
And that you doubt that the curly headed private who
dances so well has private means. It's too bad that the lieutenant is plain and awkward, Angela;
He has already broken two twenty-dollar bills.
Business before pleasure, eh, Angela?
—*Camp Reynolds, PA, Pfc. Edward Chandler Manning*

ALL AFTERNOON THE AUTUMN LIGHT

All afternoon the autumn light
Pours through the elms: the promised frost
Remote upon this lucid air
Drifts from the millpond, and the bright
Discursive peace that you had lost
Moves like a ghost through the warm square.

The girl was lovely, too, you say:
And gentle, like the mourning dove
By the green pond, her colors sad And pretty.
But she mourned all day,
Troubled about the course of love,
And the sweet sounds that made her glad.

But if she gave you hope, the will
You found in her was cool and strange;
And all she chose to do was walk
Down town, or lonely, on the hill
To stare at the mild season's change;
And all she promised you was talk.

September gave you little time
For the sweet flesh and the soft hair;
But the warm will and the earth's prime.
The indolence upon the air
Intransigent and primitive.

But so you knew her, too, and found
All of her passion strategy still
With the late ripeness that the sun
Pours now upon the autumn ground
Before the first obdurate chill
Gathers along the deep mill-run.

You see her now where the wind stirs
The burning leaves, or where you turn
To see the pond break into fire.
The light flares, and the water blurs.
She is there still, so you may learn
Something about love and desire.
—*AAFBU, St. Louis, Sgt. Samuel French Morse*

ALEUTIAN LAMENT

We've all got dollies;
They're pinned on every wall,
From a pistol-packin' mama
To luscious Lucille Ball.

We always find 'em waiting
True as any pearl,

But we'd trade our paper dollies
For a fickle-minded girl.

They've got no animation
Though posed to hypnotize,
Displaying dainty breastwork,
Hips and knees and thighs.

We never have to worry
About 'em doing wrong,
They're only paper dollies
Like that one in the song.

We're getting out of practice
At winking flirty eyes:
We need some real live dollies
To make us flirty guys

But we pin 'em up as often
As we find a shapely lass,
And cuss the Frank Sinatras
Enjoying all that class.

We'd take our chances on losing
A dolly that was real:
A blonde, brunette or redhead
Would have the same appeal.

We are no longer choosy—
For a short one, fat or long,
We'd trade our paper dollies
To the guy who wrote the song.
—*The Aleutians, Cpl. James R. Gardner*

ANYBODY HERE WRITE MUSIC?

The day I finally went away,
She swore she'd hold all other guys at bay,
But a bar jimmied open what a yardbird couldn't sway,
AND MY LOVE DONE MARRIED A SHAVETAIL.

I guess the contrast helped a lot,
A gent in the hand beats a bum in the pot,
When the gent is a looey, the bum's not so hot.
SO MY LOVE DONE MARRIED A SHAVETAIL.

My heart is kicking up a storm
I wish she'd chosen a Mormon
It can't be just the uniform
Or she'd have gone for a doorman.

But it's the shame that leaves me cold,
She swapped a healthy private for a bar of gold,
The pasture's now deserted where a colt of love was foaled,
CAUSE MY LOVE DONE MARRIED A SHAVETAIL.
—*Fighter Command School, FL, Pvt. Robert D. Kemper*

ABOUT LOVE

Each little bird and bee
Has a he or a she, but me.
I'm all alone,
No ringing phone, No she.
Ah, sad to say,
Each night and day
It's I, not we.
Ah, me!
—*Pope Field Propwash*

PREVUE?

Go home and tell your mother
That I hate her very looks.
The only homelier I've seen
Have been in comic books;
But the thing that gripes me most is,
Every time she draws my eye,
I am dismally reminded
What you'll look like by and by.
—*AAB, Ephrata, WA, Sgt. William R. Carty*

CALL TO ARMS

Please won't you be my Jezebel?
Give me thy evil eye!
I'm fuller fed then I can tell
Of virtue sweet and shy.
I want no gingham-fronted fright,
No braided-haired gazelle.
This is the hour: this is the night;
Please be my Jezebel!
—*Ephrata AAB, WA, Sgt. William R. Carty*

BEFORE THAT ROSE WILL DIE

I placed a red rose in her hair,
And said, 'twixt kiss and sigh,
That I would stroll to London Square
Before that rose would die.

And stroll by London Square I did,
But passed the taverns by,

For I must go and claim my love
Before that rose can die.

And I returned to claim my love,
But never dreamed that I
Would find my love had flown away
Before that rose did die.

Then died my heart a thousand times
Before that rose died one.
(But mine will live a thousand more
And that poor rose is done.)
—*New Mexico State College, Pvt. Ira Jackson*

LADY OF THE SERPENT'S TONGUE

There is a lash he can't escape,
There is a goal that will not slack,
There is a vengeful female shape
Busily blistering his back.

For sting her sharp strokes cannot lack
While blood is warm and hearts are young
And potent words a wallop pack---
His lady of the serpent's tongue!

Whenever he thinks to break and scat
And hide for safety in the attic,
Or if he sneaks his hat and coat
To stage an exit diplomatic,

The echoes of that voice despotic
Of every vagrant breeze are rung,
In accents frigidly hypnotic---
His lady of the serpent's tongue.

Sir, may your skin remain,
Your breath never wheeze
A pain-wracked whistle---

His lady of the serpent's tongue!
He reached for a rose, but
He plucked a thistle.
—*AAB, Ephrata, WA, Sgt. William E. Carty*

ON THE WAY

Another day spent out,
And I lie on the hatch
Feeling the propeller beat
Like a wild heart.

And I think of you
Everywhere I look
I see you; in the rigging
Taut with the wind; in the sky,
The solitude of space.

Nothing is so lost
As a ship at sea;
No man so lonely
As a sailor.
—*Australia, Cpl. George Kauffman*

OUR BASE

All day long we fight the Gnats,
And then at night, the vampire bats.
Nobody knows the hell we had
And to think, I thought Scott Field was bad.

All day long we wade the sand,
Nobody lends a helping hand.
I have to share my bunk with three---
Mosquitos, sand-fleas, gnats and me.

The only town is down the river.
The women there would make you shiver.
Don't know which is the worse I've seen,
The big and fat, or the long and lean.

Maybe some day I'll go back.
I'll hit New York in full field pack.
I'll sit down in their best café,
And what I'll order won't be hay.

I'll eat a steak with all the trimmin',
Then full, I'll go and find some women.
Though they may help me to forget,
It'll take a damned long time, I'll bet.
—*British Guiana, Sgt. James Bartlett*

ON THE ROAD TO (CENSORED)

By the lazy South Atlantic
Lapping languid at the beach,
There's a nut-brown gal a-settin',
And she's not a Georgia peach.
The wind is in her tresses,
And the love within her eye
She would not trade for all the world---
No other lad than I.
At the famous Bar of Wonder

Just above the river scene,
That's where she made her living,
As a naughty strip-tease queen.
She is not exactly luscious
As a Georgia peach would be.
She is short and there are bulges.
 But she certainly isn't "green."
I met her there one afternoon
 Around the hour of 3;
She came around to say hello
And sit upon my knee.
From there---well, things got out of hand;
"Twas love, indeed, at sight,
Dear Lord, please give me back my strength
To just forget that night.
On the hilltop, in the palm trees,
 In a South Atlantic breeze,
I ask her to forgive me
And let me please be free;
 For yonder waters call me
To my home beyond the sea---
I can't be stayed by naughty dames
Who sit upon men's knees.
—*Brazil, Pfc. Richard Brookshire*

ON BEING SINGLE

I am no longer able
To gaze at Betty Grable,
Both Hedy and Miss Lake evoke a groan.
For when this war is over
And others roll in clover
Here's one GI who will still sleep alone.
—*Chanute Field, IL, Cpl. David Troup*

NURSES? CURSES!

Sing us a song of pain and penance---
Army nurses are all lieutenants.
Whether they're blondes, brunettes or titans,
The hell of it is:
They have commissions,
And privates, creatures of low degree,
Can dream but never hope to be
More to the nurses that win their hearts
Than pulses, temperatures and charts.
—*Fort Banks Digest*

MY LOVE

My love is tangible to me,
A thing I feel, a thing I see;
A springtime thing I always wear,
Like lilacs, tangled in my hair;
A living thing, forever warm,
Exciting as a summer storm.

Like vapor trails that mark the sky
When early-morning bombers fly,
My love has left a mark on me;
An everlasting melody!
—*AAFBU, Miami Beach, FL, Pfc. Catherine Murray*

MILITARY LULLABY

Jeeps tumble over hot bogs.
Sky suffers one great yellow blister
Which bursts at noontime
And drenches the camp with pus-like heat.

Dust rides the heatwaves,
Nullifies all color,
Clothes all images entering the eye.

At last the strained hours loosen
Like tired muscles
And the day's ration of sleep is issued.

In the deepest hour of night
They are wakened by the rain's soft body
Hurled against the tents.
And one lies thinking
How a girl woke him thus in the night
With her crying.
—*Manila, S. Sgt. Troy Garrison*

MIDSUMMER METAPHOR

When I saw the pretty white clematis curl
Its tendrils round the pump-house lattice, and unfurl
The pointed leaves that last year broke the aged wood
 with heavy greens
I knew what happens to a weathered man who loves a
young thing in her teens.
—*Ft. Bliss, TX, Pvt. Thomas Langner*

MAUD, MORT, MERDE

'Tis man's enjoyment man to kill;
Many men against their will
Were forced to shriek their last alack
As twisty wheel and groaning rack
Did free the spirit volatile.

Men were often gently pressed
Within the Iron Maiden's breast.
They fed them there with Paris green
And washed them off with gasoline;
The flames did clean up all the rest.

But man to man I'll soon confess,
Although with women I'm obsessed,
The sex called male is much more human
Than the so-called sex of woman.
'Tis not because I am repressed.

Now Mabel, Dorothy, or Gail
Is crueler far than any male.
Forceps, pincers, the fiery stake
Are simpler tortures for men to take
Than passion old and passion stale.

And if you think that I malign,
Observe her movement gelatine.
Her skin is fair, her glances free,
But still that fruit is not for thee;
The other guy is on the brine.

She knows the torture congruent;
Now blood runs high, now passion spent,
To every man his own receipt;
Delight the wight with sweet conceit
but to the gent be violent.

By God, those doxies make you pay,
Or in the heart or in the hay,
And if you would these ardors please,
Your legs become parentheses;
Your bones will soon decay.

So, dunk me in some strong concrete
And drop me in the river sweet.
You'd think that I'd have learned my lesson;
Another blonde has got me guessing.
I think that I'll repeat;
Please prepare the winding sheet.
  —*Keesler Field, MS, Cpl. Howard M. Rosenfeld*

MALARIA

I dream of shadows,
Sweet and mysterious,
Of darkling shapes in
Revelry delirious.

In this continuous night
Of coarse desire,
Only you can keep me
From the fire.
  —*Lincoln AAF, NE, Pfc. Samuel Napsrstek*

MAKE MINE A MARTINI

A soldiers dreams (or so I hear)
Are of the simple things held dear.
What time he rests from toil and strife
And plans upon his post-war life;
A cottage first with lawn and trees,
A garden plot to spade and rake,
The songs of birds, the drone of bees,
A glimpse of woods and distant lake.

(But I'll take a duplex with a built-in bar
And bathrooms which number four or five.
When a yearning comes for gardens
I'll hop a cab for Marden's,
And look back from the Hudson at the Drive.)

A sweetheart from his childhood days
To make the cottage into home;
The girl whose simple loving ways
Will still his last desire to roam.

(Well, make mine a gal who can shine like a star
At the Colony, the Stork, or 21;
A self-sufficient brat In a Lily Dache hat
Who adores "Forever Amber' sort of fun.)

The luscious things she'll roast and bake
Bring glowing pictures to his eyes;
The summer corn, the chocolate cake,
The juicy huckleberry pies.

(But this guy craves some blue points or a bowl of caviar,
Some vichysoisse, a pheasant under glass,
A flaming crepe suzette,
And---"Garcon, don't forget!"---
Some Courvoisier afloat on demitasse.)
  —*Camp Crowder, MO, Pfc. Ralph H. Chapman*

GI BEER SONG

Translucent are the windows of my soul
And fogged the panes that open to my brain.
Attained at last the long awaited goal.
For beer is sold in the PX again.
Wherefore I smite the lyre anew for thee,
Adenoidally my croaking voice is raised
In nasal paeans to the absentee
Still visible to optics blank and glazed.
Absent in flesh, but ever in mind,
And what a place that is, love, I declare,
For one so chic, so well-bred, so refined;
You really have no business to be there;
By any code, its conduct unbecoming,
A gentleman to take a lady slumming!
—*AAB, Ephrata, WA, Sgt. William R. Carty*

FOR YOU AT VALENTINE'S

I set a candle burning in the wide
Deep casement window of my soul for you
At Valentine's, and there it shines beside
A world that holds an evening star to view
From iridescent windows of the sky:
The world is good and tells a wond'rous story
Of friends, of faith, of love that shall not die
But ever shine transcendent in its glory
So shines my candle with its rays for gleaming,
No night is dark when faith is near at hand;
Still shines the evening star, my heart is dreaming
The dreams that only lovers understand.
The simple faith that will establish love
On earth as Venus smiles her blessing from above.
—*Newfoundland, Sgt. Loton Rogers Pitts*

DENIAL TO CYNARA

I do not promise always to be true
Or swear unceasingly that we won't part.
I say that you are precisely…..you.
And that your tenderness disturbs my heart.
I do not offer you unswerving faith
Or timeless vows, or anything save this;
I shall sometime go stalwart down to death
With the remembered guerdon of your kiss.
—*Camp Claiborne, Pvt. Thomas F. St. John*

DEAR SGT. ROOT
(In re: "White Lies," Yank, July 22, 1942)

We took that trip through Port of Spain----
Admit it was a peach,
But have you been to You-Know-Where
Where the girls live on the beach?
These lovely maiden's skins are white---
As white as white can be---
As white as blackout in the night---
As white as ebony.
But they are lovers of the sun,
And spend their idle hours
Roasting like a hot-cross bun
Out in the sandy bowers.
This turns them to well-done brown
That verges on the black.
It colors them from golden crown
Down to their lower back.
The soldier here's not color blind---
No more than he is wealthy.
The major problem on his mind Is
"Why are the girls so healthy?"

L'ENVOI

He likes the whiskey, likes the beer,
He likes the tropic atmosphere.
But there's a constant growing fear,
"Where are the snows of yesteryear"
—*Caribbean Area, Capt. Victor Strauss*

DAY DREAM

In a little Algiers garden
Fringed with heaven's fragrant dew,
Where the weeping willows sigh,
I would like to be with you.

We could watch the drifting sky,
Smell the perfumed flowers, too;
But, my darling, that's not why
 I would like to be with you
In a little Algiers garden.
—*Fort Benning, GA, Sgt. Leonard Summers*

DATE BUREAU

I had always thought the date bureau a very handy adjunct to any organization,
But I confess that recently my opinion of it has not ascended much. This is the situation:
I asked what a certain date was like, and the date bureau replied this girl's qualification
Was enhanced by the fact that she was extremely capable of intelligent conversation.
To be quite terse:
Who wants to converse?
—*Sheppard Field, TX, Pfc. Marv Lore*

CONTAMINATING THE CLASSICS

She was a phantom of delight
I'd only see when I was tight.

I fear thy kisses, gentle maiden,
For lipstick may not be all with which they're laden.

My heart leaps up when I behold---
But on second thought you needn't be told.

She is not fair to outward view;
I leave the rest for you to construe.
—*Puerto Rico, Pvt. Louis Fisher*

LINES TO A CENSOR

I've got a girl so far away,
And she is sweet and frail,
But how can I send my love to her
When the censor reads the mail?

This girl is, oh, so very sweet---
I love her willy-nilly,
But how can I tell her of my love
When in print it looks so silly.

I hate the thought of those tender words
Being read by stranger's eyes:
The soul-writ words for her alone
The lies and alibis.

So, read my letters gently, sir.
They are not meant for you,
But for a girl so far away,
I scrawl this silly goo.

But when you read my letter, sir,
And laugh with profound delight,
Remember, sir, that another censor
May laugh at the letters you write.
—*India, Sgt. John Purcussia*

LINES TO A BRASSIERE

A bit of pink, a scrap of lace
A strap to fasten it in place,
You wreath of femininity
Taunting my integrity.

Behold! It waves and flaunts its grace,
Before my eyes and eager face---
Swaying, laughingly and mockingly,
Alluring in its symmetry.

What wonders might its flounces hold,
Gather, shape and firmly mold
Such selfish sensuality!
Entwining all---and none for me.

A scrap of lace! My heart decries,
What time and space between us lies,
Yet I remain---but hopefully
Thinking, dreaming, wishfully.
—*Williamsburg. VA, Frank Frederick SK2c*

LINES FROM A FILIPINO GIRL

If every GI told the truth
When making love to our fair youth,
These tender words might make me vow
To live with thee and serve thy chow.

But every GI on our streets
Makes love to every girl he meets,
And love to you is just a word
That all of us have often heard.

You hold our hands, look in our eyes
Before we fully realize
What's happening, you're gone, and then
We wonder if you'll come again.

Next thing we know we get a note.
Where from? You're not allowed to quote,
Or so you say---and what is more,
You're in the first wave on some shore.

But we stroll down to Santa Fe,
And there beneath a mango tree
We find you lying, full of charms,
Another girl held in your arms.
—*Leyte, T/Sgt. Sidney Haralson*

LEDO ROAD AGAIN

I must go down to Delhi again
To see all the Wacs and Waafs
And all I ask is a ten-day leave
And some travel-time, perhaps;
And the wind will blow and the scotch will flow
And the chow will be steak, not spam,
And the sack will be soft and the floor not dirt.
If I'm late, who gives a damn?

I must go down to Delhi again
Where there's no such thing as mud.
Where the streets are paved and the men are shaved
And the girls are as many as men.
And all I ask is a long, cool drink
And a pretty girl by my side
And a long good-by and a drawn-out sigh
As I take the Road in stride.
—*India, Cpl. Irv Marder*

JERSEY JILL

Someday when I gaily march back home
After dating a Samoan maid
Rich in ornaments of blue-green jade
Or a fire –blooded belle from Rome
Or a ballerina, beautiful
In her jeweled boots and ermine wraps,
Or *senora*, passionate---perhaps
Jersey Jill will seem a little dull.

Foreign janes can easily beguile
Me with colors and perfumes which drug
All my senses just like zombies, while
Jill can only cut a wicked rug,
Burn with kisses, rouge a bit; so she
May seem dull to some---but not to me!
—*Fort Benning, GA, Sgt. Leonard Summers*

IT'S SO MUCH MORE

It's hard for her to think anything
But that I want to take her into my arms
And make violent and passionate love
To her.

It's hard for her to think anything
But that I want to crush her to me
And paw her
And breathe with difficulty.

It's hard for her to think anything
But that I am lonely for the love of a woman---
For that and nothing more,
Or that the evil animal within me seeks an outlet---
Only that.

And yet
It's so much more
And there is no way for me to tell her
That I want but to talk to a woman
To hear the voice of a woman
Friendly, trusting:
"Hello, Stan, How are you?"

I want only understanding to quell the emptiness I feel;
But how can I tell her that to me she's a touch of home,
A touch of Ocean Avenue?
How can I tell her that I like the way
She walks across the room;
I like the way she crosses her legs?

To her I'm but a khaki shirt and trousers
And GI shoes,
With lust on my sordid brain.
And I am lonely and want to say pretty things;
I want to tell her about the farm
And how I miss it in the hot summer.

And this will be no more
Than the countless other times
I've looked at and admired pretty girls,
"I wish he'd stop looking at me," she'll say.
"These soldiers think of only one thing."

And at about eleven o'clock
I will return to the barracks
And as I lie unsleeping on my bunk
I will try to fill the emptiness inside me
With thoughts of home and Louise.
—*Drew Field, FL , Pvt. Stanley Swerdlow*

IN YOUR ABSENCE

Innumerable times
Throughout each day
Similies regarding you
Occur in my mind.
Some are corny,
Some are plagiarized,
Some are fair
And some are of a nature
That at the present state
Must await fermentation
Of that thing called Eros.
When the thought,
"She Is the incarnation of some
Grecian goddess," comes to
Mind for a moment I think
That I've got something,
But the briefest spell
Of time oxidizes it.
Sometimes after some
Rhetorical thought
Has been rejected I
Find myself saying,:
 "She Simply defies description."
And a short while afterward
The afterthought arrives:
"That would be more pertinent
 About five or six years
 Ago." And so on and so on
 Throughout the day until
Reality does away with it.
—*Puerto Rico, Pvt. Louis Fisher*

IN THE SUN

If you feel the warm day coming on,
You step up to the sun and touch it,
 You touch it slowly, let it drip.
You like to know that it is warm
 And the sun is on your face.
Sometimes it is closer than that:
It is rolling down your back:
It is a hoop, and a hand
Out of the blue section of the sky
Is pushing it on and on.

She will come to you
 In the warm sun and the hot earth
 And the hungry days,
She will be touching you
And you will feel naked and humble
Beside her,
And her eyes will be blue,
Her skin will be fair,
Her fingers will not tremble,
But you will hold them
And feel them, soft and firm and warm.

This is a perfect day for a dream
Or something like that.
You are that, soldier:
A person away from the city.
You are thinking of the plum pudding,
Or the corner street light,
Or the bottle of soda, or the schoolroom.

Come, take the sadness from me.
I am waiting here, I am touching you
And, as I kiss you, I hear you say
That the warm sun is in my face,
And your eyes blink
Because I am in every ray.
—*SU, Philadelphia, PA, Cpl. Sarge D. Sterling*

IDLE OBSERVATION

There's a certain kind of whistle
That GIs are prone to use
When a gal is modeled nicely
From her fanny to her shoes.

There's another type of whistle
That you'll recognize in cases
Where a soldier's roving eyeballs
 Come to rest on pretty faces.

But the most *wholehearted* whistle
(If you'll take the time to check)
Greets the gal whose curves are fullest
In between her waist and neck.
—*Scott Field, IL, Cpl. Hal Chadwick*

INTERIM

My love was a beautiful dream,
But dreamers, alas, must awaken.
I thought it was peaches and cream:
How could I have been so mistaken?
My faith in romance is quite shaken:
Hearts and flowers are not what they seem.
If it's true Cupid brings home the bacon,
He must pitch for the opposite team.

(My soul is sad
My heart is sore.
I won't be glad Forevermore;
My psyche won't sing,
My eyes won't dance.
It's a pleasure thing
To unromance.)

This morning I thought she was mine.
Tonight I am laden with sorrow,
But I mustn't forget not to pine
Any longer that evening tomorrow.
Then, somewhere, a tenner I'll borrow.
For I have an engagement to dine,
And I'll hide from the clutches of sorrow
In the joys of flirtation and wine.

(For a bubbly glass
And a new romance
And a fresh young lass
And another chance
Are the surest token
To keep intact
A heart not broken
But slightly cracked.)
  —*Camp Van Dorn, MS, Cpl. Alex Drogichen*

IN INDIA

Oh, in India, in India
All the cows walk in the street
And the air is oh, so sweet;
But if you're wise, you'll be discreet— In India

Oh, in India, in India,
Fortune-telling fakirs dwell,
And the lies they sell sound swell.
But if they're true, I'll say farewell---
In India.

Oh, in India, in India,
Pretty women wear a veil;
Thereby hangs a mournful tale
Because the veil is not for sale---
In India.
  —*India, Cpl. Leo Liebman*

HAUNTED SPRING

How strange to think that you
Who made me so aware
Of every living thing
Will not be here to share
This spring;
To watch the blossoming
Of hedges and of trees,
To hear the blustering wind
Turn to gentle breeze
Heavy with scent of lilacs;
To answer with a smile
The shy and friendly glance
Of pansies as we hurry past;
To watch the tiny daisies dance
Across the field.

How strange to think that you
Who loved so much
The gentle rain of spring
Cannot now feel its touch,
While I who wait
And listen for your call
Must carry in my heart
Unending fall.
  —*New Guinea, Sgt. Kathleen Nealis*

SUZIE ON THE WALL

Bugbee's the guy on the bunk next to mine,
And Bugbee's got Suzie and Suzie's divine.
Suzie smiles down from our communal wall,
Smiles sweetly at me and at Calvin and Paul.
O Bugbee's near frantic and Bugbee's near mad,
And deep in the green in the eye of the lad;
He threatens to tear Suzie down from the wall,
But Suzie demurely still smiles on us all.

Dear Bugbee, rest easy, the maiden is yours,
And when you come marching home from the wars,
Attired in honor, triumphant for truth,
Resplendent in glory and shinning with youth.
Suzie will smile from her doorstep through tears
And smile for you only throughout the years.
  —*Dale Mabry Field, FL, Pfc. Sidney Mason*

STORM LOVE

When the wind rose and bent the slender trees,
And lightning gave life to the driven clouds
With delicate veins of fire;
You seemed to draw the passion of the storm
Into yourself.

The rain,
The quietly insistent rain,
Was all the sound we heard.
And I kissed your young mouth,
Young with desire and bewilderment,
And saw briefly your green-flecked,
Swimming eyes in the momentary spurt of
A match flame.

Next day in sunlight you were changed again.
You said, "It was the rainstorm."
Perhaps it was; and I could wish
My life be spent in everlasting storms
Of freshening wind and fire-flash
And running rain
If such things made you love.
   —*Maxton AAB, NC, Sgt. Philip R. Benjamin*

SPRING FEVER IN AFRICA

My buddy said that you would be
A peachy girl to write to;
He says that you're a lovely thing,
And even fairly bright, too.
(She's probably as dumb as hell
But she's a girl, at least---oh, well.)

In these respects you differ much
From local girls available;
The native sisters of this town---
Descriptions are not mailable.
(The nurses are restricted for
The aristocracy of war.)

But what to write you puzzles me
Because I never knew you;
You probably don't care about
The things I like---or do you?
(Why did I start this silly letter?
A crap game would have killed time better.)

Suppose we call the whole thing off
And each write to a friend.
It may be duller, but at least
It serves some useful end.
(My Godfrey, how I waste my time;
At least I've made the damn thing rhyme.)
   —*Central Africa, M/Sgt. Harold E. Shipley*

SONNET TO MARIANN

Oh, I remember what I thought of you
In bygone days. I thought you were mean,
Indescribably nasty, rude, obscene,
A doggoned dirty, double-crossing shrew.
Oh I remember how I watched each new
And clever trick you played upon those green
And unsuspecting men.
"Well she's the dean Of rats,"
I cursed, as men are wont to do.

But that was very, very long ago,
And now, with tears, I emulate the thinker
And visualize the past—the past I know
So well. And like Cervantes in the clinker,
I judge the world with thoughts as pure as snow;
But even so---I think you're still a stinker!
   —*Ft. Benning, GA, Sgt. Leonard Summers*

SONNET TO LAURA

When I am dead (each soldier sometimes savors
His obit from the view of the bereaved)
I'll be one of those popular cadavers
Of which the people hear with smiles relieved.
As though to say, "Well, now at last he's quiet.
I knew him when he was possessed somehow;
If any mischief brewed, he had to try it
Just once too often! Hmph! Where is he now?"
Whatever ill they say---it will be ample,
All based on glaring fault of mine---
I fear they'll miss my single good example
Of long, sincere devotion at your shrine.
But if they do, it will be nothing new;
The first one to forget it, was you.
   —*AAF, Ardmore, OK, S/Sgt. William R. Carty*

SONNET FOR MARGIE ANN

I ask: In the maelstrom yet to come,
When by the rushing tides I am hurled
To twist from dark to dark, from dumb to dumb,
Alone and breathless in a turning world.
In those quick moments when I try to hold

Myself in changing balance, uselessly
Struggling for retention in the mold
Of what I am, and what I want to be;
Then let the swirl of happenings subside,
And I will cast far, far into memory
For a lake, and a walk and evening's tide,
And you in the sunlight, and you with me;
But when the pause of memory is done,
My hands will clench around my heated gun.
—*Fort Eustis, VA, Pvt. Perry Wolff*

SONNET FOR CHARLOTTE

Be with me always in the days ahead
When I shall doubt that loveliness remains.
That truth and beauty live in all this pain.
Let me remember little things you said.
The way you laughed and how the shadows fled
Before your smile; the haunting strains
Of songs you sang, and warm September rains.
Let me remember moments all too quickly sped,
And though I leave the dreams I called my own
To walk apart in some distant land
Fighting to hold the happiness we've known,
Your love, your courage will beside me stand
Till in the midst of battle all alone
I call to you and reaching, touch your hand.
—*South Pacific, Pfc Dudley M. Shoemaker*

SONNET

This mute inexplicable universe,
Upon whose floating crust I stand aware,
Whose son I am, who gives me tears and air,
And who to me these pleasures does disperse,
Has moved again and we are gone apart
In silent movement and unshuddered pain
To lands where each the other shall sustain
By flickered recollection's backward chart.

Yet this I see of you: quiet grace,
Your fingers resting in my hand,
The tints of color in a fair, fair face;
I see all this, and seeing understand;
This universe can imperceptibly
Revolve again and bring my love to me.
—*Fort Eustis, VA, Pvt. Perry S. Wolff*

SOIREE

You sing a song or two
And you have a little chat,
You make a little candy fudge
And then you take your hat.
You take her hand and say "good night,"
And sweetly as you can.
Ain't that a hell of an evening
For a great big healthy man?
—*USN, Doug Wilson Y1c*

SMALL TOWN

No place to go,
Nothing to do;
Here there is no
Band that plays blue.

Dissonant notes
Or music by Liszt;
One only dotes
On things that are missed;

Art by Monet,
Women in tights,
Russian ballet,
Big-city lights.

Under a brooch
Of stars, on the grass,
I have some hootch
And I have a lass.

Here at my side
Marigolds sway,
Wind is a bride
Excited and gay.

But here there is no place
To go for diversion,
No circus, no show place
Or moonlight excursion.

No ball game or fight club
Or place one can dance,
No beer joint or night club---
Just booze and romance.

No couvert or fee
For table or cork;
Here love is free---
To hell with New York.
—*Fort Benning, GA, Sgt. Leonard Summers*

SHY

Tonight was any night
And yet I stood entranced,
A dreamer by a moor,
You did not choose to glance,
But still I waited there,
And wistfully debated
If I should run or stand.
I came near choosing; then,
For fear of losing, fled,
And stumbled out the door.
—*Galveston AAF, TX, Cpl. Thomas Matthews*

SHORE LEAVE

The eager sailor chafes the rail,
Looking shoreward.
His state is ecstasy.
After a long voyage at sea,
He looks to the woman as an
Englishman Looks to his tea---
This cup I'll drink! Says he……..
—*Italy, Sgt. Harold O. Wang*

SEDUCTION

A woman smiles,
Entrances, beguiles;
Mere man succumbs
To feminine wiles.

Events transpire,
Repressed desire
Sears the soul
With consuming fire.

With the dawn
He is gone;
Woman glorious, ever victorious,
Slumbers on.

Could I but see
What bewilders me;
Who is conquered,
He or she?
—*Sioux City AAB, Iowa, Pfc. R. G. Smetana*

SEA SHELLS

I walk along the shinning windswept beach
And see the vaulted blueness of the sky,
The rippled dunes of sand, the stones and shells,
And hear the marching waves, the sea gull's cry.

We once walked here together hand in hand
With flying tangled hair and foam-clad feet,
Our pockets filled with shells, our throats with song;
The gods were good to us and life was sweet.

The long white waves still thunder on the shore
And on the wind above the same gulls glide.
The sky is still that singing blue. I turn
And half expect to find you at my side.

You walk with death across the land and sea
But you will hear the waves again with me.
—*Fort Monroe, VA, Pvt. Jane Murray*

REPLY TO BETTE DAVIS

I'm neither too young nor too old,
I'm just about right for a real romance.
But no little chick ever throws a glance;
No female tries to charm me
Since I am in the Army.

I'm neither a wolf nor a dope,
But nevertheless there's no hope.
I used to think that I was Heaven's answer to a dame
But once you're in a uniform all soldiers look the same.

It's wasteful to leave me out here in the cold---
I'm neither too young nor too old.

I'm neither too young nor too old,
I still have all my teeth, and my hair's my own,
Yet every tomato leaves me alone;
My arms will not enfold her---
She wants bars on the shoulder.

I'm not an old fool, nor a punk,
But still all my chances are sunk.
I begged to have a uniform, but you can have it back;
I'm not a conqu'ring hero; I'm a most unhappy sack.
The Draft Board will tell all who need to be told,
I'm neither too young nor too old.

I'm neither too young nor too old.
I'm not just a schoolboy nor yet a seer.

I've got enough dough for the gin and beer.
What does it ever get me? No gal will ever let me……

I'm not in a wheelchair as yet;
The backs of my ears aren't still wet.
The reason I am on the shelf---two letters tell you why;
They're not BO---you should have guessed---they are, of course,
GI. A rifle is not what my arms want to hold
I'm neither too young nor too old.
   —*AK, Cpl. Lester Asheim*

RELATED COUPLETS

I like a girl who knows
How to hold on to her beaux.

I dislike girls with an education
For the reason that they're all conversation.

Come live with me and be my love,
And baby, you know what I'm thinking of.
   —*Camp Crowder, MO, Pvt. Louis Fisher*

REASSURANCE ON THE HOME FRONT

My heart is yours and immune to theft,
Since sizing up the men who are left.
They all are old with creaking knees
And soon catch cold under apple trees.
So calm your fears, beware of the WAAC;
I belong to you till some men come back.
   —*Robins Field, GA, Sgt. E. Blackwell*

RANK INJUSTICE

My brother is a captain
In the Field Artillery.
My roommate is an ensign
On a battleship at sea.

My cousin is a major
With the big guns on the coast.
I've a pal who signs the passes
On an eastern Army post.

My friends are all commissioned,
But I never cared before
That I was just a private,
Though I've served a year or more.

But now I'm plenty troubled
And I'm deep in misery.
Last week my girl friend joined the WAACs,
Now she's a PFC.
   —*Middle East Air Force, Ray Gleason*

RANDOM THOUGHTS ON WEDLOCK

Some men wed for a widow's mite,
Some for a brief caress;
Some get caught when a sweetheart's "might"
Becomes an urgent "Yes!"

Some men marry to have an heir,
Some men marry for fun;
Some wed with but two weeks to spare,
While Papa holds a gun.

Some men like a swanky affair,
While others despise it;
Some go ahead without a care
And let time legalize it.
   —*Camp Swift, TX, T/S John W. Greenleaf*

PUTTING ON THE SQEEZE

In other days, when lace and stays
Adorned milady's torso,
She yearned to be as willowy
As Venus---only more so;
She didn't spare her derriere,
She made her clothes include it---
It may have pained to be restrained,
But, womanlike, she dood it.

Now, willowy or pillowy,
A dame is still a dame;
We men don't care what women wear,
We love them just the same.
If fashion's whim decrees them slim,
So be it---they are thin;
But thin or stout, we'll take them out
Whatever shape they're in.

But Sal and Sue are subject to
Another sort of squeeze---
They'll fret and pout and go without
Their rubber BVDs;
This war of nerves is tough on curves,
But easy on the eyes---
When we have peace, will women cease
To hide their shape and size?
   —*Camp McCain, MS, Cpl. Alex Drogichen*

POST-WAR EMPLOYMENT

There seems to be some fine hair splitting
About women working or quitting
When the war is ended and our men
Return and want their jobs again.
Some feel that he ladies, having tasted
The fruits of labor, will think wasted
The time spent parboiling hubby's stew.
I hope they're right in this point of view.
I do not plead for the status quo,
When I earned and women spent my dough.
My manly instincts might be outraged,
But I think that they could be assuaged.
I'd learn to loaf in easy stages
For a trim gal who earns good wages.
      —*Robins Field, GA, Sgt. Nathaniel Rogovoy*

PORTRAIT OF A DEBUTANTE

Surrounded by magnificence galore
She lounges on a couch and dangles
Expensive jewelry: her upturned hair
Is perched like clustered claret clouds before
The storm descends in gold and silver banners.
She wears a silk brocaded chartreuse gown;
Her lips are tipped vermillion, lashes brown;
Ah, rich her varied ornaments and manners,
She shows her richness in the stilted book
She reads, the snobby way she likes to carry
Herself; she shows it in her glassy look,
In each licentious night-club sex safari
And in the contents of her pocketbook---
She's just the kind of girl I'd like to marry.
      —*AAF, Hyde Park, NY, S/Sgt. Henry Lefer*

PERSONAL INSPECTION

His blouse was too tight
And it sagged to the right
While the collar bulged out in the back;
His trousers rode high as
They stretched on the bias,
Because of his large lower back.
Yet his sweetheart,
Miss Nashing, Cried,
"My, you look dashing."
      —*Santa Anna Army Air Base, CA, Cpl. Ray Duncan*

PASSION NOTE

The styles will change, my dear, I know,
As fashions always do.
The red nail polish you adore
Tomorrow will be blue.
You'll wear your hair tucked up, or down,
And you will probably vary
The length and cut of blouse or skirt---
Be modishly contrary.

I do not ask that styles mark time,
That you shun the latest fashion.
I only hope when I return
You'll wear the same old passion.
      —*USNTC, Bainbridge, MD, Don Marshall*

TRANSITION FLIGHT

Rocking and swaying in this steaming coach
And in a mellow mood---yes, schblitzed anew---
I feel that age-old atavism encroach
Upon me in the constant need for you.
All history is repetitious, so
From out subconscious labyrinths you float,
Like Venus, in a warm and golden glow,
To bring a strangling lump into my throat.
This primrose path with you in just a state
Of mind---sweet dalliance with my love!--- (Why, yes,
I'll have another of the same!) It's fate,
Beyond a doubt, Marie; but I confess
One poignant, bitter fact is all too clear;
I cannot woo a memory my dear!
      —*Ardmore AAB, OK, Sgt. William R. Carty*

TO THE ONLY ONE

With you, though we've not left this land,
I've traveled far and high.
I've crossed
The endless clouds of stars that fill
The cold, dark reaches of eternal space.
I've trod the sun- and wind-swept wastes
Of the Saharan plain, and have seen
True beauty in smoke-smudged towers of cities
Big and small.
And I have heard music
Where all was noise and discord once before---
Before you came.

My soul, once a philosophic configuration
Of my mind, was born full-grown

When first you crossed my way
So long ago.
 I did not realize or, Still better, was not able then
To know how to walk with head
Above the clouds that mask all reason
And all thought in every earthly striving
Toward a goal.
This you have done for me.
By being you.

And so with pen in hand I sit
And try with all the power I have
To find the words to speak for what I feel.
But those mere words cannot express such
Deep emotion. It must be felt
By one who too can see
Beyond the walls of this, our ordered life and see the
beauty of the commonplace
And hear the music where all was noise before,
And such a one are you.
—*Camp Campbell, KY, Pfc. Arnold Kirschner*

TO THE GIRL I LEFT BEHIND

Oh, I could write and say I miss you so,
That I have traveled far and never found
A rose to match the radiance of your glow;
A voice to touch the music that you sound.
Oh, I could tell the nights I have not slept
And cursed the space that kept us far apart,
And I could count the silent tears I've wept
But could not soothe the aching in my heart.
Yes, I could name the many girls I've scorned
Who held soft invitations in their eyes,
And all the sweetness lost and never mourned
Of aching tenderness and melting sighs.
Oh, I could pledge my love until eternity,
But darling what a liar I would be.
—*Chanute Field, IL, Sgt. Edward Schapiro*

TOMORROW

When the brass begins to tarnish and the gold begins to fade,
When the gabardines are wrinkled and there's dust upon the braid,
When the rosters have been posted and you've had your final say,
Will you speak to me tomorrow as you spoke to me today?

When we meet upon the corner in our customary clothes,
Will your attitude be lofty?
Will you still look down your nose?
Will you curse me as you did when in my weary steps I faltered?
Or will you speak more kindly be the circum- stances altered?

When you've made your final error and we've taken all the blame,
When we've reached civilian status, will your manner be the same?
Just what will be your thoughts when we have gone our different way?
Will you think of me tomorrow as you think of me today?

Will you still be just as quick when asked to demonstrate
    your knowledge,
Or will I do your problems when we both get back to college?
If I meet you on a dance floor or when strolling on the lawn,
Could affairs be vice versa? Will I be the one to scorn?

Perhaps we'll meet tomorrow with a slightly changed relation:
I'm sure that it will be a most amusing situation.
I'm quite convinced that it will be a most un-
pleasant day
If I think of you tomorrow as I think of you today.
—*Newfoundland, Pvt. Lauriat Lane Jr.*

THOUGHTS WHILE SITTING IN A PERS. OFFICE

Pvt. Smith, the last we heard,
To far off Bali was trfd.
And to a local Bali maid
Most marked attentions Smitty pd.

This gal was pretty. Shapely? Very!
But motives strictly mon.
She wore no stockings, wore no garters,
Was awfully bare in certain qrs.

But, suddenly w/out permission
Smith's family had a new add.
A tan and white 8-pound descendent---
A Balinese C1 A dep.

For just a moment's rec.
He shells out cash for the dur.
For he who's tempted by a beauty
Must pay for what's N L D.
—*Fort Jackson, SC, Cpl. John W. Donahey*

THOSE GALS IN OLE AUSTRALIA

When the boys came back from "Parlevous,"
They sang praises of a maiden.
She was magnish,
Their favorite dish,
Ya shoulda heard them ravin'.
For this maiden fair they named a square,
In the heart of every town.
She'd never wear,

Fair Armentieres,
For her glory was renown.
But in forty-two, a Yankee crew,
Arrived in the land down under.
They were amazed
And then left dazed
To gaze about in wonder.
The gals down there were worth a stare,
For in truth they were a wow!
And Armentieres
Could not compare
With the beauties we saw now,
The old AEF, if there's any left,
Can sing of their French tomato.
But what the hell!
We swapped mademoiselle
For those gals in Ole Australia.
— *Australia, Pfc. Jerome T. Baller*

THE WIVES

Bless the wives,
They fill the hives
With little bees and honey.

They ease life's shocks,
They mend our socks---
But don't spend the money!

When we are sick,
They heal us quick---
That is, if they should love us.
If not, we die;
And yet they cry,
And raise tombstones above us!
— *Army War College, WA, D.C., Pvt. Hayden E. Williams*

THE SOLDIER SPEAKS A RECORD TO HIS WIFE

Though, darling, we are under stars
While praying at night, the heaven there as here
Allows no margin that our thoughts can't shear.
The abyss you recognize is only hours;
And just to think the abyss is to have crossed it;
Air stirs the grass with prints of this belief.
And emptiness dies on which prescient reef---
 Ours, ours alone, because an aeon lost it---
Pulsates, is priming, like the tongue of men
(Which shapes its future answer rimmed on time,
Shapes too the interval set here in rhyme,
Itself a shape, no shape---a pen, no pen),

Where love, like prayer, will brook the chaos ever,
Quite as a song once sung is sung forever.
— *Hawaii, Cpl. Jon Beck Shank*

THE CHIEF'S LAST GOODBYE

An old chief lay on a bed of pain;
All hope had passed, his life ebbed fast,
Oh ne'er would he rise again.
"Have you no gal so fair and true,"
They whispered over his bed,
"To whom you would tell a last adieu?"

The old chief softly said,
"There's Betty back in Bremerton,
Juanita in Mexico,
There's Sally in Seattle town
And Beatrix in Bordeaux.
At Hampton roads there's Harriet,

 Whom I must surely see,
And Nellie too at Newport News;
Please bring them back to me."
The death watchers stared in wild surprise
And then they said once more
"Come tell us pray, without delay

The girl that you adore,
The girl to whom you have sworn to love
 And bring both wealth and fame,
To whom you have promised your life and hope,
Quick, chief, tell us her name!"
"There's Lilly at Long Beach," he said,

"And Daisy dear in Diego;
There's Lucy in Los Angeles
And Pauline in San Pedro,
 Barbara dear in Brooklyn,
And Susie in St. Paul."
The old Chief sighed,

"It's time I died; I've sworn to wed them all!"
— *New London, CT, From U.S. Submarine Base*

THE ARMY WAY

Call it love or something cheaper,
Call it sex or something deeper,
Tell me it's the sweetness of her face.
Say it's physical attraction,
Psychological reaction.
Tell me it's her simple, youthful grace.

Say I like the way she dresses,
Say I fell for her soft caresses,
Tell me it's the love light in her eyes.
Call it willful lust for pleasure,
Or her soul, eternal treasure,
Say it's just the fire that never dies.

Go on, ask your foolish questions,
Make your asinine suggestions,
Dwell upon her virtues by the score.
Guess what made her my selection,
How she gained my deep affection,
Tell me why I'm hers forever more.

But here's the truth, as clear as water:
My loved one is the CO's daughter.
  —*Columbia AAB, SC, Cpl. David A. Traylor*

THAT'S HOW I'M WITHOUT YOU

Like a fish without gills.
Like a nurse without pills.
That's how I'm without you.
Like a fleet without boats,
Like a song without notes,
That's how I'm without you.
Oh darling, all my success will be less.
I'll confide, I'm just a mess
When you're not by my side.
Picture war without noise.
Picture kids without toys,
That's how I'm without you.

Like a show minus girls,
Like a court without earls,
That's how I'm without you.
Like Lamour without looks,
That's how I'm without you.
Oh baby, Hedy Lamarr would be tame.
I would bet,
Compared to the thrill of that night we met.
Think of Hope without howls.
Picture guys without gals,
That's how I'm without you.
  —*Camp Bowie, TX, T-4 Jay M. Goldberg*

TELL ME SOLDIER

Tell me, soldier.
Tell me confidentially.
What it is you miss so much
While in this foreign land?
With this he knelt
And held forth in his hand
A portion of the soil of Persia.
This, he said, is much the same
As dirt in California.
And the Orontes over there
Beyond the town of Hamadan
Resembles the mighty Sierras
That I so often I have seen
From my back yard in Montebello.
And my shadow casts
The same extended sketch
Upon the ground of any nation.
And this same sun,
Artist of my shadow
Slipping through the window of my home
At dawn,
Dissolves the darkness of that night
Much the same as here.
But back there,
Near the window at breakfast time,
Illuminated by the sun,
A countenance with golden hair
Smiles across the table;
And confidentially, soldier,
It is she I miss so much.
  —*Persia, Cpl. Ralph Viggers*

WHY BOTHER?

You cloak yourself in sables,
 Wear the latest style in frocks;
A foreign male beautician
Coifs your auburn locks.
You're quite the height of fashion,
So elegantly elite;
The finest of the booter's art
Is for your dainty feet.
You want me to admire you
(At least that's what you say);
You want me to be proud of you,
Hence all this gay array.
But why bother with such fineries?
You could dispense with those,
For when I do, dear, dream of you,
You're in your birthday clothes!
  —*Camp Lee, VA, Pfc. Charles F. Kirby March*

WOMAN IN WHITE

Step up men and I'll tell you a tale
Of a vision in white and a misfortunate male.

My story begins. and that day I curse,
When I fell in love with an army nurse.

I caught my breath as she walked through the door
This marvelous maid from the Medical Corps.

My pulse increased, my blood pressure dropped
When she took my temp, the thermometer popped.

She called the doc, and a guy walked in
With a Milwaukee chest and a double chin.

He said, "My boy, you don't look well."
I lay back and grinned like an imp from hell

And looked deep into that nurse's eyes
As blue as the blue in Irish skies,

And said to the doc, "Don't call the hearse,
I'm just in love with an army nurse."

The weeks flew by, as I lay in bed
I vowed this lovely nurse I'd wed,

But little I knew that as I grew well
I was doomed to a fate far worse than hell.

For this government gal with eyes like stars
On her shoulders wore two golden bars,

While I, in the Army too, by cripes,
Was only wearin' a couple of stripes.

Oh the Navy's in training out on the lake
And a naval commander is feeding her steak;

So I curse the day she looked at me
That G.I.gal from the ANC.
—*Overseas, Cpl. John A. McAllister*

VICE VERSA

Though Kipling knew ladies and life in the East,
What he learned about women, won't help in the least.

His poem called "The Ladies" made quite a big hit, But
there's one little part that doesn't quite fit.

He said with great frankness, and no doubt was right,
"The things that you learn from the Yellow and Brown
will help you with the White."

I got along fine with a pale-faced gal I knew in my own home town,
But I can't understand (that poem failed to show) her connection with "Yellow and Brown."
—*New Guinea, Cpl. Thomas Hawkins*

THE NURSE FROM BUTTE, MONTANA

I've crossed the rivers of the earth,
The Nile, the Susquehanna;
I've roamed the seven seas, and been
From Guinea to Guiana;
I've been in a thousand towns or more
From Chungking to Savannah,
And had a girl in every town
From Fez to Texarkana;
But the prettiest girls I ever saw
Was a nurse from Butte, Montana.

Some girls have lips with the scent of spring,
And some with the taste of manna;
Some girls converse in a throaty tone,
And some in clear soprano.
Some girls are flighty, some are very calm,
And some like Zola's "Nana";
Some girls may be, like Venus, warm,
And some cold, like Diana;
But the temperature that I like best
I found in Butte, Montana.

I saw some girls in a harem, once;
I've been in a fine senana;
But my taste runs to the Occident;
I like Americana.
You can have your geisha girls, my friend,
And your brown maids from Havana---
I'll call things square, if I can get
The nurse from Butte, Montana!
—*Camp Shelby, MS, Sgt. Grant A. Sanders*

THE LAST HOUR

Give me this one hour
Alone in the silent room
With you.
Heat or the lack of any warmth
Matters not,
For the air is charged
With a fire of farewelling,
And sorrow buried
In a pile of great anger
Burns at the hidden wick
And ashes mount in the room's stillness.

Carry the hollow, hardened stones
Out into the cold of today
And they will melt into great drops
That flood my shoulder's burden
In a blinding stream.

Walk with me now
And let no murmur
Disgrace your lips
But only
Let hands clasp our message.
—*Camp Richie, MD, Pfc. Lee Richard Hayman*

WHITE LIES

Let's take a trip through Port of Spain…..
The city fair and kind;
Where every soldier from the States
Is growing color-blind.
See the damsel standing there
Whose skin's---well, rather tannish?
I asked her what she was, last night.
She answered: "Boss, Ah's Spanish!"
And see the little girl on the Square?
Say, she's a comely wench.
And if you ask her pedigree,
It's: "Honey chile, I'se French!"
And pipe the gal with the corporal there?
She has a delicate touch.
I overheard her say to him:
"Oh, Yassuh, Boss---I'se Dutch!"
And note the broad with the vacant stare?
She has such shapely knees.
She whispers low to have you know
That she'am Portuguese!
Let's venture to the Country Club
Where all the white folks meet;
Where entrance gained by soldier boys
Is quite a noted feat.
Oh, gosh! Oh, Gee! Just looky there!
Standing in the shade!
Never yet into my life
Came more attractive maid!
I steal across the velvet lawn
As softly as a kitten.
And the first darn thing I hear her say:
"Ah sho does miss Great Britain!"
And so it goes with Port of Spain……
The city fair and kind;
Where every soldier from the
States Is growing color-blind.
—*Sgt. Hardy Root*

WE LIVE TO LEARN

Did you know
We wandered today by a creek bed,
You and I,
Along a weed-entangled path?
Murmuring shade of silver elms
And drooping branches of red oak
Concealed and cooled us from the sun.
Silvered water trickled quietly.

After a while we rested
By a grass encircled spring,
Watching butterflies and ripples over rocks,
And puffs of clouds
And etched green leaves against blue sky,
And bees,
A tender breeze,
Warm and midsummer afternoon,
Toe-danced across the fields to kiss us.
In my lap you laid your head,
A piece of grass between your teeth,
"Ah," you said, "this is peace!"
And you sighed and then were silent. I said, "Yes,"
Thinking you would go to sleep,
For you were tired from our walk.

But you spoke: "We live to learn,
And thereby comes our universe,
Our wars aren't fought in vain,
By them we grow unknowingly
Into a molding whole.
This war reached out
Encompassing all lands
And people we never thought of.
We touched them with our culture.
It, too, will flower from this

With tolerance, perhaps,
Born out of understanding
That association brought us."

I listened quietly,
And watched your face.

You closed your eyes.
"Death can't take our life away It is here---
With you, with me, with love," you said.
And I believed you.
    —*Fort Des Moines, IA, Pvt. Judith Bridge*

WAIT

Think not too much, just now, of me
Nor dwell too long on what has been
Or is to be,
But, darling, teach your heart to wait and hunger not.
The days are long that
I'll be long away,
And longer still the nights when memories will mock
Your every thought and silence will enclose you
In its tomb.

Sweet longings for the days to come
Will not conceive, nor nurture them to life.
And memories that are to be
May not be worth the memories that are;
So trust them not.
Be free of all that is, or was, or is to be.
Be patient, and instruct your heart to wait,
My love;
Think not too much, just now, of me.
    —*USMA, West Point, NY, Cpl. Thomas C. Carrol*

"Hey, catch!"

Section Four
Humorous Poems

AT EASE!

There's a sergeant out our way,
Where the dot and dashes play
And the spread antennae hum like bumble bees,
Who, when it's time for class, sir,
He's our own G.I. professor
When he says, and boys, he means,
"By gad, AT EASE!"

"Now, this here's a generator,
That'n there's an oscillator. . . "
"Sarge, at what potential will it bat the breeze?
What's its tonal variation?
How does sun spot infiltration. . ."
The sergeant scowls, he means,
"By gad, AT EASE!"

"What equation of resistance?"
Ask the student with insistence,
Punctuating with North Carolina wheeze,
"Haven't you the least propensity
To compute the gaseous density. . .?
The sergeant booms, "I said,
"By gad, AT EASE!"

"But in gases radioactive
Seen through spectroscopes refractive
Like we worked on in physics lab'rat'ries."
"Say, d'ya wanta teach this class?
If ya do, get off yer seat!
Now I said, and' by gad I mean, I said, AT EASE!"

Well, at last the day is done,
And the honey-dripping sun
Is sinking fast behind the gilded trees;
Stand retreat, chow, movie---bed!
Get my pillow 'neath my head;
I say, and by gad I mean, Sarge, I'm at ease.
    —*Casual Det. OCS, Fort Sill, OK,*
      Cpl. Edward M. Bershtein

A SAD SACK'S LAMENT

How happy they who 'mid life's toil and strain,
Can sit and chug-a-lug a dozen beers,
Can get themselves so fried they feel no pain
And leave their woes behind them like the years.
For these, the chosen few, life holds no dread,
For they can drown their sorrows in their wine,
Can get themselves well oiled and go to bed
And wake up three days later feeling fine.

For me, there is no peace in Baccus' cup,
No thrill in pouring down those potent brews.
I take a drink and promptly flash it up;
In short, I find that I can't hold my booze.
And so, when I feel low and need a shot,
My motto's "Pepsi-Cola hits the spot."
—*Columbia Army Air Base, SC, Cpl. David Traylor*

ARMY TIMEPIECE

Dear Mom: Your letter was a welcome lift
But do not send the watch you plan to buy,
Betimes it would have made a useful gift,
But that was in civilian days gone by.
Now time has lost its urgency, and so
I need no watch to mark what hour's fled.
There is a gift that you might send me, though:
Please send a pocket calendar, instead.
—*Herbert Smart Airport, GA, Cpl. Nathaniel Rogovoy*

A RESERVED SEAT

A soldier at the pearly gates,
With face quite worn and old,
Meekly asked the man of fate
For admission to his fold.

"What have you done," said St. Peter,
"To gain admission here?"
"I was in Company L, 129,"
Said the soldier, drawing near.

The gates swung sharply open,
St. Peter rang a bell.
"Come in," said he,
"Take up your harp,
You've had enough of hell."

There were beautiful angels everywhere;
His peace had come at last.
Then thought he,
"My company---
I'll get them all a pass."

So he turned to old St. Peter,
Saying, "sir, could one more favor be mine?"
May I reserve this area for
Company L,
The pride of 129?"
—*South Pacific, Pvt. Carl Grabig*

BULLY BEEF

Far beyond the broad blue ocean
There's a land of heat and damp
Where the forbidding jungle
Starts just at the edge of camp.
It's a land of many scourges---
Ants, mosquitoes, jungle rot---
And 'twas there I got acquainted
With the worst scourge of the lot.

You can boil it, stew it, fry it,
Serve it cold or piping hot;
You can mix it with the gravy,
You can leave it there to rot;
But however you may fix it
You will always come to grief,
For no matter what you call it
It will still be bully beef.

You can talk about your Frenchmen
Eating slimy snails and frogs;
You can mention dusky natives
Frying crickets, roasting dogs;
But the most repulsive foodstuff
That exists on land or sea
Is the tough and stringy canned meat
Which the Army feeds to me.

You can eat it with your eyes shut
And a clothespin on your nose;
You can eat it in a mess hall
Or out where the *kunai* grows;
You can serve it up in dishes
Camouflaged beyond belief.
But no matter what you call it
It will still be bully beef.
—*New Guinea, Pfc. Jacob Richardson*

BEER RATION IN NEW GUINEA

Dig your ice box, Make your plans,
Drink your beer, Smash your cans. Go to bed
In a mellow haze.
Wait another Thirty days.
—*New Guinea, Pvt. Jack H. Steinmann*

BEEP PEEP THE JEEP

A jeep is a beep is a peep
That runs with a kangaroo leap.
It hops in a bound
Six feet off the ground,
That jittering jiving jeep.
Many's the obstacle course
Not run by man or by horse.
The jeep without wheeze
Takes each in a breeze,
To only the driver's remorse.
There's nary a job jeeps shirk;
They'll work like creatures berserk.
Their big job I guess
Is giving the press
Some news when the censor's at work.
—*Huntsville Rec. Area, AL, Sgt. George P. Johnston*

BED CHECK

The first time I get bed check,
I find it's quite a bother;
I'm pacing hard the latrine floor
And worrying like a mother.

"Where are my blund'ring boys tonight?"
Oh, wild I am with woe
They must be in by 12 tonight
Or down their names must go.

What must my mother have gone through
When she'd wait up for this lout.
Alack! I know now how she felt
On her jaunts to bail me out.

Eleven o'clock and all's not good---
There's 20 bunks still empty.
I'm pacing hard the latrine floor
(Ahboomp, ahbimpety, bempety!)

Eleven-thirty and what do you think?
There's only one guy missing!
If he's not in by 12 tonight,
His name will be listing.

He'll get some extra duty sure---
They'll make it tough for him!
With a half hour more to go,
He'd best start coming in!

"He'd best start coming in,"
I muse. "One empty bunk, by heck!
One empty bunk, one empty bunk,
One empty bunk to check."

I'm pacing hard the latrine floor
While sleep is on me creeping;
I sit me on a latrine bowl---
And bye and bye I'm sleeping!

The blasted bugle wakes me up,
The latrine's bright with shine.
More to my woe I later find---
That empty bunk was mine!
—*Camp White, OR, Leonard Guardino*

BALLAD OF PVT. JEEP

At last the fateful day arrived,
The weather was clear and fine,
And John J. Jeep his rifle grasped
Right on the firing line.

"Ready on the right, ready on the left,"
And the flag began to sway.
The Jeep felt glad as he saw the flag
Only 200 yards away.

"Call your shots," his coach cried out
As John his piece did raise;
The flag is up, the flag is down,
And the Jeep began to blaze.

His first shot killed a pigeon,
His second struck a crow,
And down in the pits, watching for hits,
Were the markers lying low.

As his rifle roared, his scorer snored,
But the Jeep kept right on firing,
Fifty shots without a hit,
And he showed no signs of tiring.

The captain snarled and gnashed his teeth
As he watched how the dirt would spurt
For the shots that didn't explode in the sky
Were sure to go off in the dirt.

When the Jeep withdrew as the whistle blew,
You could hear the officers rave,
For instead of a 5, or a 4, or a 3,
They saw nothing but red flags wave.
When pressed for an explanation,
The reason for his flaws,
The Jeep would only answer

He wanted to see Maggie's drawers.

They threw him in the guardhouse,
But he uttered never a peep,
For what could you expect from a horse's neck
With a name like John J. Jeep.
　　　　—*Camp Davis, NC, Sgt. Stuart Gray*

BALLAD FOR BEATING THE CENSOR

I feed my horse bran.
On shipboard I spit a-lee,
Disembarked at_
And then went to_____.

The girls shun brassieres,
The trees aren't maples;
Took off from__
And landed in__.

Now, where to from here?
It's a cinch it's not home---
Not for some months, I fear---
But it's not bad in_____.

And our final spot
(Just take it from Harris)
Is now pretty hot,
But we'll love it in_____.
　　　　—*Italy, Pvt. Burt Harris*

BACK TALK

Indulge your rash impulse to row
With brass—say nothing clever;
 "You may be a second looey now,
But his war won't last forever!"

Show your top-kick who's in charge
The worst, most so-and-so one
Gives in to; "Just---a minute sarge,
 I don't take that from no one!"

You'll never know what you've been missin'
(Fun which ends in blissful stupors)
Until you've countered with;
"Say, lissen Just because you're paratroopers………."
　　　　—*Fort George Meade, MD T-4 Willis Conover*

A VET'S LAMENT

I've had eight weeks of training
As a Army first –aid man.
I've learned to drill with bandages
And mastered a bedpan.

The treatment of a gas attack,
They drummed into my head,
And how to save a bloody mess
And how to mark the dead.

I've drilled in close formation,
And I've stood my trick at guard;
Most of it was simple,
But some of it was hard.

And when they taught me all they knew
Of treating injured men,
They packed me off to Washington
To go to school again.

For 12 long weeks I sweated through
The veterinary course;
Instead of first aid to a man,
I learned first aid to a horse.

The Army Veterinary School
Will teach a man to tell
The quality of sides of beef,
Simply by smell.

They gave us our diplomas
On our graduation day,
But they gypped us of our furloughs
And sent us on our way.

To a land, they say, that God forgot,
Where sidewalks are a path,
Where the Okies tramp barefooted
On the sour "Grapes of Wrath."

So, I'm here at old Fort Reno,
My diploma packed away;
When I'm not feeding horses,
I'm shoveling it away.

Here's to the U.S. Army
And to all the Army schools;
But damn the man who sent me here.
To wrestle crazy mules.
　　　　—*Fort Reno, OK, Pvt. M.K. Lynds*

ALWAYS A FIRST-CLASS PRIVATE---NEVER A PRIVATE FIRST CLASS

He struggled and sweated through basic,
Taking the worst that they had.
He mastered the gas, grenades and the rest,
And his record on guns wasn't bad
(But the damned galoot never learned to salute,
So promotion he never had).

In Europe our man was splendid:
His record for Nazis was high;
He got every medal for valor,
Was really a rugged guy
(Yet the stupid boor never learned to say "sir,"
So ratings all passed him by.)

At home they gave him a party---
The mayor and some of the crowd.
He even inspired the workers,
And the babes around him were proud
(But I must admit, his clothes didn't fit---
Promotion for him: Disallowed).

He was always a first-class private,
Never a private first class.
He had a way with an engine
And he knew his guns and his gas
(But he never could get Army etiquette---
He remains a private, buck-ass).
—Camp Gruber, OK, Cpl. Jack C. Bell

AR 615-26

Oh, they've got a little index in the Army,
And it's known as AR 615-26.
It's the damndest little index in the Army,
The very brightest thing in Army tricks.
There's the nicest little number just for you lad---
The kind you'll get in heaven when you die.
It stands for all the things you did back yonder
Before the good Lord branded you G.I.

Now take the case of Elmer Jones, embalmer---
079, that's him! And what is more,
He's counting packing boxes at the freighthouse,
Assigned and joined, the Quartermaster Corps.
Or maybe it's Sylvester Oats, the lucky barn boss, 210,
they call him now, the lucky guy!
He types endorsements for the CCO
And hopes to be file clerk by and by.

While Horace Whimperwell, the erstwhile poet,
Who charmed New York with neat and naughty fables,
Was indexed 288, and promptly sent
To GHQ to tend the general's stables.
Oh, they've got a little index in the Army,
But believe me, boys, the damned thing's all in fun,
For they put you where they want you in the
Army, And they want you most of all behind a gun!
—Fort Douglas, Utah, Pvt. Charles Todd

A SAGA OF THE RUGGED NORTH

"You are aging, Sgt. Williams," the corporal said,
"And your hair has become very white;
What's more, you incessantly stand on your head---
Do you think that your mind is quite right?"

"You are new to this Alaskan land,"
The sarge was heard to state.
"Another year and you'll understand
That I'm bucking for Section Eight.

"You are aging," said the lad, "as I mentioned before,
And have circles under your eye;
And you turned a back somersault in at the door---
Pray, woudst explain to me why?"

"In the States." quoth the sarge, as he flipped his slack lip,
I oft would go out on a date;
Two years have passed since I saw a svelte hip,
And I'm for Section Eight."

"Thou hast stripes," mused the boy, "so one would deem
As wise as the law alloweth;
Yet you stumble about as if in a dream,
And sometimes froth at the mouth."

"Ere the war," said the sarge, "a tippler was I,
With a taste for whiskey straight;
Now two arid years have passed me by,
And I'm prime for Section Eight."
—Alaska Pfc., Wilfred L. Andes

A PRAYER TO ST. BARBARA

Please, St. Barbara,
If you can,
Make me again
An Artillery man.

Make me a guy
Who eats greasy chow,

Who pushes around
The end of a How.

Put me on a hill
And I'll be the dope
Who squints all day
Through the end of a scope.

Let me ride in the rain,
Let me ride in the dark,
And I'll not complain;
Just let the guns bark.

Let me hear once again
As I wade in the dew,
"Cease fire! Close station!
March order! We're through."

At any rate
Let me be
Anything else
But a___MP.
—*Fort Du Pont, DE, 1ˢᵗ Lt. Ellsworth A. Warner*

AN UPTON GRADUATE

Two months I spent at Upton.
With basic I am through;
My major letters I have won,
I wear the old C.U.

I learned to drill at Upton.
I'm trained to kill the Hun.
But ain't it sort of funny
I never shot a gun?

At right flank march I'm snappy.
Close drill to me's a trifle,
But why is it at Upton
You never saw a rifle?

Duck walk and boxing I had,
Six weeks without surcease;
You lug a gun at Upton,
But never shoot the piece.

I f I am sent to battle
And some foe tries to kill me,
I'll point my gun and shout "Bam! Bam!"
If he ain't dead I will be.
—*Pvt. Jim Burchard*

A MINOR POINT, PLURAL

Texas women are fair and lovely wenches,
To deny that I wouldn't dare;
But, alas, there is a minor flaw:
Their chests! There just ain't anything there.

Texas women are like Sammie Brand
(The lad that's penning this rhyme).
Yes, we're alike in one respect:
Flat---busted all the time.
—*Randolph Field, TX, Pvt. Sammie Brand*

ALOYSISUS

A loud rookie by name Aloysisus,
To his sergeant, who that day fell vysius,
Bragged he'd only be seen
In a job that was clean;
So he spent the whole week scrubbing dysius.
—*Army Flying School, Marianna, FL, T/3 Abraham Stern*

AFTER KP

Here's to our first cook---
May he writhe in pain.
May he hang himself
On his dog-tag chain.

May his GI shoes Stick to his feet.
May his arms drop off
As he stands retreat.

May his sun-tans tear
While he cooks the peas.
May the moths consume
His best ODs.

May he drink the tea
That he serves, I hope.
May the cup be full
Of GI soap.

Let him be confined
With a smokers cough.
Let him serve 12 meals
On his Sunday off.

May he scar his throat
On his daily steak.
May it be his arms
When he takes a break.

poems are made
By fools like me.
But let me have
Him on KP.
    —*Camp Murphy, FL, Pfc. E. Klavan*

A BROTHER'S COMPLAINT

Sis is going with a sailor,
At first it didn't faze us;
But now the family's talk is full
Of sailor's salty phrases.
We found it rather hard at first
To follow his speech,
Since talk is different on board ship
Than it is "on the beach."
When talking during dinner,
He talks like other boys;
Except he calls the lettuce "grass,"
And celery just plain "noise."
His "salty" talk is slangy,
And hard to understand;
He calls the canned milk "iron cow,"
And sugar he calls "sand."
The spinach he calls "Popeye,"
And Grandma always squirms
For when we have spaghetti,
He says, "Throw me the worms."
He sat beside my father,
And needed elbow room;
He looked at dad and said:
"Say, Mate,
Rig in your starboard boom."
We finally caught on, though,
And now are doing fine;
We say "six bells" for 3 oclock
When we are telling time.
When Ma goes to the city,
Or runs down to the store,
And someone asks us where she is,
We say she's "gone ashore."
Sister call a floor a "deck,"
To hear her talk is sport;
To her, a roof's and "overhead,"
A window is a "port."
Then, too, if someone gets "fouled up,"
Or some new trouble comes;
And Dad starts to complain,
Ma says:
"Now, Pa, don't beat your gums."
When pappy goes to work just now,
We say he's "turning to";
Whilst Mother "swabs" and never scrubs,
As she used to do.
The place sure has gone salty,
Which makes me lots of trouble,
For when Ma says,
"Come here, 'chop-chop',"
 I go there---"on the double."
I wish that "tar" would "weigh his anchor,"
And do what I oft' think;
"Point his bow" and "trim his jib,"
And go jump in the 'drink."
    —*The Bulldozer Camp Endicott, R. I., USN*
     Training Center

THE PRIVATE'S LAMENT

There is a tavern in the town
(In the town),
Most plainly posted out of bounds
(Out of bounds)
Where grim MPs with arm band, mace and sneer
Search longingly for privates drinking beer.

CHORUS

Good-by, likker, I must have thee,
Sadly though the parting grieve me.
For authority has left no place where we can meet.
Adieu, vermouth and vodka, too.
(Yes, adieu),
I cannot take my cheer with you
(Cheer with you),
The only places left for likes of me
Serve coffee, soda pop and sometimes tea.

Although I walk the street all day
(Walk all day),
There's no place I can blow my pay
(Blow my pay),
All joints are labeled
"Officers Only Here",
Go elsewhere, elsewhere, private for your beer.
    —*Middle East, Stars and Stripes*

LATE TO RETREAT

Those aches and cares that torment me,
How small beside eternity!
The eyes that looked through time with fate
No longer frown, 10 minutes late:
The mind that traveled far-flung space

Can disregard a yard-lost race.
Or so it almost seemed to me,
Immersed in grave philosophy,
Until I woke to a sergeant's glare
And now potatoes sadly pare.
—*Fort Warren, WY, Pvt. Roland A. White*

TO AN ARMY STEAK

Oh Army steak, I somehow feel
You ought to be more ample;
Are you sure they meant you for a meal?
You look so like a sample.

And if by chances you should be shunned,
Take heart and do not sorrow;
Like Phoenix you shall rise again;
You'll be croquettes tomorrow.
—*Oakland Fighter Command, CA,*
Cpl. Thomas W. Kraseman

ARMY CLASSIFICATIONS

Case No. 1

He was a lad who was never at peace
Unless he was covered with oil and with grease.
He loved taking motors and engines apart,
Just a twist of his hand---presto, they'd start;
Motors diminutive, motors titanic,
The one wasn't built that could phase this mechanic.

At classification he took every test
To find just the job that he could fill best;
Though with paper and pencil he proved quite a jerk,
The Army just rated him company clerk.

Case No. 2

He was one of those cultured and literate birds
Who always used polysyllabical words;
A wizard at math, and ace at logistics,
He could juggle and balance the most subtle statistics.
Though an expert on Shakespeare and Einstein and Freud,
On motors and engines his mind was void.

Now after a battery of test after test, IQ and aptitude and all of the rest,
The Army decided his gargantuan brain
Was best fitted for greasing a truck or a plane.
—*Charleston AAB, SC, Cpl. Carl Fenichel*

GI DAYDREAM

I sat upon a lonely knoll and looked up at the sky,
Where shapes of clouds took on forms of those that never die;
There fierce-eyed Zarathrustra stalked, and yonder was his cave,
 And all the gods of Homer walked with Wagner's mighty brave.
While high on fancied Pyrenees stood Roland calm and sure,
With trumpet and brave Oliver to meet the treacherous Moor.
But I ask you to envisage my displeasure if you can
When I saw midst all those faces my drill sergeant's saintly pan.
—*AAB, Sioux Falls, SD, Pfc. Bernard Kaplan*

NOISE

I can take the quake
That dive bombers make
When they blast the earth to hell;
I can steady my ear
To the sounds others fear of torpedo and mine and shell;
I never lose poise
At the loudest of noise
That 's thrown at a soldier of war;
But I'm driven insane
By that frightening strain
When a barracks mate starts to snore.
—*AAB, Charleston, SC, Cpl. Carl Fenichel*

THE SAVAGE BREAST, PIANISSIMO

(A professor in Denver has condemned the army's reveille because psychologically, the bugle is all wrong, and advocates a change to something in waltz tempo on the violin.---News Item)

The bugle blows too harsh a note
From blaring, brassy, shrilling throat;
Than thus to jar the boys each morn
With rasping toot of army horn.
Far better 'twere to substitute
A soothing violin to suit
The sleepy mood of reveille;
And while you take such liberty
With old tradition, so brass-bound,
Why not thus soften all the sound?

Select the sergeants for the croon
With which they call the army's tune
And let the KP publisher try
His larynx at a lullaby;
Adjust the cadence as we roam
To dulcet sweep of metronome.
Then tune the bombers deadly roar
To key of C, symphonic score;
The same for rifles, cannons too,
And leave out all the notes of blue.

This army life does have its faults---
Perhaps it ought to be a waltz;
So send us men to lead in tones
Of soft, caressing baritones.
Then when I lay me down to sleep,
Be it foxhole, inches deep.
Send me a noncom just to croon
A tuck-me-in, sweet good-night tune;
Insert the perforated score,
Piano player's song *d'amour*
Into machine gun's off-key bark
And play "M1, Hark Hark, the Lark!"

If we must have such things of war,
Let's harmonize it in three-four;
O sweep the barracks fox-trot time
And issue bulletins in rhyme;
Revise the uniforms to pink,
Put perfume in the GI ink
And fear no foeman's waiting breath---
They're sure to laugh themselves to death.
—*Fort Warren, WY, Pvt. Roland A. White*

TOO MANY POINTS?

Be-dewed, be-dipped, befuddled and be-beered,
I sit here thinking, absent love, of thee
In idioms in which I have been reared---
The ultimate in numb civility.
When in recorded time did that evoke
The slightest trace of a responsive fire?
What could such rheumy romance do but choke,
Before its birth, the wellspring of desire?
Ah, devil a heart was ever won this way,
And devil a heart by verses such as these.
So, slowly I bestir my maudlin clay
And drain my glass down to its very lees.
Then in the dregs I see your face a-glow:
I say, "You ought to diet, sweet, you know."
—*Ephrata AAB, WA, Sgt. William R. Carty*

AS HOLLYWOOD WOULD TYPE ME

I'm a cussin', swearin',
Rip and tearin',
Mean and vicious hound,
Just a two-fist slammin',
Bangin', damnin'
Filthy bag of sound:
I'm a bottle-clinker,
All day drinker,
Soaked in gin and rum;
I'm a hot and boilin',
Dame despoilin',
Lewd and lecherous bum;
I'm a low IQer,
A smutty sewer,
The Army's Si Legree;
I'm a rortin', snortin',
Hell-cavortin',
Dem and deezer,
Guzzling geezer,
Soldier-hatin',
GI satan,
Son of a b-------that's me!
Special Order No. 261 just made me a sergeant.
—*AAB, Charleston, SC, Pfc. Carl Fenichel*

ORDERS OF THE DAY

(News item: American soldiers must not speak to Moslem women.)
Order: Yanks at Casablanca
Will commit no hanka-panka.
Order: In far-off Oahu
There must be no *tohu-bohu*.
Soldiers shall not shilly-shally
As the drive the Japs past Bali.
Even along the quiet Rancocas
Orders are: no hokus-pokus.
Other restriction, fella, follow
For men who hail from Walla Walla.
—*1st Decontamination Unit, Pfc. Y. Guy Owen*

ON RECEIVING A LETTER FROM YANK

Some happy day when I return
To civilization, I'm going to burn
The cubbyhole that houses Yank
And turn the place into a blank---
With hand grenades and Lewisite,
And bayonets and dynamite;
But first of all I'll strangle the drip
Who sent me that rejection slip!
—*FPO, San Francisco, CA, Meredith Ray Davis*

ONLY THE BRAVE

With bayonets they tortured him,
They tied him to a tree,
Hot coals they placed beneath his feet,
And pulled his fingernails free.
They hung him up, just by his thumbs,
His brow was damp with sweat,
But he refused to tell them where
He'd hidden his cigarettes.
—*Britain, Pfc. Albert Dellinger*

ODE TO OD

No more we'll hail our snowy undies
Hanging from our lines on Mondays.

Farewell to doughboys clad in white
Shirts and shorts; they're much too light.

Now olive drab will camouflage
Us from the enemy's barrage.

So proudly hail our OD undies
Hanging from our lines on Mondays.
—*HQ VII Air Corps, Jacksonville, FL, Sgt. Jack Harig*

OBITUARY

Under a friendly tavern spigot
Lay out my grave and write my ticket.
My life was raw but always cricket
And Bacchus my partner and guide.

This is the verse that you grave for me:
"Here lies a GI where he longs to be
With a flask on his hip and a blonde on his knee
And a quart of shellac in his hide."
—*Camp Gordon Johnston, FL, S Sgt. Franklin M. Willment*

NOSE, MEET ARMY

Since I've entered into service
Various odors haunt my days,
Wafting through my little tent flap
With each vagrant breeze that plays.

At one end of our battalion
Breathes a sump pit, dour and dank.
If the wind should change it brings me
Burning garbage, just as rank.

Just before the tar-clad warehouse
Where our company street ends,
Flies commune about some shacking
That the very air offends.

One thing, Army, one thing only
Makes this life not bad to bear.
It's my tried and trusty gas-mask,
Built for twenty-four-hour wear.
—*Pvt. Al Hine*

NOMENCLATURE OF AAF DETAIL

Guys in the Air Force no longer are Joes
We're mess attendants, as everyone knows;
Though we peel and we scrub like other GIs,
We're mess attendants who fly through the skies.

Infantry, Cavalry, Artillery men
Wind up on KP again and again,
But we in the air Force, though we don't get it less,
Are perfumed and polished *attendants de mess*.

And while we are at it, we may as well blush,
Our latrine orderlies are *attendants de flush*.
—*Lowry Field, CO, Pvt. Charles Lehman*

NOISY YARDBIRDS

It's 9 o'clock and all is well,
The lights are out—so now I'll tell
Of the queerest noises in the night
That come from characters on my left and right.

The wheezers wheeze their sad refrain,
The burpers burp and relieve a pain,
One overnight guest lets out a yell,
Another yardbird cries, "This is hell."
Never again will I go AWOL,

A dogface on my left gives forth a moan,
Awake with insomnia I let out a groan,
The guys with asthma pant and gasp,
Another yardbird's cough sounds like a rasp.

They touch my heart, they're yardbirds in pain;
When you think they're through they start again.
I murmur, low and deep,
"Shut up, dammit; let me sleep."
—*Nashville, TN, A/C Ira Katzman*

NIGHT BEFORE CHRISTMAS

'Twas the night before Christmas, and all through the pads,
King Kong and sweet reefers were all the cats had.
Their boots were laced, they were really in there,
So far hipped, St. Nick was no where.

Then out of the dark, ole Santa fell in,
Adrape at the front, pegged tight as skin;
He was tagged this time in some hard-cuttin' brown
And the glare from his konk brought all the cats down.

When he fell to his benders and opened his sack,
The glitter and glamor drove all the cats back.
The old hipster rose, with his gauge brewing hot,
And the cats came on: "Hip us, Santa, just what ya got."

"Shuck all cases, and 'step on a snake,'
Never, ole boy, give a square lane a break!
When your gauge is low and you think it won't last
Just as I do---blast, man, blast.
Now, my story is fine and you'll agree
There isn't a stud that's quite hip as me,
Frilly is my play, now take it slow---
Skin me once, ole man, and rut 'Let go!'"
With these hip words, he can't thin this slammer,
And that's the last the cat's dug ole Santa.
—*Australia, Pvt. S. Feinberg*

MY FRIEND GARAND

I'm told the rifle is a man's best friend,
To have and hold until the bitter end.
The dog was once the only candidate
That you could count on to protect your fate.
But now it seems my rifle is to be
My dog, my confident, my family.
My rifle is a friend, I must agree,
But how it could bake pies I cannot see---

The sergeant told me if I had to choose
Twixt mother and my rifle that she'd lose.
Now lately I've been spending much time thinking,
Just when my rifle might prevent my drinking.
—*Pfc. John Hay*

MY FOUR-FOOTED FRIENDS

I had a little horse
And his name was Chief,
But now he's on the menu
As barbecued beef.

I had another little pony
And his name was Sam,
But now he's disguised
As sugar-cured ham.

So it's ashes to ashes,
Dust to dust;
If the glue factory didn't get them,
Then the butcher must.
—*Morrison field, FL., T/Sgt. Richard K. Greene*

MY FAVORITE PATIENT

"Ward boy!" he shouts (I'm his personal maid),
And his voice is annoyingly firm;
He's a tyrant accustomed to being obeyed,
And he gloatingly watches me squirm.

His is the cry that revulsively near
I must heed in my subjugate state---
Slave to those pills with pain in his ear
Who is green from some pickles he ate.

It's never the boy with the real Purple Heart
Who's demanding his pie with ice cream;
It is always this desk-calloused little upstart
Who comes out with that insistent scream.

Simon Legree with his whip and his hounds
I'd forgive and invite to have tea,
Only I wish I could fight twenty rounds
With this guy who shouts "Ward boy!" at me.
—*Cushing General Hospital, MS, Sgt. James Rice*

MOTHER GOOSE, 1942

Rock-a-bye Troopship
On the wave's top.
When the surf rolls
The Troopship will rock;
When the surf breaks
The Troopship will fall
And up will come breakfast,
Dinner, and all.
    —*Australia, Pfc. Dan Laurence*

MONDAY MORNING TYPIST

UGly little gremlins wonLt you goawzy/
Monday istn' like Ab ordinary daay.

I s aw you move tge wpace bar
And jjam those keus besides.
Ufly lirtl grimlens
Damn yoru little hides!

Beat it, scram, bwfore mi
Fingers starrt to itch
To tear you ilmb frlm lmib---
Oh, You goffzj)#(-*%"&'$#?
    —*Turner Field, GA, Pvt. Robert D. Nesbitt*

MEMO TO A MEAT PACKER

Oh, stop to think while on your way
To rake in GI cash,
That soldiers up Alaska way
Get awful tired of hash.

I've eaten lots of funny things
For breakfast, lunch and dinner,
But never thought I'd fill my gut
With last year's Derby winner.

Do you eat all the steaks yourself.
Or are you really slipping,
That you must send us frozen swill
And second-handed drippings?

You have us where you want us now,
In spite of our digestion.
We have to eat the stuff you sell,
But let me ask one question:

Just what would happen to your dough
If the GI proletarian,
When he gets back, should in revenge
Go all-out vegetarian?
So think of that before you pack
More hash for ocean crossage;
Try sending us some real chow,
And less Vienna sausage.
    —*Somewhere in Alaska, Pvt. Raymond E. Lee*

ME GUSTIBUS

I like the old field rations,
I honestly do,
With unaccountable passions
For salads and stew;
There's a tang in a ham hock,
A thrill in smoked butts. . . .
Hey! Don't go away, doc,
I'll convince you I'm Nuts.
    —*Gowen Field, ID, Pfc. Irving Kraut*

MAIL CALL

This is something worth writing a poem about,
This is something big with a capital B,
This is laughter and death,
Sorrow and joy, misery and ecstasy.

This is everything that life is,
Plus something like a miracle.
This is all the poetry in the world---
Yes, and all the music too---

Carefully folded up in odd-sized envelopes
And handed out with a heart-jumping yell;
"Atkinson! Balubowitz! Kelly!
Jones! Johnson! Schwartz!---
Every name called,
And every name conspicuously not called.
A poem.

Yes, by God, a real poem,
Try this:
Melt all that poetry that ever was
In one great sum of metric beauty
Go ahead.
It won't hold a candle to this.
This bright thing,
This magic paper,
Unbelievably touched by known hands.
    —*India, Pfc. John R. Cook*

GZCRZCHIEWSKI

I'm in this man's army
At least tow mont's more.
I met a lot of fellas
That I never knowed before.
I call them Jones and Murphy,
And Cohn as' Antoinette;
Yet all them guys what knows me,
My name the just forget.
Gzerzchiewski.

Now what's wrong wit' those fellas,
Ain't they never was to school?
Or can't they read plain writin';
Or are they just plain fool?
Now I pernounce Jones Jonesie,
And I pernounce Smelt Smelt,
Yet they never get my name right
And it reads just like it's spelt,
Czrzchiewski.

But get us on the drill field.
Th' whole thing's mighty strange.
Cause every thing is dif'runt,
An' wat a funny change,
If some one's out of step or line,
If some thing goes wrong,
You hear them pack of non-coms
Sing out in one loud song,
Gzcrzchiewski.

There's plenty of K.P. detail,
And plenty soldiers too.
There's guardin' and there's garbage,
Boy, there's plenty work to do.
Each night that topkick sarjint
Makes out the next day list.
He never can pernounce it
But yet he never missed
Gzcrzchiewski.

Some soldiers crave for womans,
An' others for their pay;
Some guys want just be sarjint,
An' some to ship away.

Now me, I don't like vodka,
Or cards or any game.
I have just one big longing
It's just to change my name
To Smith.
—*Pvt. Harry Hemmendinger*

GREENLAND'S WOE

We sat on our bunk
In a blue sort of funk
(It was only our second night here).
For someone had said
With a shake of his head,
"Like I say, there's no women or beer."

"No women?" we said
With our eyes growing red
From tears and a horrible fear.
"Yep, it's all true enough
And sounds pretty tough,
But there just ain't no women or beer."

So it's a sad sort of thing---
Maybe someone can sing
And maybe somebody's conscience is clear---
But Greenland will be run
And the war will be won
Without the help of a woman or beer.
—*Greenland, Cpl. John Fisher*

GO AHEAD, TRY TO INFECT ME

Oh, whiskey is a potent brew,
A virile alcoholic dew;
It does amazing things to you,
A snifter or a shot.

But shots of corn are not as rough
As shots of certain other stuff.
Oh, please dear Lord, I've had enough;
My arms have gone to pot.

An ultimate in brutal crime:
My record's lost the seventh time!
The viruses within me climb.
They've got me on the spot!

Go ahead, try to infect me.

With typhus I'm on friendly terms,
I'm intimate with smallpox germs,
My corpuscle in anger squirms---
It's jealous like as not.
Oh, gentlemen, in pity view,
An antipathogenic stew,
An antiseptic sot.
—*Robbins Field, GA, Cpl. Sheldon Harnick*

GPLD

One thing, sir, has puzzled me;
Who washes clothes in your laundry?
Be it pixie, brownie, witch or elf---
Some bandit gang? I ask myself.

I stack my clothes on Tuesday night,
Recheck my list to make it right.
I tell you, sir, I truly try,
And then---I kiss the bag goodbye.

Time passes. . . .two weeks, say
And then arrives one happy day.
My luck has turned, the world's not black---
I miss KP, my laundry's back.

But then, snafu! I grunt a groan.
Are these the goods I once did own?
Are these the clothes worth so much pelf?
Are these the socks I darned myself?

What vandal's inked such hellish blots?
What trickster's tied such fiendish knots?
Were bottoms smashed in moron's fits?
Who chewed my shirt to little bits?

Laundry folks are not like rabbits.
Producing's not among their habits.
Reduction seems more in their line.
They mark the loss with a careless sign.

I cry my grief to sergeant stony.
I plead and sob; he snarls, "Bologna!"
Who donnit? is the question posed.
My clothes are gone. The case is closed.

My Christmas wants are truly frugal.
Don't need a gun. Don't want a bugle.
And since rich gifts I cannot hoard,
Please send me an old washboard.
  —*Fort Jackson, SC, Cpl. Thomas E. Sayles*

G.I. SOAP

Oh, G.I, soap, of thee I sing,
You're chemically an awesome thing:
Concerning you my thoughts are rife,
You dominate my G.I. life.

You take the grime from barracks floors,
You shrink my long, gray woolen drawers,
You peel the grease from pots and pans,
And chew the skin right off my hands.

You eat holes in my cotton jeans,
You sanitize G.I. latrines,
You're in my hair, my clothes, and now,
I even taste you in the chow.

Your powers of destruction seem
The answer to a chemist's dream.
You look as though you're meant to be
Just soap. Inside, you're TNT.

The War Department isn't wise
To waste time on inventive guys,
All G.I. soldiers have the dope.
Our secret weapon's G.I. soap!
  —*Fort Devens, MA, S/Sgt. S.E. Whitman*

G. I. NURSERY RHYME

Little Miss Muffet sat on a tuffett,
eating her curds and whey;
Along came a soldier
and looked at her bolder
Than any youth of her day.

She put down her sandwich,
and in plain G.I. language
Asked him what he wanted---and when.
He said he was coming for some good old home cooking---
So Miss Muffett is finished with men!
  —*Daniel Field, GA, Pvt. George Daniell*

GI MOTHER GOOSE

Cpl. Jill ran up a hill
And soon was in hot water
Ermine wraps for after taps
Were fine---until they caught her.

Mary served a little Spam;
Her guests were GI gents.
The case was tried by Uncle Sam;
The verdict: Self Defense.

Pvt. Peter Punkineater
Had a wife but couldn't beat her.
Took up Judo; never wins.
Damn civilian rolling pins!

I see a ship a-sailing,
A-sailing on the sea,
And that's me at the railing
Fresh from POE.
—*Ft. Leonard Wood, MO, Sgt. John W. Greenleaf*

G.I. HOME MAKER

The homely arts
This Army has taught
Should come in handy
When peace is wrought.
Necessity trained us
Tricks of going
At needle and thread
On vital sewing.
Buttons off here,
A chevron there,
A rip in skivvies
And simple tear---
Are nothing!
—*England M/Sgt. Larry McCabe*

"GEEI"

I looked long and lovingly at her
And touched her gently with care.
Gee, she sho' is a beaut!
The answer to a soldier's prayer!
My heart beat very strangely;
I just had to feel her!
"Hey soldier, come over here
Look, and electric spud peeler!"
—*Fort Myers, FL, Pvt. Ralph Alford*

FULLISHNESS

'Twos a brillig daye in sumbah,
Andt tha skye wahs filt wuth bairds.
Whin a bloomin bewgler ops anndt bulows. . .
Sum knots in forths ande thirds.

Waal, noe whon rilly kares hute
Jist wot tha hale hee blayes,
Bot whin hee ops ande blowt a floot. . . .
Hee wuss bairied in thrae days.
—*Camp Crowder, MO, Sgt Mark R. Curilovic*

FIELD PACK

Devised by Satan (or was it Poe?),
This tool of torture is our worst foe.
Combining the garrote, the stake and the rack,
And presented to us as the innocent pack.

Harnessed, weighted, strapped and slung,
One is surely headed for the iron lung.
This walking depot, this one-man safari,
Will soon be fit to tie---or bury.

Please don't construe this as complaint,
'Tis merely a plea, in voice grown faint.
Heed the crying need, this woeful lack,
Of a motorized, mechanical, self-propelled pack.
—*Fort Robinson, NE, Pvt. Edward Bayer*

FIELD CONDITIONS

First you take the air around you in the woods that do abound,
Then you mix it up with nothing and you stake it in the ground,
And you think of all the scout knots you were tying when a boy,
Then you tie this nothing up as if it were a Christmas joy.

Now you waterproof the canvas that you know just isn't there,
And you bring the sides down tautly till you've rigged it good and square,
Then you bring all the fixtures requisitioned months ago
That were promised you by people whom you "simply have to know."

And though you do not have them and you're sure they'll never come,
You sit your fanny on them just to keep from looking dumb;
Next you call your section leader on a phone that doesn't ring
And tell him very calmly you are set for anything!
—*India, Pvt. Barney August*

FAMILY ALBUM----1960

Dear father, is that your martyred demean---
The one with the visage that's slightly green?
How pale and worn you seem to be;
What a horrible wound is "housemaid's knee."

Now, really, did you go over the top
Armed only with that trusty mop?
I'll bet the enemy saw his doom
When you charged him with your deadly broom.

Are tanks and mortars hard to bag
With a bar of soap and a dirty rag?
A strategic point must be hard to defend
When your only weapon's a "plumber's friend."

At the risk of arousing paternal ire
I'd venture to say, my valiant sire,
From the pottery background plainly seen
You fought the war inside a latrine.
—*Camp Wolters, TX, Sgt. W.C. Allison*

"FALL IN"

There was the guy, defective of ear,
A cannon could roar, but he couldn't hear.
Rejected and home, he'd always complain,
Of the neighbors upstairs, their kids playin' train.

There was the man, defective of eye,
They showed him a chart he never could spy.
Back on the street, some sweet thing in pink,
Would pass 'neath his gaze, he'd give her the wink.

And lastly, the one, whose molars were shot,
Chew, no siree, he simply could not,
But show him a steak as tough as they come,
He'd stow it, my friend, he wasn't so dumb.

But all of these guys are due for a hitch
Examining boards have made a slight switch.
They're not so severe (New Army Decree).
They'll teach him to bite, to hear and to see.
—*Sgt. G. S.*

FAIRY TALE

Little Miss Muffet decided to rough it
In a cabin both old and medieval;
A soldier espied her,
And plied her with cider,
And now she's the forest's prime evil.
—*Sherman Field, KS, The Shermanic*

EVADER ON HORSEBACK

You, too, may have heard of the lad 28
Who was classified in the draft as 3-A.
This sorrowful sack, I make haste to relate,
Is no longer listed that way.

He wrote down one charge he was bound to support;
A 2-year-old female dependent,
As a result of which he is now in court
Reclassified as a defendant.

For while the statement was technically true
(He could certainly prove every word---
She was female and just had turned 2)
The lad is no longer deferred.

The draft board checked on his questionnaire
And found to its utter dismay
The charge was in fact a prancing young mare
And as the man says, that ain't hay.

Criminologists say they may miss one clue,
Which fills them with bitter remorse;
He could not have done what he hoped to do
Unless she had been a draft horse.
—*Herbert Smart Airport, GA, Cpl. Nathaniel Rogovoy*

EGGS

Oh, I've never had much money,
Though I've never had to beg.
But, I've never known a thing as scarce
As one doggone fresh egg.

At home we had Rhode Island Reds
And chickens with white legs.
And we always had enough of
Those precious things called eggs.

Yes, at home we had a-plenty
And never had to pay,
But on this confounded island
The hens refuse to lay.

When I return from this darned place
I'll eat my fill and then,
Just to top the whole thing off,
I think I'll eat the hen.
—*New Hebrides, Pvt. Malcolm Wyman Reynolds*

EDUCATION

The Army can teach me a technical trade
Or how to kill in a commando raid;
To handle a carbine or use a knife,
To protect my airport with my life,
But here's one thing they'll never do---
Teach me to relish GI stew!
—*Port of Embarkation, Pfc. John M. Hickman*

EARLY WORM

The moralists may all affirm
The earliest bird should get the worm
That, to my notion, is absurd;
The early worm should get the bird.

For had he longer lain abed
His cousin, and not he, were dead.
Some day the early worm will learn
How seldom early worms return.
—*Camp Shelby, MS, S Sgt. Grant A. Sanders*

DON'T ASK FOR CIGARETTES

Gilfrigen was big. Gilfrigen was threatening.
Yet he couldn't intimidate
Iona Packortwo, the PX Beauty.
Gilfregen would howl, long and loud.
For cigarettes, Iona
Would sell him candy, cough drops, eye drops,
But not cigarettes.
To Gilfrigen this was discouraging,
So he tried trickery.
One day Gilfrigen entered the PX
Disguised as a butt can.
Iona Packortwo was puffing lustily on a cig.
She threw said cig out the window
And deposited the wrapper of a marshmallow bar
On Gilfrigen. He was PO'd
That Iona had thrown her butt out the window.

Then Gilfrigen tried bribery.
He gave Iona a steak swiped from the mess hall.
He gave her a gas stamp, and he gave her his GI shoes
For ashtrays, his helmet liner for a flower pot.
Finally the supreme moment came
As supreme moments will:
Gilfrigen asked Iona to give him a pack
Of cigarettes---the long slender kind.
She gave him a dirty look and sold the last pack
To a feather merchant who drove the coke truck.
So Gilfrigen burned and burned.
He knew he had made an ash of himself.
—*Clovis AAF, N. Mexico, Pfc. Robert Rieker*

DIM OUT

It was three a.m. in the early brights,
And the joint was loaded with darks and lights.
A G.I. square was lapping Saki,
Hep to his jive, a Kat in Khaki.

A prima donna caught his eye,
Fine as wine and three quarters high,
"Whatever she wants!" And this creola
Ordered her up a big rum cola.

He eased over to this Queens's table
To soft gum beat her a bedtime fable;
"Baby, you're really the town's sensation.
You rate A-1 in my classification."

This here now cat was a bogus creeper,
Oiled to catch an unbooted sleeper,
A Harlem hipster, sharp from the city.
He thought he could trick this small-town kitty.

"Look here, chicken," the G.I. spelled,
"You're with the man that runs this field.
My raiser's got him a seat in the senate.
The stripe on my arm means first lieutenant.

"And babe, I've got a top B.S. plan.
I'm the smartest kat in this whole land.
I make my money playing cards.
Don't need no pass; I jive the guards."

As they sat there lushing and having a ball,
Our boy didn't know he rode for fall.
He mugged her lightly; she said, "Please stop."
And dunked his drink with a knockout drop.

When our G.I. square began to think
He was back on the post in an M.P. clink,
And his country chick, in her village flat,
Was splitting his gold with a country kat.
—*Tuskegee Army Flying School, The Hawks' Cry*

D DAY

"What did you do on D Day, daddy?"
I'm thinking of the little laddie
Who perched upon my post-war knee,
Asks this question then of me.
And I will say, with visage green:
"I was cleaning the latrine."
—*Sheppard Field, TX, Cpl. Marv Lore*

COMPLAINT TO AN EMPTY PURSE

I used to dream that *Harpers*
Would plead to get my work,
While I'd shrug off each offer
With a supercilious smirk.

Each editor from each mag
From pulps to slicks on through
Would plead with me to condescend
To send a line or two.

I wouldn't look to *Esquire*---
It's quite beyond the pale---
Though maybe the *New Yorker*
I'd favor with a tale.

And now and then the *Satevepost*
Might get to print my stuff,
But that was if—and only if---
Their checks were large enough.

My income from writings would overflow the bank---
But now I'm glad to settle for A squib---for free---in
Yank.
—*Alaska, Cpl. Lester Asheim*

CHOW-LINE SERENADE

I sing of the fellow who serves me my food
And the way he dumps cake on my pork.
Such finesse---it's a dream! What an artist Supreme!
Did he learn at the Waldorf or the Stork?

Not a surgeon can equal his delicate touch
As he sprinkles baked beans on my pie.
With a swallowlike swoop my dessert's
 In my soup---How unerring, how steady his eye!

Like your salad with gravy? Or stew on your fruit?
He will fill up your tray to the brim.

So, three cheers and a bow for this Maestro of chow!
For they named the word "mess" after him!
—*Truax Field, WI Pvt. Auerbach*

CONFESSION

From my day of birth I've blotted out mirth,
Plagued minds that were at ease;
I'm approached with fear, and as men draw near
There's trembling in their knees.
I bring scowl and frown, cursing up and down.
I'm the devil's own, oh Lord!
For GIs through me learn they're on KP
--- I am a bulletin board.
—*AAF, Greenville, SC, Sgt. Benton Berman*

CLASSIFICATION

They said to Jim, "Say can you type?"
He said, "I can---what luck!"
He's covered now with axle grease
And runs a two-ton truck.

They said to Joe, "What did you do?"
He said, "I drove a truck."
They put him at an Underwood
And made him squadron cluck.
—*England, Cpl. Stanley Ferber*

CHAIRBORNE

Corporal, T-5, sergeant, tech,
Specialist first class, pain in the neck
Push a pencil---make the grade.
Pull a trigger---underpaid.
Stateside, homemade, furlough, pass
Make your rating kissing brass.
Orders, records, requisitions
Get you ratings and commissions.
Back from Asia, ETO,
TS, boys, but the T/O----
—*Camp Craft, SC, Pfc. Joseph Piro*

(CENSORED)

We used to think, in days of peace,
When cobbers got together,
A good opening for friendly talk
Was mention of the (censored).

Thermometers rather suggest
(If I may be so bold)
That temperature sometimes go up,
And often it's quite (censored).

There's something I cannot quote,
Although it comes to mind:
If (censored) comes, Shelly once asked,
Can (censored) be far behind?

And now that you have read this verse,
You can't write, don't forget,
That (though my humor may be dry)
My doggerel is all (censored).
—*Australia, Sgt. Clyde Kenneth Hyder*

CAMP SHOW

As I recline upon my seat
Of dirt and cushioned stone,
The curtains part, a cheer goes up.
The Camp Show has begun!

And now we see some magic tricks
Controlled by farce and thunder;
Houdini hadn't a thing on him,
Why he's a perfect wonder.

And now four guys come strutting out,
All spangled in black pants:
They trip the light fantastic
In a soft-show shuffle dance.

And now two gagmen, now a stooge,
And now the endless drone
Of two men playing mightily
Upon a xylophone.

But while these acts are going on
There comes a mighty shout:
"Where in hell are all the girls
You advertised about?"
—*Sheppard Field, TX, Pfc. Marv Lors*

LOVE SONG FOR CLERKS

To lv on fur feels strange, my dear;
I hope there's been no C, my dear,
And that I'll find you still atchd,
And that we're still warmly mtchd
As when I left that other year.

I burn to see you once more jd.
Has anyone your heart purloined?
If you say no, I'll feel reld,
forget the months I was so peeved
At ltrs briskly, briefly coined.

I've been most true to you, my lass;
To me no other's in your cl.
When flirts asked what my shoulder patch meant
I always answered with det
And let the cheap temptations pass.

I WP at half past ten.
In three days I'll ar and then
I hope you'll meet me at the st
For 10 full days of jubilation
Before I must dep again.
—*LAMA, Leesville, VA, Pvt. Daniel L. Schorr*

LINING, SILVER

Nobody cares if
I'm bitter;
Nobody cares if
I'm low.
To the hats with the brass
I'm a name on a pass,
A serial number, a joe.

Nobody cares if
I'm desperate;
Nobody cares if
I'm sunk.
But the gist of it all
Makes me happy withal,
Because nobody cares if
I'm drunk.
—*Greenwood AAF, MS, Sgt. Robert W. Cahoon*

LINES TO THE CREATOR OF THE FATIGUE HAT

Nerts to you, GI modiste,
Be you living or deceased,
Who contrived this grotesque lid,
Under which my charms are hid,
Wearing which my wolfish glance
Would kindle laughter, not romance.
—*Seattle, WA, Pvt. W.L. Woodhouse, CA*

LINES ON MUTTON

Come landlord, fill the festive bowl,
Yet harken before you do.
By the hilt of my knife, you forfeit life
If you fill it with mutton stew.

O give me a home where the buffalo roam,
And give me a six-gun true.
Then dig a ditch for the sonovabitch
Who offers me mutton stew.
—*England, Pfc. J. Murphey*

LETTER TO SANTA CLAUS

This may sound like a strange request,
But it is quite sincere.
Please send me just a brand-new heart,
That's all I need this year.

The one the Lord provided me
Was either second-hand
(It broke so easily) or else
Was of a fragile brand.

So send me one of some sterner stuff,
Of a resilient grain.
Asbestos, now, might do, and wrap it,
Please, in cellophane.
—*Hendricks Field, FL, Pvt. Ralph E. Marcellino*

LEST WE FORGET

Many a mound this war has seen,
In distant lands and near;
Many a spade has clawed the earth
Midst shot and shell and fear.

Many a man has gazed upon
That hollow wide and deep,
Some with blistered hands,
And some I did see weep.

Many a man will ne'er forget
As he silently tread by,
That there once stood his comrades---
Men like you and I.

And when the strife is over,
The soldier and marine
Will ever see before them
That field G.I. latrine.
—*Australia, Cpl. Herbert Seligson*

LEAVE ME BE

To release a man for line duty
Is the purpose of a WAAC.
That is so kind of the little cutie,
Let's give her three cheers and a smack!

Who told the lady I'd rather fight
Than remain in my present station?
The battle line is for men of might;
Let me goldbrick for the duration.

War can be fought minus women, I guess,
So, away with this undue abasement!
Where lives the WAAC with enough finesse
To rate a goldbrick replacement?
—*Alaska, Pvt. Frank J. Mickey*

LADIES, ETC.

Ladies ethereal
Are not WAC material.

Ladies who the asphalt tread
Would much prefer to lie abed.

Ladies who are bookish
Are not always good-lookish.

Ladies whose eyes say "Come hither"
Get many GIs in a dither.

Ladies over 40
Are not generally sporty.

Ladies with bars on their shoulders
Are sometimes built like boulders.

Ladies who drink whiskey
Are apt to be frisky.

Ladies on the make
Are easy to take.

Not all spies
Have mascaraed eyes.

A homely maid or a fatherly gent
May have a pro-Axis bent.

After the war, a general
May find his commission ephemeral.

I would like to see the private journal
Of some Tahiti-stationed colonel.
—*Truax Field, WI Pfc. C.G. Cappo*

KITCHEN COPS

I think that I shall never see,
A job as sloppy as K.P.
K.P., where greasy arms are pressed,
with pots and pans against the chest;
K.P., where stand the chefs all day,
Barking orders at their prey;
K.P.'s, who may in evening wear,
A spot of gravy in their hair;
K.P. where all the yardbirds hop
To nonchalantly wield a mop
Poems are made by fools like me
And so's the list for that damned K.P. Pvt. D. D. in
  —*Brooklyn Bay Breeze*

KP JABBERWOCKY

'Twas dawnish, and the sloplich prive,
Did toil and spicker in the kitch,
A-polixing the fork and knive,
The plat and cup, no matter which.

"Then never goldbrick here, my son,
 "And never loaf upon the job;
 "This kitch, it is no place for fun---
 "And messy sarges will play hob!"

He took the vorpal mop in hand,
Long time the grimish floor he mopped;
He peeled the spuds to beat the band,
'Till on his tiredy back he flopped.

And, as a-goldbricking he lay,
The messy sarge, with eyes of flame,
Came shuffling in to start the day,
A-whistling lightner as he came.

"Well,well! Well,well! What have we here?
"A goldbricker upon his back!"
The messy sarge's face did leer---
He took his gig list from his pack.

"So, hast thou been a bad goldbrick?
"I'll gig thee now, my beamish prive!
"Take up thy mop, now do it quick!
Thou sluggard! Let thee look alive!"
'Tis nitish, and the sloplich prive,

Still toilet longly in the kitch,
Peeling the spud, shinning the knive,
Mopping the floor, no matter which!
  —*Fort George G. Meade, MD, Cpl. Dick B. Gehman*

KEEP IT CLEAN

Oh, let your songs be silent
And be your voices mute;
A soldier's not an opera star,
He's just a bloody brute.
A song may lift the sagging heart
And wing the flagging heel,
But pass the order down the line
And there'll be no appeal.

Civilian ears are tender
And soldier songs are crude,
And if some woman heard you sing
She'd think the Army rude.
So button up your lips, my lads,
And trudge along unheard;
A soldier's just a bloody brute,
He's not a blasted bird.

Though singing cuts the miles in half
And speeds the hike along,
"Mademoiselle from Armentieres"
 Is not a moral song.
Choose something safe and sacred,
A soldier must not smirch
The Army's honor with a song
Unfit to sing in church.

Oh, the ghosts of other armies
That filed into the past
Will listen to your choruses
And stare at you aghast.
For a dumb and songless army
You lads will have to be
Unless church hymns and lullabies
Will set your voices free.
  —*Camp Shelby, MS, Sgt. Grant A. Sanders*

KEEP 'EM FILING!

When I'm decrepit and mellow,
A white-bearded old fellow,
With my grandchildren crowding at my knee,
All asking for a story
About my feats of glory
In this war that's making such great history . . . .

65

Oh, how shall I explain,
Oh, how shall I refrain
From telling them the truthful situation?
That their granddad was no ranger,
No commando in grave danger,
But a clerk who pushed a pencil for his nation.
—*AAB, Ephrata, WA, Cpl. Bernard M. Wolpert*

ISLAND HAPPY

Gee, but I love to see coral,
Gee, but I love to see sea,
Gee, but I love this little isle
And every coconut tree.

Dehydrated food for me,
I hate potatoes you must peel;
I'm crazy over Army Spam
And couldn't live without my veal.

I like to see the movies
Produced when I was born;
Existence would be empty
Without old-fashioned corn.

I want to stay here all my life
'Neath a Melanesian sky,
For I've become what we all call
An "island happy" guy.
—*South Pacific, Cpl. Kenneth S. Davidson*

INDIAN HARA KIRI

There was an old man from New Delhi;
When asked would he fight he said, Well, he
Thought maybe not.
You know what he got?
A Japanese knife in his belly.
—*Somewhere In the Caribbean, Capt. Victor Strauss*

I WANT---

I want to cuddle with the colonel
When I'm feeling sad and blue,
And let him dry my tears away
Like my mamma used to do.
I want a sympathetic captain
Who will take me on his knee
And read me bedtime stories
Till I'm sleepy as can be.

And I'd like a gentle sergeant
Who would tuck me in just right
Then bring me a glass of water
And wish me "nightie-night."

If the army should consider
These requests a little queer,
Then please, commanding general,
Can't you bring my mamma here?
—*Camp Wolters, TX, S/Sgt. David R. Mclean*

INSPECTION

All of them grabbed the bus into town:
Some of them went for the dance,
Some of them went for the bottled stuff,
And a few just to press their pants.
But they all had somewhere they planned to go
For drink, or dance or confection.
But I stayed in, went early to bed:
I got gigged at inspection.
—*Camp Robinson, AR, Pvt. Max Goodman*

HOW NOT TO INCREASE YOUR CIRCULATION

Toward those uncounted millions,
Those well-fed civilians,
We guys can feel no envy, to be frank
Let them drink their Scotch at bars,
Let them drive their motor cars---
But we're the only ones who can read Yank.
—*Chanute Field, IL, Cpl. David Troup*

HEAVENLY DISCOURSE

He had no escort to the pearly gates,
A colonel in a jeep passed him by.
"I'm sure a guy with single stripes still rates
A better guide to heaven that his feet."
Said private Joe, "I figured dying means
The end of blisters and those army beans."
He got there feeling like a worn out rag
And asked Saint Peter where he had to go
To park his feet and shed his barracks bag.
"And how about those angels, pal?" he asked.
"Now just forget the angels," Peter said.
"They have to please the living, no the dead."
"Before you can come in we first require
Your previous occupation and your name.
Then we'll assign you to the heavenly choir

And issue you a pair of GI wings.
Your diet is restricted, since you will train
To help the members of the Chaplain Corps."
"Oh Lord!" moaned Private Joe, "no angel dates,
No drink, no fun, no sleep past reveille.
Oh well, I still recall some hopeful baits;
The devil shoots a wicked pair of dice."
The moral is: don't hope for milk and honey,
They might not even lend you any money.
—*Pfc. John Hay*

SUPPLY

Back in Texas where I took my training,
I had no galoshes when it was raining.
Straight to supply and down on my knees,
"No soap," said the sergeant. "It's all overseas."

Then in England we finally sailed.
"No supply troubles now," I wailed.
Went to the sergeant with my song and dance,
"TS, my boy, It's all in France."

Someday soon I'll cross the Rhine,
Everything then should really be fine.
The supply angle will be terrific,
When I get there it's in the Pacific.
—*France, Pfc. Bob Timrick*

STRENGTH REPORT (LAST RESORT)

Down in steaming Moresby,
They still bomb it just for sport,
I'm sweating and I'm worrying
 Over a screwed-up strength report.

Now I'm the guy that's supposed to know
Where every outfit is---
Where they are, how many there are
And what the hell's their biz.
Before I lie down to sleep at night,
I first get down and pray;
Make the strength report be right,
Oh, Lord, help me today!

Although I know the darn things wrong,
 There's no use for me to cry,
And neither do I sing a song
 When the ratings pass me by.

Now, how I got these corporal's stripes
I'm sure that I don't know,
And I won't be so much surprised
To see this rating go.

When I turn in the strength report
The major smiles with glee;
He knows it's wrong before it starts
And he brings it back to me.

Tomorrow's Monday once again
 And I'll try it one more day.
Then if I'm short just 15 men
I'll go jump in the bay.
—*New Guinea, Cpl. Dudley E. Bramblette*

SPAM

Jackson had his acorns, Grant his precious rye,
Teddy had his poison beef, worse you couldn't buy.
The doughboy had his hardtack without this Army's jam.
All armies on their stomachs move, and this one moves
on spam.

For breakfast they will fry it, for supper it is baked,
For dinner what a delicacy, they have it pat-a-caked;
Next morning it's with flapjacks or maybe powdered eggs.
Where the hell'd they get it all? they must order it by the kegs.

Surely for the evening meal they'll cook up something new,
But these cooks are sure uncanny; now it's in the stew.
And thus the tireless cycle goes, it never seems to cease;
Spam in the stew, spam in the pie, spam in the boiling grease.

We've had it tucked in salads, with cabbage for corned beef,
We've had it for and entrée, perhaps aperitif,
And we've had it with spaghetti, with chili and with rice;
I remember such a happy day, we only had it twice.

Back home I have an angel whose name I'm going to change.
I'll buy her a fancy home with a newfandangled range;
But marital bliss is sure to cease if I ever ask for ham
And find my eggs are looking up from a slice of cursed spam.
—*Morocco, Cpl. Mark F. Quigley*

SONG OF THE DESERT RAT

Day after day in the desert, Sun, sun, sun.
Day after day in the desert, Wind, wind, wind.
Day after day in the desert, Dust, dust, dust.
Monotonous, isn't it?
—*Somewhere in the damn California desert, Sgt. Dave Berry*

SNOW JOBS

Oh, I'll stick near
When they chew my ear
About all the millions
They made civilians.
It doesn't matter
When they start to chatter
How they can take their drinkin'
And never get stinkin'.
But brother I go, I really do blow,
When they say it ain't the stripes
That they want, but the dough!
—*Fort Hamilton, NY, T-4 Irving Rockmore*

SKIS

I think that I shall never see
A board as tricky as a ski;
A ski whose slippery side is pressed
Upon the earth's soft snowy crest.

A ski that ends a perfect schuss
But leaves me lying on my puss;
A ski that makes me hope and pray
That I will live another day.

I fly through space, I'm fancy free,
And ricochet from tree to tree.
My bones are cracked, my flesh is torn,
I wish to hell I'd not been born.

They scooped me up from off the snow,
'Twas to the morgue I thought I'd go.
The doctor spoke these words to me,
"In tougher shape you could not be."

"Your skis were found a mile away,
As for your poles I cannot say.
Your pack was hanging from a tree,
Your teeth were spread from A to Z."

"We'll patch you up as best we can,
But let me tell you, man to man,
That if you do not 'bend zee knees'
You'll never learn to ride your skis."

Today I am a wiser lad,
I've gathered from the spill I had
That poems are made by fools like me,
And fools should never try to ski.
—*Camp Hale, CO S/Sgt. Harold J. Gust and
Sgt. John C. Decker*

RECONVERSION

The war is over,
and we're all reconverting,
But one small problem remains disconcerting;
What will happen to the playful little moron
Who always said, "Don't you know there's a war on?"
—*Sheppard Field, TX, Pfc. Arnold Wolf*

RANK REFLECTION

I vow that I
Would never gripe
Could I but wear
Just one more stripe.

But then again
It seems to me
I felt that way
As pfc.
—*Camp Atterbury, IN, Cpl. G. G. Dowling*

QUERY

Should the Nazis make use
Of electrical juice
To power their blitzkrieg advances,
Could we possibly say,
As they roll on their way
That the Nazis have amps in their panzers?
—*Beloit College, WI, Pvt. John W. Sullivan*

PVT.

You can talk about *amoebae*,
Or whatever you elect. The lowly *protozoa*
Really earns profound respect.
There's a one-celled hairy monster,
Paramecium, by name;
You'll find him venerated
In the Science Hall of Fame.
You can throw in all the microbes,
Wherever you may tramp:
I can go you one step lower
Without stepping out of camp,
And I can prove it by my looey
That my candidate is champ.
Go on, name all the old bacteria
With which the world is rife,
But the jerk they call the *private*
Is the lowest form of life.
—*Camp Wallace, TX, Pvt. Henry B. Weisberg*

PRAISE THE SILK

As I sat in the plane with my chute on my back
I was frightened as could be.
The jumpmaster was ready in the door---
I knew, for I could see,
The boys on the ground looked like bugs from afar,
The ground it looked so black.
"Stand up, and hook up!" the jumpmaster cried,
And I found myself on my back.

When I stood on my feet like a leaf did I shake
As my knees were beating a tune,
But bravely I said "Move over men,
Move over and give me room."
I stood in that door with a prayer on my lips,
Wondering why I was there,
When I saw the jumpmaster leave the plane
And sail out into the air.

Then out I went into the blue
With my face as white as could be;
I tried to count and check my feet,
But God, why couldn't I see?
I opened my eyes and my chute finally opened,
My knees, they even stopped knocking;
I looked up above and saw my true love,
Made from----400 *silk stockings*.
  —*Fort Benning, GA, Pvt. Irving E. Taffel*

POST-WAR PLAN

I would like to go to Paris
And see the Eiffel Tower.
I'd like to view a church or two;
Improve the shining hour,
For a trip to modern Paris,
Guidebooks say, one shouldn't miss.
But to my mind another kind
Of tourist jaunt is this:

I'd like to see Vienna town,
But not to dance its dances.
And my mental state would likely frown
On Viennese romances.
(Perhaps, if you would rack your brain,
Then you yourself might ken a
Valid reason, very plain,
For visiting Vienna.)

I would like to go to Roma
And see St. Peter's Square.
I understand the things on hand
To see are myriad there.
Yes, a trip to ancient Roma
Is a rubbernecker's must,
But I've a thirst for one trip first
That I will take or bust:

Oh, I'd hie me to Vienna, not
To sway Strauss' tunes
Nor to feel my blood beat fast and hot
Beneath Danubian moons,
But to take some TNT in hand
(A ton would suit my quirks),
To set it with a time fuse and
Blow up the sausage works!
  —*France, Pvt. Charles Petterson*

POOR PVT. QUACK

God moves in a mysterious way,
But the Army has him beat.
To prove my point we'll take the case
Of Pvt. Joe McTweet

He joined up with his Uncle Sam,
'Twas just a year ago;
They sent him straight to Scott Field
To study radio.
He started school with Pvt. Quack,
And egocentric lug;
But just two weeks thereafter Poor Pfc.
Quack washed out.

Joe learned his code and theory, too,
And never once held back
So help him God, he'd not flunk out
Like poor Pfc. Quack

Four months have passed in this sad tale,
And never does he slack;
He knows now that he will not fail
Like poor Cpl. Quack

Now Pvt. Joe is out of school,
Degrees he does not lack;
He's thankful that he made the grade
Unlike poor Sgt. Quack

Pvt. Joe now pounds a key,
In a land where all are black;
While in St. Louis at the USO,
Sits poor Staff Sgt. Quack.
  —*Austtralia, Pvt. Herbert A. Hanley*

POEM FOR A T/SGT., WAC

Fat little woman,
I love you good,
Love to scrape when
I could be rude,
Love to watch you eat your food
At noon.

Wherever you go business is fine,
You could turn vinegar into wine,
So slick like a fender is your line,
So sweet your tune.

Lady executive, on top of the list,
Ten to one you've never been kissed
Under a willow pale as mist
Under the moon.
—*Swannanoa, NC Pfc. Gloria Marchisio*

POEM

I'm a Japanese jerk
From Japan.
I work and I work
For Japan.
I get eight cents a day
(Which isn't much pay).
If the Axis wins out
I'll get 10 cents, no doubt;
So, "Onward to glorious triumph." I shout,
And meanwhile
I'm reading a textbook about
How to speak German.
—*Camp Wolters, TX, S/Sgt. David R. McLean*

PLEA TO A PX BARBER

Barber, barber, hold those shears;
Life is short and fleeting.
Save your brawn for later years;
Spare my scalp a beating.

Clip gently up and down my neck;
Forget those gooey lotions;
Don't leave my head a total wreck.
Cease your sales promotions.

I came to you in fettle fine
With outlook bright and rosy;
I leave you like some Frankenstein
Or even worse, Lugosi.

Barber, heed my plaintive song
It's such a simple task;
A decent, smooth and not-too-long
Haircut is all I ask.
—*Sioux Falls AAF, SD, Pfc. Leslie Waller*

PLAINT

The colonel had his eagles,
The captain has his bars,
The major has an oak leaf,
The general has his stars.

And if you're counting chevrons,
The topkick has a slew,
The bugler has a single one,
The corporal has two.
The marksmen have their medals,
Technicians have their 'T,"
There must be some insignia
For everyone but me.

I'm not marked out in any way
And that's why I don't see
How all those gol-durned chiggers,
Can head right straight for me.
—*Camp Wolters Longhorn*

PILLS

The Army doctors have a cure
They use for all your ills;
No matter what the case may be
They always give you pills.
A man can well be dying,
Still, no matter how you fret,
They throw a flock of pills at you.
And soldier, you're all set.

I've taken pills for everything
From broken legs to gout;
I've even put them in my shoes
To keep the water out.

One time we were in battle
And we ran plumb out of lead.
We needed ammunition, so---
We used those pills instead.

Well, sir, you won't believe me,
But a lie I never tell;

The enemy couldn't take those pills---
They're all dead as hell.
—*Camp Adair, OR, Cpl. George Hindberg*

PENNILESS SERENADE

Fort Bragg, N.C., August-----
Fort Bragg recently began
a three-months experimental plan
of non-credit, cash-on-the-line,
no canteen books, etc.

Under the spreading fiscal blight
The Ninth Division stands
Bereft of credit, pockets light,
And nothing in its hands;
And solvent soldiers, flush with coin
Are scarce as rubber bands.

The rainy day is here at last,
Migawd, how it doth pour!
The day of canteen checks is past,
The wolf is at the door.
No credit, trust or "on account"
At any G.I. store.

The early part of every month
(The War Department states)
You get your dough and out you go
Quite rich (at Army rates).
But don't forget, oh Croesus new,
That dough---it circulates.

No more the friendly canteen book,
To yank you out of hock,
And thirty leering days await
To limp around the clock,
With seven hundred hours of
Disbursements by the flock.

Young man of substance, wampum, pelf,
Some grim retrenchments lurk;
Two strikes have you just been called on you
To lessen paperwork;
And credit now is down the drain
To spare the audit clerk.

Oh, thrift and care and saving-ness
Economy and lack,
Are things you'll need to make ends meet

Till pontoon books come back.
  (Until when, you pony up;
  Yes, you will hold the sack).

Dust off those double entry-books
Take stock of all your kale;
Credit, debit, balance up;
Recheck the dreary tale;
Move over, Churchmouse, little pal,
It's either you or jail!
—*Pfc. J. Don Peel*

TWENTY-FIRST BIRTHDAY

I sit here in my cozy cell;
My heart is filled with joy,
For I am twenty-one today---

My folks and friends remember me
With gifts and revenue;
How did the Army celebrate?
CQ.
—*Brooklyn Army Base, NY, Pfc. Daniel Waldron*

TUNE FROM TUNIS

Dirty Gertie from Bizerte
Hid a mousetrap 'neath her skirtie,
Strapped it on her kneecap purty,
Baited it with *Fleur de Flirte*,
Made her boy friend's fingers hurty,
Made her boy friends very shirty.
She was voted in Bizerte "Miss Latrine" for 1930.
—*Camp Lee, VA, Pvt. William L. Russell*

PASS

At night
We write
Our name on pass;
But night and pass
Erase too fast.
—*Fort Sheridan, IL, Pvt. Irv Rosenthal*

PARTIES

I prefer going
To parties stag
For the reason
That you can
Make a pass
At every lass

And then too
If you do
Get stuck
With some bag
Who refuses to
Do anything but
Chew the rag
You can always Say,
"Pardon Me a minute,"
Which of course
Becomes indefinite.
—*Camp Crowder, MO, Pvt. Louis Fisher*

TRAVEL NOTE

From London to Tahiti,
From Attu to Port of Spain,
From Bougainville to Martinique,
You'll hear a new refrain;
From Frisco to Pearl Harbor
The legend will appear
That during World War No. 2
Mrs. Roosevelt slept here.
—*Southwest Pacific, Sgt. Jack N. Carl*

TO THE ENDS OF THE EARTH

The jeep is well known to the ends of the earth,
And has left its impressions thereon.
On the fronts of the war it has proven its worth;
On the rears it has battered the brawn.

It's put many a bruise on a broad British butt,
Or a calloused Canadian can.
It has reddened the rear, as it lurched in a rut
Of the Russian artilleryman.

There is many a seat that was made in U.S.
That has winced at its shattering blow;
And the Fighting French think its thumping caress
A test of their love for de Gaulle.

And even "down under" the tale is the same
(A little bit battered and sore);
While rugged Chinese make it into a game,
With patches on pants as the score.

Wherever the world-renowned jeep make its way,
There's a new batch of blisters in birth;
So now you know what we mean when we say,
It is known to the ends of the earth.
—*Camp Swift, TX T-5, John W. Greenleaf*

TO A NONCOM I KNOW

The Romans had a word for you---
Three words, I should say,
No single word could comprehend
A noncom, anyway.

They are: *non compos mentis*
(Words which quite embrace
The thing you are)---nuts, insane,
A psychopathic case.
—*Hendricks Field, FL, Pvt. Ralph E. Marcellino*

TO A HEP CAT

Ah, Jack, to wear our English drapes once more
With fifteen cuffs and twenty-eight-inch knees,
To let our hair flow freely in the breeze
And wildly jump across a solid floor,
To wear deep purple flowers in our coats
Of light tan Bedford cord and sport a pair
Of brown suede shoes, while blatant trumpets blare
And gutbuckets thump out their rhythmic notes.

Oh, we could scream and rave and gaily leap
To boogie beats and frolic to and fro
Like and excited, crazy GI jeep.
This then is our most sacred dream, I know,
But right now I would like to catch some sleep,
So will you please turn off the radio?
—*Fort Benning, GA, Sgt. Leonard Summers*

TO A CENSOR

Out here in the tropics
There aren't many topics
Concerning which a soldier may expound,
For the censor military
Is a fellow very wary
Who chases every rumor to the ground.

He's a master at omission
When he swings into position
And there aren't many statements he condones
No use to howl at his derangement
If he ruins your thought arrangement
As he adds a couple phrases of his own.

At expunging he's proficient
And he runs his beady orbs across the script;
From your gossip and your gaff

He takes the wheat out from the chaff
And leaves your finished letter neatly clipped.

Just a hint of army ration
Will set his teeth to gnashin'
As he snips it out with hot and bated breath;
And a bit of soldiers data
Is bound to be *non grata*,
And is sure to meet a fate that's worse than death.

And though it may be all fair weather
When good fellows get together,
You can't transmit the fact to kith and kin;
For though it's only now and then, sir,
If you sneak it past the censor,
You're a better man than I am, Gunga Din.
  —*Hawaii, Pvt. Herb Kraus*

THE U. S. NAVY BEAN

From the mess halls of the boot camp
To the dreadnaught *Tennessee,*
We feed our country's Navy
On the land and on the sea,
First to greet the gob at breakfast
With an appetizing scene,
We are proud to claim the title
Of the U.S.Navy Bean.
We're a pest in old Cavite,
Or the ditch at Panama;
When the crew is very needy
Of a meal, they get us raw;
For we're on the *Shenandoah,*
And the lowly submarines,
And not a gob has pushed a swab
Who hasn't eaten beans.
Here's health to you and all the ship's cooks
Whom we are proud to serve;
We get them many dirty looks
And yet they keep their nerve.
If the Army or Marine Corps
Ever look on heaven's scenes,
They will find the tables loaded
With those U.S. Navy Beans!
  —*USS Moffett, Bozo*

THE TOOLS OF WAR

The cannons roar, the rockets soar;
Are these, you say, the tools of war?
Ah no, not so, it cannot be!
The tools of war they gave to me,
With which a better world to make,
Were these: A mop, a broom, and a rake!
Point of Embarkation
  —*Pf. John D. Hickman*

THE SHORTS OF CAPT. L.

We have been in situations that would make the bravest flee,
We have known the many dangers of the man who goes to sea,
But all of the sea's vast horrors, there is none that leaves us---well,
More ready for a keeper than the shorts of Capt. L.
We would rather face torpedoes than to face the gruesome sight
Which has often waked us screaming in the middle of the night;
More ghastly view, it is our vow, no mortal ever saw,
And although they're not, they should be banned by international law.

Yes, we know they're patriotic and will save much needed cloth,
For they're cut so brief they wouldn't feed a wan dyspeptic moth,
But although they may be wonderful to brave the tropic breeze,
We are sure they weren't intended for a pair of knobby knees.
They are covered o'er with rust spots---'tis said they once were bright,
But now we rear they could be classed as anything but white.
And when the captain wears them, 'though we never make a complaint, We would think he'd be embarrassed by the places where they ain't.

If worn by bathing beauties we would have no cause for grief,
For they contain the goods to make just one small handkerchief,
But when the captain puts them on, and then declares he's dressed,
Instead of sighs of rapture we give sighs of vast protest.
Now seamen all are wicked and we haven't lived so well.
We know that when on earth we're done we're sure to end in hell.
We will try to face the torments that we find in Satan's ports,
But God grant that we're not tortured by the sights of L. in shorts.
  —*U.S. Merchant Marine, Leonard F. Joslyn, Radio Officer*

THE DIAL TWIRLER'S LAMENT

I wish the Army kindly would do me a simple favor
 And raid these guys who use a fancy 'lectric shaver.
Why can't they be like most of us, as even you and I,
Who rise each morn and scrape our china with a razor, plain GI?

If this keeps up I do confess that I shall rise some a.m.
And go and search these culprits out and perhaps commit mayhem.
For nothing seems to burn me more, with this I am emphatic,
Than turning on my radio and getting all this static.
So will the Army kindly grant this small and simple favor
And confiscate this curse of mine---the fancy 'lectric shaver?
—Camp Rucker, AL, Sgt. Fred M. Rogers

THE COLONEL

"My battalion is formed," said the Major,
"In a manner prescribed by the book."
:Will the Colonel please come look them over?"
Said the Colonel: "I'll look."

"They're a fine bunch of men," said the Major.
"Not even one case of V.D.
I think you will find them most sturdy."
Said the Colonel: "We'll see."

"They're rarin' to go," said the Major,
And spoiling to get in a fight.
They're the best group of men in the service."
Said the colonel: "All right."

The battalion moved over the parade ground.
The captains and first sergeants roared
Out commands while the Major looked happy.
Said the colonel: "I'm bored."

The battalion marched over the parade ground,
And damn it, they marched very well.
The Major puffed up like a pigeon.
Said the Colonel: "Oh, hell."

Said the Colonel: "I'm sick of reviewing."
The colors and standards all drooped.
"To be frank with you men---and I mean it,"
Said the Colonel: "I'm pooped."
—Pvt. John Buoy

THE CENSOR'S WOES

I am a censor, and oh! what a curse:
Of all of my jobs, this is the worst.
I read these letters till far in the night,
And one in a hundred is probably right.
I hack and I cut with my trusty blade
As on through the mountains of mail I wade.
There are letters to sweethearts, friends, and wives;
It's strange to know intimately so many lives.
I read of their 'plaints, ambitions and dreams,
Of their sorrows, loves, and of their schemes.
Here I must cut for he mentions the rain.
Another slice out for he talks of terrain.
Another deletion---he wrote of a date!
Must cut again; says "shipments are late."
Enclosed is a picture that cannot be sent
For in it there shows one G.I. tent.
The letter's in ribbons---it's cut full of rents;
To whom it's addressed, 'twill never make sense.
Hundreds of letters I sign, seal and stamp;
At the end of the day, I've got writers' cramp.
I've done my job well, at least so I feel,
But gad! Here's another I have yet to seal.
I'm tired and I'm weary. I'll give this one hell;
Who'd write such drivel? Please pray me tell.
Well, this letter's censored, in full, goodness knows,
All's gone but "dearest" and "with love I close."
This is the worst I have seen in my life.
What's this? Ye gods! From me to my wife.
—Australia, 1st Lt. George A. Gillespie

THE BUZZY-WUZZY FLY

When my brogans hit the lumber and I close my eyes in slumber
And my thoughts go back to Brooklyn and a quart of Seagram's rye,
Who comes crawling with his footsies on my undefended tootsies
With a beastly buzz of boredom and an arthropodic sigh?
Yes, an arthropodic sigh
In my quart of Seagram's rye---
It's the grisly ghoul of Guinea; it's the buzzy-wuzzy fly.

I can twist my foot or thump it, I can bang my foot or bump it,
I can wiggle it and jiggle it and shake it till I die;
But, to flies who have no feeling, human feet are most appealing
And I know I won't discourage him, no matter how I try.

I can try and try and try, I can try until I die,
But there's nothing quite so stubborn as a skinny Guinea fly.

He'll be messy if I crush him, so I gently, lightly brush him
Then I scratch my foot and back upon my bed of thorns I lie;
But the Guinea fly is chummy, so he crawls across my tummy
And he buzzes his defiance at the starry Southern sky.
And I look up at the sky, As upon my bed I lie,
And I roundly curse the parents of this prickly, tickly fly.

Oh, my only life-ambition is to make and expedition
To a college lab where fifty thousand Guinea flies I'll buy;
And my heart will fill with gladness as I tickle them to madness,
As I pull their wings to pieces and I buzz their brains awry.
Yes, I'll buzz their brains awry, And a Mason jar I'll buy
And in Ration C I'll pickle every lousy, frowsy fly.
    —*New Guinea, T-5 Norman Lipman*

TASTE IT

The origin of G.I. soup
Will perhaps forever be
Secret to a soldiers mind,
Shrouded in mystery.

Last night I thought it bean
And dug down deep,
Even strained it through my bread,
But found no beans to keep.

Then I thought of celery
And stirred around for leaves
But even if I'd found some there
They might have come from trees.

It couldn't be tomato,
The color wasn't right.
And besides there were no seeds
To be found in there last night.

I'd almost given up until---
At last! Don't be a dope!
As any fool can plainly taste,
It's made with G.I. soap!
    —*Lincoln Air Base, NE, Sgt. K. V. Lamoreux*

YOUR NOSE KNOWS

M-1

How to tell the Gases
Grandma smelled geranium,
Started feeling kind of bum
Sure you guessed the trouble right.
Grandma whiffed some Lewisite

PS

Don't you find my odor sweetish?
Said flypaper to the fly.
I smell just like chloropierin,
And you'll think you'd like to die.

CG

Maud Muller on a summer day,
 Smelled the odor of new-mown hay.
She said to the Judge who was turning green,
"Put on your mask! That there's phosgene!"

CN

Apple blossoms, fresh and dewy?
Normandy and romance? Hooey
For the charming fragrance then known,
Now is chloracetaphenone.

HS

Never take some chances if
Garlic you should strongly sniff
Don't think Mussolini's passed,
Man, you've been mustard-gassed.
    —*Fairfax Downey, Major Field Artillery*

WITH APOLOGIES TO A CERTAIN SONG

Down lay the soldier;
The time was getting late.
Down lay the KP;
Short sleep would be his fate.
Up rose the CQ,
Kitchen Coppers he must wake,
Rousing all the KPs
With a horrible swift shake.

Shouting:

Scrape the lard and pass the dirty dishes.
Scrape them hard, all those dirty dishes.
Don't retard the line of dirty dishes,
Soldiers on KP.

Disregard your inmost natural wishes.
Don't bombard mess-sergeants with the dishes,
Just discard what's left of steaks and fishes.
It's your day, KP.

The pusher reported it.
The mess-sergeant ordered it,
You'll never ever finish KP.
Singing:

Scrape the lard and pass the dirty dishes.
All food discard no matter how nutritious.
Faster, pard, although it's repetitious,
Soldier, you're KP.
—*A.A.F.C.C. Nashville, TN, A/C Gordon M. Low*

WHY I GET KP

If the sergeant says, "Fix bayonets!" he means the words he spoke,
And doesn't like your answer when you holler, "Mine ain't broke!"

When he says to you, "Sling rifles!" and you throw yours a mile,
Do you wonder why the poor old sergeant never wants to smile?
"Order arms," he told me yesterday, so like a crazy guy
I went and ordered a pistol from the boys at supply.

I'm always in hot water and always in a rut,
And I'd be a better dogface if I'd keep my big mouth shut.
—*NY, Sgt. Robert J. Evans*

WEATHER REPORT

While jungle fighting in New Guinea
It must be cooler to be skinny.
Alaska is another matter
For there it's warmer to be fatter.
When temperatures are minus zero
It's tough as hell to be a hero,
And so is intrepidity
In spite of the humidity.
So take the hint, each fighting man,
The weather's pleasant in Japan.
—*1st Decontamination Unit, Pvt. Y. Guy Owen*

THE KEE BIRD

Oh, I've heard the squeal of the trolley's wheel
When the brakes are applied too fast,
And the fright'ning scream that is made by steam
Of the locomotive's shrill blast.
I know of the fright that comes in the night
When lions and tigers roar,
But I'll ne'er forget and always regret
The cry of those birds that soar
O'er the Arctic ice. Oh, it isn't nice
To remember those cries that I've heard,
So, listen, and well, to the story I tell
Of that terrifying Kee Bird.

This bird is as big as a full-grown pig
With wings as wide as this---
His neck is as long as his beak is strong,
And his talons never miss
When catching a seal for his daily meal
(For he eats but once a day).
It's a horrible sight to see him at night
Lying in wait for his prey,
But strong men quiver, animals shiver,
At his raucous cry, so bold,
For he seems to say in his Kee Bird way,
"Kee-Kee-Keerist, but it's cold!"

Oh, the Eskimo in his hut of snow
And the huskies in their den
Will quickly awake and begin to shake
At this terrible nightly omen.
The Mounted Police will suddenly cease
Their travels through the cark
And stare at the sky with shuddering eye
For this bird isn't a lark.
Each man at this base will conceal his face
'Neath the covers, quite shameless, I'm told,
When this bird on high does utter his cry,
"Kee-Kee Keerist, but it's cold!"

Some day, I'll be home, ne'er again to roam
Away from that land to the South.
I'll live where it's warm and frost doesn't form
On the whiskers around my mouth.
I'll go to bed and there rest my head

Close to my loved one's arms.
They'll be peace and rest; I'll be one blest,
Content with connubial charms.
But sure as I dream, I'll wake with a scream
Recalling those nights of old,

When that ------ ------- bird could always be heard,
"Kee-Kee-Keerist, but it's cold!"
—*Baffin Islands, Canada, A/C Warren M. Kniskern*

THE GUY WITH THE SQUEAKY SHOES

I rather like a good long hike,
But there's one thing that gives me the blues:
It's to suddenly find I'm right behind
The guy with the squeaky shoes.

"Fall in, fall out," some noncom'll shout,
And each man follows these cues,
Except,---well, you see, they were drowned out for me
By the guy with the squeaky shoes.

So, I'm bawled out, called a fool and a lout,
Man, I take plenty abuse,
Oh, why must it be I, who is hounded by
The guy with the squeaky shoes.
—*Camp Pickett, VA, Pvt. Hy Yanowitz*

Section Five
Poems about Military Life

FELLOW COUNTRYMEN

I am whatever you are:
Your friend and brother,
Your drinking companion.

If you are Italian and proud,
Then I am proud to be an Italian,
And when you ask me
I will tell you that.

A Scandinavian might see,
In my brown hands and sailing ways,
A fellow countryman. I am that.

Because I have a dark swarthy look,
A Greek will say, "You are Greek!"
A brother has eagerly recognized me,
And I am glad to be a Greek.

Some may guess me Hebrew, Slavic, Spanish.
Shall I deny my Spanish, Slavic, Hebrew decent?
I am all of those valiant comrades.

A savage wrack-brain of my company
Insinuates against the Negro's equal manhood
I quietly explain his error---
Or spit in his eye.
Negros are not ashamed
Naming me one of their own.
I am proud.

I am whatever you are, You no less than I.
    —*Paris Island, SC, Pfc. Lewis Arthur, USMC*

GREAT SOUTH BAY

The red-brown marsh grass glints beneath the sun,
A signal and a warning that the autumn has begun.
A straggling line of thistles is marching down the field
Wearing sturdy, stubborn courage as a buckler and a shield.
A white gull is penciled against the turquoise skies,
And on the surface of the bay a saffron sunset lies.
The restless, surging water mocks the stillness of the land,
And taunting waves roll in to break in laughter on the sand.
A cloud of wings goes swiftly by---a lonely crane in flight.
In the wind's voice is a warning of the coming of night.
    —*New Guinea, Sgt. Kathleen Nealis*

BLANK IS THE CANVAS

Blank is a canvas,
Blank as night,
The unexpressed
In want of light.

I need my brush
To splash the hues,
Viridian, sienna,
Ultra blues.

Give me hues,
I cry in vain
To lash the hills
Beneath the rain.

The vibrant greens;
The wind-brushed field;
A man, a hoe,
The earth, sun-peeled.

Crude water-wheels
Maintaining order
In a winding, tangling
World of water.

Geometric
Patch of earth;
God-made patterns
Seek rebirth.

O, what a fierce
Aesthetic call!
My brush! My palette!
My paints! My all!

Give me these
That I may borrow
Light---and seal it
For tomorrow.

Wait and cry
And howl and wail---
The paints and brushes
Are still in the mail!
—*China, Pvt. David Attie*

BASIC TRAINING, WAC

In Georgia there are clouds and trees
And clay, of course, and birds and bees.
We sit indoors while people talk
Or else we walk;
March out of doors, with stern resolve,
Strong faith and sober feeling,
Horizon limited and a strictly zero ceiling.

Hair on a woman's neck
Above the collar, very neat;
Hat set square; beyond, more heads,
More hats and nice big serviceable feet.

Eyes front. Eyes right.
We march. Now watch it there and keep that beat!
Above all drift the clouds so white,
Rolling with laughter down the round sky.
Above us sleep the giant pines
Marking time till we have passed,
Taking with us our noise,
Our regulation tears and joys, our massed
And patterned, quite GI
Insanity.
—*Swannanoa, NC, Pfc. Gloria Marchisio*

BARRACKS TWILIGHTS

Barracks twilights are lonely;
Faint blues and dimming reds of sunset
Up the long, straight avenues; yellow
Lights aglow in the gaunt windows
Lonely we wander, men without women,
Tired of harsh, male voices
Hearing adolescent curses, we, slovenly
In shapeless fatigue hats, or burnished
With brass buttons in new uniforms,
With no women to admire them.

Barracks twilights are lonely;
Wrenched from out lives, we
Wander in groups, boast in high tones,
Turning our memories of little home towns
Back in our brains. Barracks twilights
Are lonely; yet more lonely by far
The men not in the barracks, cursed
With greater loneliness, unseen,
Feeling the pull and clutch and pain
Of a war that has passed them by.
—*Philippines, Cpl. Hargis, Westerfield*

BARRACKS

It is just an old shack
Made of wood and steel,
And how in a high wind
It will rumble and squeal.

It is hot when we're gone
And it's cold when we're here,
And a darned poor hide-out
When those details are near.

We cuss it and we damn it
From pillar to dome;
Be it ever so humble
There's no place like home.
  —*North Atlantic Command, Pvt. Earl W. Post*

BAR, MOSQUITO

Some Quartermaster master mind
Put in for one more star
Because he is the father of
The famed mosquito bar
But to the end I'll still contend
The bar is overrated:
You see, my canvas cot and it
Are very much mismatched.

For I have yet a night to see
When sound asleep I seem to be
And my mosquito bar is tucked in,
A damned mosquito hasn't ducked in.

It seems that as I soundly nap
Away the blacked-out night,
Somebody's feet jerk out the sheet
And make my bar untight.
No matter how I fix the thing
It never fails to happen:
When I arise, yawn, rub my eyes,
I see the edges flapping.

My atabrine I'll gladly take
By twos or by the jar
And toss aside the QM's pride---
The brown mosquito bar.
  —*Australia, Sgt. F.H. Boslett*

BAKSHISH

Bakshish, that's all you hear in India, bakshish.
When you go walking down the street
A thousand beggars you will meet
And each with sad expression
Will chant the same confession:
No mamma, no papa, bakshish.

If you decide to take a gharry ride, sahib,
You state the price that you will pay.
The driver nods his head okay
And when you pay he'll grab it,
Then say with the force of habit:
No mamma, no papa, bakshish.

From six to sixty they all shout,
No mamma, no papa, no sister, no brother.
And if you should linger, they'll tell you another
But not before they tug at your sleeves,
For the charge will be two annas, please.

Bakshish, that's all you hear in India, bakshish.
No matter where you chance to be
You're followed till you pay a fee.
 And once you do they've found you,
And they will gather round you, and hound you;
No mamma, no papa, bakshish.
  —*India, Cpl. Leo Liebman*

A T-5's TRAVAIL

I have a buddy who wears two stripes,
A corporal, that's easy to see.
I have two stripes on the sleeve of my shirt,
But unfortunately mine have a "T."

We draw the same pay, and he's a swell guy,
One of the finest alive.
But he's a buck corporal, a line NCO,
And I'm just a goddam T-5.

Back home, on furlough, at dances and such,
The girls didn't know what "T" means.
But here in the Army he lives like a king,
While T-5s are scrubbing latrines.

My letters say "corporal," the same as my pal's.
And when we fall out to get paid
The exalted line noncom gets not one cent more
Than the lowly technician fifth grade.

Some day we both hope to better our rank,
And when this event comes to pass,
Let him be a sergeant with great big stripes;
I'm bucking for private first-class.
—*Australia, T-5, Arthur M. Ross*

ASSIGNMENT---BY THE NUMBERS

Before the war I practiced law,
And argued points much mooted,
Now this is how the Army saw
I'd end up best suited.

For ten hot days I chopped the trees,
And strung my nether ham.
I cut my arms and skinned my knees.
Did my sergeant give a damn?

In the sun I mixed concrete,
Used to floor a new latrine.
I think it would be more discrete
To use not me but a machine.

Yesterday I joined the 'line',
There we service all the planes,
I must have acted mighty fine---
For now I'm washing window panes.

Tonight I walk interior guard,
And watch the hangars and the planes
To swim my post would not be hard.
It's full of holes; it always rains.
—*Greenville Flying School, MS, Pfc. Joseph L. Abraham*

A MOMENTO

Like silent sentinels the barracks' double-decked bunks stand,
Empty of their laughing occupants;
The last have answered the call.
The temporary dwelling has served;
Vermin will take over and will crawl
Until all human scent and parcels of food are gone;
Then they will depart, as now
The rain runs down the rusty beds to the rotting floor,
Sunshine streams through the broken windows,
A passing deer approaches silently and looks in.
Rusty are the beds, lonely the room, buried the secrets.
—*Fort Sill, OK, T-4 Emil Hess*

AND SEE THE WORLD

Much have I traveled in the realms of gold
Of which poetic tongues have often told;
The pathways of romance I've sailed along
Through fabled seas apostrophe in song.
A varied voyage mine? Forego the notion,
For what do you think I saw? I saw the ocean!

Water, water everywhere; water day and night.
Water, water all the while and never land in sight.
A tropic scene with swaying palms the morning sun may rise on,
A magic land within my grasp, but it's over the horizon.

So every day I sit and stare at the never changing sea
And try to picture land near which the ship's supposed to be;
But since land is anathema to crowded transport ships,
The storied world lies just beyond my outstretched fingertips.

For all I see of foreign lands as round the world I roam
I'd learn much more from a travel book on my own front porch at home.
—*China, Pfc. John L. Van Der Voort*

ALEUTIAN JOY

Nothing daunted by perpetual chill
In his avid search for some tasty swill,
The raven dives at a moment's detection
Of a suitable dump of tainted perfection.

Shrilling, cawing, loud and brash,
On spotting a juicy pile of trash,
Down he swoops with corvine greed,
Soon joined by friends in noisy feed.

The extermination of this ravished ruck
Is soon announced by contented cluck,
As he homeward wheels from his diurnal glut,
Serenely happy with a bulging gut.
—*Aleutians, S/Sgt. Leroy A. Metcalf Jr.*

A SIMPLIFID TAX PLAN

The tax bill this year, as you must know, was passed this year when congress grew weary;
It's a cross between pay-as-you-go and Einstein's Relativity Theory.

Einstein can prove that time and space are fourth-dimensional equations,
That two and two make four some place, but not on all occasions.
While Rumi believes in forgiveness now, skip a year is his plan,
You see, my friend, why milk the cow when you can buy milk in a can?
Thus opposite forces converge in debate and brought forth a compromise pact
That's neither fish nor fowl, I venture to state, nor based on fiction or fact.
Behold, rare formulae and figures abound to amaze the mightiest seer;
You calculate round and round and come out, I think, I hope, out here.
Yet while I'm bewildered and slightly amused, one thought unwrinkles my brow;
The tax collectors, too, are mighty confused and are attending a school to learn how.
The day will come, as it surely must, when my simplified plan will be used;
Mine is the way to less painlessly bus the public so sorely confused.
My plan may be thought by some as too rash, and make them hot 'neath the collar,
But it's simpler to let Uncle Sam take our cash and pay us 10 cents on the dollar.
 —*Herbert Smart Airport, Macon, GA, Cpl. Nathaniel Rogovoy*

ADVENTURE

Each wispy cloud piece
That breaks away from the herd
To drift the uncharted way
Takes with it a part of me,
For I have followed the call
Of the wind.
The adventurer and I
Are forever one.
The rivulet which shuns
The river, to run its course
Alone, receives my tender love.
 —*Lincoln AAF, NE, Pfc., Samuel Naparstek*

A DOGFACE IS NO SEA DOG

In the garrison we were happy
But now they've got our goat,
'Cause they've got us bag and baggage
On a damn banana boat.

On the desert, in the mountains,
We're as happy as could be
But we're having lots of trouble
Since they sent us out to sea. . . .

Where the left side is the port side
And the toilet is the head,
Where you bang your skull in the hatchways
Till you wish that you were dead,
Where a chow line ain't a line at all
But just a milling bunch,
And you finish up with breakfast
Just in time to start with lunch.

And you hit the hay in layers
Like pre-war layer cake,
With bunks four high, that touch the sky;
Oh, what a chance you take.
Each time you wish to turn and toss
Amid your fitful slumber,
You have to warn the other guys
And do it by the numbers.

The drinking water's salty
And if you should need a shave,
Your buddies gladly wish you luck
And bid you to be brave.
You'll know exactly what I mean If you've been on a boat,
For the chances are 50-50,
When you shave you cut your throat.

When the weather's nice and sunny
They keep you down below,
But you'll guard guns upon the deck
If it should rain or snow.
We've heard that on the bounding main
All things are pretty swell,
So let the Navy have their boats,
And let them go to hell.
 —*Fort Ord, CA, Author Unknown Submitted by Cpl. Ray E. Thomas*

AACS LAMENT

They call us the AACS
Dit happy guys are we.
We copy the sigs for the weather,
And dog rob for ATC.

We're stuck in far off places,
From Maine to Timbuctoo.

In climes of all descriptions
We get our traffic through.

Hand-me-down parts for equipment,
Most of it borrowed or stole,
Some shacks are tin-covered lean-tos;
Others use a bombproof hole.

We're scattered from hell to breakfast,
No knowing our own CO,
Attached to a hundred outfits,
We're orphans wherever we go.

Our guys don't ever get medals,
For this we don't give a damn.
For we are the guys that they call on
When an airplane gets in a jam.
    —*Caribbean Command, M/Sgt. J.C. Keyser*

THOUGHTS ON A HOT NIGHT

Oh, to be stationed in Iceland,
With temperature 40 below;
I'd find paradise In an igloo of ice
And sleep under a blanket of snow.
Oh, for a transfer to Iceland,
With an iceberg or two for a base,
Where all good GIs
Feast on Eskimo Pies
While icicles grow in your face.
    —*Charleston AAB, SC, Cpl. Carl Fenichel*

EVENING TRANSPORT

He waits until the sun has lost its lance,
And in the coolness all the troop is still.
It's only then the soldier finds his chance
To dream his way to any place he will,
One liquid motion of the weary eye
The lid is dropped: the private curtain falls
Against the marching and the time to die,
Against the firing and the bugle calls
Then let the cadence of his war increase
And injure all his body but his eyes
Still he may close them: he will be at peace
For he will ride his transport to the skies.
This one departure when the day is done,
Is rich and final as the set of the sun.
    —*Camp Crowder, MO, Pvt. Darrell Bartee*

LAND SAILOR'S LAMENT

It seems like such a shame
That I don't know the name
Of any of the parts of a ship.
I've been given the word
By a yeoman who heard
That they're sending me out on a trip.

I shiver to think
Of that shimmering drink
With the wind and rain and the squall;
And a bo'sun mate's pipe
And a stomach to gripe
At the constant rise and fall.

It's been so much fun
When the work is all done,
Drinking brew when I get into town;
It's sad, but I fear
That they won't give me a beer
When I really have troubles to drown.
    —*Naval Air Station, Norfolk VA, Irving Feldman Y2c*

ODE TO A GUARD

The guard patrols his lonely post,
Finding comfort in the boast
That he alone of all his station
Bears the burden of the nation.

Hears a crunch upon the ground,
Quick as lightning turns around
Then he grins and feels absurd---
His own footsteps he has heard.

Getting sleepy, names the states.
Whistles snatches, recons dates,
Counts his steps and counts his turnings,
Figures out his yearly earnings.

Cheer up, sentry, after war
You'll be trained for jobs galore.
Summons server, tax collector,
Postman, cop, or bank protector.

I can see you walking floor
For a big department store;
Running wife's errands maybe,
Walking round the room with baby.

And if you should get restless for
Certain features of the war,
Button up your collar tight
And walk around the block all night.
  —*Fort Custer, MI, Pvt. Martin Weldon*

ORDNUNG

Blankets are folded just to a T,
Still reeking of sweat.
Shoes smell of ole dubbing,
But tie up the laces;
The leather need rubbing.
This fungus infection
On feet half-demolished
Will pass inspection
In shoes that are polished

Minds are conditioned
Just to a T.
They're reeking with hate
And the smell of old bias.
But lace up your thoughts,
Praise the strong and the pious!
With brains half-demolished
By morbid routine,
They'll pass for good soldiers
(Till peace strips them clean).
  —*Fort Bliss, TX, Pvt. Thomas Langner*

OPEN RANKS

We'd never been inspected;
We never had suspected
That anyone would even want to look us up and down---
When all at once they sprang it
(With our stockings crooked, hang it!)
And the State Guard looey really went to town.

We haven't kit and rifle
Or any other trifle;
We've only got our uniform and the chassis which it's on.
But it seems that that's sufficient
When the officer's efficient,
And it's just about the damnedest thing we've ever undergone.

For I wouldn't like to mention
What I thought while at attention.
We stood with rigid faces while he circled aft and fore,
But that looey's pretty plucky---
And he's also pretty lucky
That our military discipline is excellent and more.

If that looey meant to ride us
By the way in which he eyed us
(As the Guardsman in the corridor suggested loud and long),
He didn't raise a snicker---
No, not an eyelid's flicker
Betrayed that we were anything but self-possessed and strong.

But isn't it amazing
To learn such measured gazing
Is an army regulation and perfectly correct
When, to be completely candid
A civilian would be handed
A prompt and handsome shiner if he started to "inspect"?

Yes, it must be military
For it looks familiar---very;
Yes, we're learning army customs very fast,
And *nothing* will surprise us
In the way a soldier eyes us
Now we've passed our first inspection drill at last.
  —*Massachusetts Women's Defense Corps, Lt. Brook Byrne*

ON THE MARCH

After the seventh mile the men
Prefer the chanting of the shoes
To singing thrice-sung songs again---
Too little breath to lose.

A mental song does just fine
To add some voltage to the chaste
Cadence of our marching line,
And give each man his taste.

Pete in the second section, last
Platoon, squad number five,
Is beating him a rhythmic feast
Of Dixieland jive.

Out front the right guide steps alone,
Pivot of the column's tread
Drawing strains of Mendelssohn
From fiddles in his head.

Old homely hymns, tart ballads, blues
Songs of all times and recent date
Sung to the chanting of our shoes---

Silent conglomerate!

And there's a private music lingers
In the helmet of many a rover,
Of houses to be built, and fingers
Ringed when this is over.
—*San Angelo AAF, TX, Pfc. Edmund M. Zaslow*

OH, CRUEL SUSPENSE

Your three months are up
And then you guess
You'd like to try
For OCS.

Your fingers are crossed
Until when
You're notified you've got an
IQ Of a hundred and ten.

The time comes when
You praise the Lord
That at 1500 o'clock
You go before the board.

They ask you this, they ask you that,
They ask you, "What is a G.I. hat?"
They look to see that you're trim and neat,
And suddenly ask you, "What did you eat?"

They ask you how far is water from shore,
And where in the *Atlantic* is Singapore,
They ask the nomenclature of all types of rifles,
And other such tremendous trifles.

They ask you about your private life:
"Where did you work,
And what did you do?"
They stare the polish off your shoe.

You walk around weeks looking harassed,
Then suddenly get notice that you have passed.
But for the present school you're a little late
So you just have got to wait and wait.
—*NY, Port of Embarkation, Pfc. David A. Hart*

OFFICER CANDIDATE

I'm a nervous mess from OCS,
My rear it drags the ground,
And every night at 11 o'clock
In a prone position I'm found.
They cram us full of knowledge
So fast it won't digest.
I'm a candidate for Section 8
Because I get no rest.

We drill like hell all day sir,
The bed bugs drill at night;
They teach us all their tactics
Oh gosh, how they bite.
But when December 8th comes
And bars they pin on me,
I'll pray like hell for a furlough
And go on a helluva spree.
—*Fort Benning, GA, Cpl. Joseph Weiss*

OF DICE AND MEN

He who shoots craps
After taps
Responds but heavily
To reveille,
While he who is frugalier
Is up with the bugler.
—*APO 45, NY, Pfc. Carroll Johnson*

ODE TO AN ARMY SERVICE CLERK

When the half-awakened bugler
Sends forth his clarion note
And the first pale streaks of morning
Strike the brass upon his coat,
The solitary service clerk
Long since has been awake,
Thinking of those blasted forms
That he forgot to make.

They're notifications and applications
And certifications bunk...
They're designations and regulations
And consolidated junk.
There're assignment cards and charge sheets
And statements of account
He's written a thousand furloughs
And a thousand more no doubt.

There're identifications, investigations
And information rot;
There're examinations and classifications
And other polygot.
So it's write out this and write out that
And type it to the end.
And when he's dead and buried,
His death report he'll send.
—*England, Cpl. Bill Sexton*

NO PROMOTION

I have siphoned dregs of dolor
From the deepest, darkest pit.
I have quaffed the cup of sorrow;
Failed to score or even hit.

Breaks and ratings go to others
But, alas, they pass me by.
Stripes about me sprout profusely;
I am left to wonder why.

Sergeants (staff and tech and master),
Pausing briefly in their grade,
Blithely rush by to promotion;
Booted, rooted, I have stayed.

True, the war can't last forever;
Blindest fools as much can see.
But, I often sadly wonder,
Will it, maybe, outlast me?
—*San Angelo AAF. TX, Cpl. H. J. Bennett*

MY LITTLE HUT

Be it ever so humble or built in a rut,
There is no place on earth like my little green hut,
For it's flat on the bottom and rounded on top,
From the roof to the floor's an 11-foot drop.
There's a stove in my hut and that stove's kind of little;
There's a guy in my hut---one who sleeps in the middle;
His ambition's immense, for he'll kick and he'll poke,
'Till the fire goes out in a billow of smoke.
Every man in my hut will make up his own cot
Every eight or 10 days if it needs it or not,
And they'll sweep out the dirt 'til their cots look fine,
And the dirt's in a neat 2-foot pile under mine.
Though it's built in a rut about 7-feet deep,
It's a good enough place for a soldier to sleep;
Be it ever so humble or placed in a rut,
Thank the Lord there's no place like my little green hut.
—*England, S/Sgt. Gene E. Bluhm*

MOONLIGHT AT CAMP

I cannot sleep, and through the barracks door
I watch the moon with its dim, shining rays,
Bathing the camp in misty light, as o'er
Our heads in simple majesty it plays
At making mystic daylight while it may,
Moonlight at camp, and home so far sway.

In many other camps tonight throughout
The world, this moon is shining silently
Upon the many thousands who, without
A thought of self, are serving patiently;
Though in their dreams they wistfully say:
"Moonlight at camp, and home so far away."

The same moon shines upon our homes tonight,
Where loved ones wait for millions to return;
And when this saddened world is set aright,
When it has bled the lesson it must learn,
Then we shall see the end for which we pray---
Moonlight at home. We shall be home some day.
—*Camp Blanding, FL, Cpl. William P. Duggan*

MARCHE MILITAIRE

In the glaring day
The land if boring
And trucks are dusty mechanisms,
Though 'tis true
That high above the planes may climb,
Twisting and turning,
Then falling to catch the sunrays,
Like a handful of small, bright coins
Thrown by the gods.

Ah, but at night
The roads are peopled
With stubborn, coughing beasts
That probe the hillside,
Showing great white eyes
To the silence,
And against the silvered sky
Palm trees are tall women,
Their backs to the wind,
Hair blowing round their faces.

The sun, I grant
Claims the favor of fickle gods,
But darkness brings such art
That even those careful poets,
Heed the ancient song
Of the surf.
—*France, Sgt. Patrick J. O'Sullivan*

GUARD

I walk my post in lonely wood,
The echoes of the night bid heed.
They cry; The aged-leaf rustle and the whispering wind.
The black song of the crow,
The hoot of the staring owl,
The loudness of the silence in a wary brain;
The forest cries for notice.
—*Willimantic, CT, Pvt. Norman Sak*

GUARD

I stand on the crest of the hill
While below and around me
Tired soldiers are sleeping,
Their bodies relaxed,
Restoring spent energy.

Night appears,
Trailing her draperies across the sky.
In the ebony heavens a lone star emerges
Followed by others in quick succession,
A million Kohinoors Suspended in space.
Trees and shrubs harmless in daytime
Change to giants and crouching creatures.
A gossamer mist steals down the hills,
Fringing the swamp in drifts of unearthly beauty.

I am a lone spectator to a play
With nature and night as the setting.

Unexpectedly
A night-bird dips across the clearing,
Its eerie cry breaking the silence
Like the sudden sound of pebbles
Against a window pane.
As though by a preconceived signal
Lusty frogs harump themselves hoarse.
From the nearby shadows
Winged tree-dwellers whimper and scold
And a small furry shape bounds in front of me,
Its flash of movement returning me to reality.
Now nature settles back into the arms of night
While I, shifting my rifle,
Warily continue walking my appointed post.
—*Fort Sill, OK, Pvt. Gene Wierbach*

GOODBY TO ALL THAT

It won't be long, the papers say,
'Til I can join the millions
Who go their merry, carefree way;
The poor, fouled-up civilians.
No more CS, no more GI---
It's almost past believing.
KP, CQ, OD---Goodbye;
That life I'll soon be leaving.
My ribbons I can throw away,
I'm through with stripes and medals;
No more I'll hear, as of today,
That crap the sergeant peddles.
The mess hall, with its powdered eggs,
I can now leave behind me.
The rules compiled in Army Regs
No longer rule and bind me.
The shinning brass, commanding, stern
From them VJ-Day spares me.
To normal life I can return---
But, Jeez---the idea scares me!
—*Seattle, WA, T-4 Lester Asheim*

GIT UP AND GIT OUT

The bugle blows---
And why, Lord only knows.

Out of the blackness enfolding me,
Farewell to the warm bed enfolding me.
A curse on the morning night, ebony black;
A curse on the brisk breeze chilling my back;
A prayer that only a soldier knows,
"Please Lord, where are my reveille clothes?
—*Fort Taylor, FL, 1st Sgt. Luman S. Nutter*

GI JOSEPHINE

I never thought I'd care to
Have to wear my hair to
Meet a regulation.
Nor did I think that I'd enjoy
PTing so my avoirdupois
Would meet a stipulation.
I knew darn well I wouldn't cater
To Kitchen Police with CQ later, Or:
Barracks detail, Retreat and drill,
Shots and checkups, Till I'm ill.
I anticipated I'd abhor
The all too wordy A's of War,
Yet I enlisted, I'm a Wac,

With GI shoes and "Aching Back."
I stand retreat, I snap salutes,
I pull KP in GI boots,
And the gratitude I glean from this
Fills my spangled heart with bliss.
For when my weary arms are twisted,
When troubles plague my tired joints,
Some GI sneers, "Well you enlisted,"
And I recount my 13 points.
—*Minter Field, CA, Pfc. Bettianne Foster*

GI INSOMNIA

I've got tags that jingle jangle jingle
As I toss and wriggle all night long,
And their clankings softly intermingle
With the sighs, moans and cussing in my song.

Comes the dawn I'm set to grab some shuteye,
And the sarge blows the whistle loud and long.
I want to sleep and plenty of it, but I
Can hear that whistle blowing loud and long.
—*AAF, Marianna, FL, T/5 Abraham Stern*

FROM MANTOLOKING TO MANHATTAN

Pursuant to your reference to the bird's leg appended
We hereby answer you in ode and trust you're not offended.
On Friday morning, March the fifth, a morning cold and dreary,
A signalman upon our bridge found a bird, tired and weary.
The bird then was immediately brought to a bird-fancier mate
To help determine the point to which this bird would navigate.
Identification it bore not like carrier pigeons carry;
It was a homing bird, he said, that from his loft did tarry.

Nothing else was there to do. The bird was properly fed
And then released and eagerly watched as into the blue it sped.
Where it lands we do not know, but one thing we can say---
The boys of Mantoloking did their good deed for the day;
Be it small or be it great, it was true to our tradition;
The coast guard always renders aid with true determination.
Thus this bird, be where it may. . . .Greetings I'm extending
From shipmates of Manhattan Beach to those of Mantoloking.
—*U.S. Coast Guard, John K. Synovec*

EVENING AT HOME

As I lay on my cot and I stare at the pages
Of a book where the greatest and best of the sages
Has sprinkled the juiciest thoughts of the ages,

Young Roger, my neighbor in pleasure and labor,
My buddy with mop in latrine,
My field-wire reeler, potato peeler
And expert with TL 13,
Came up beside me and forcefully pried me
Apart from the muses, for aces and twoses
Were vying with ten, jack and queen.

I am not a gambler. I never had played
Rummy or pinochle, bridge or Old Maid,
But friendship is friendship and so I must trade
Two eclogues, an ode, a philippic tirade
For a pair of nines and the ace of spade.

Jack sat at my right and Ed dealt the cards,
Then Hack dealt and I dealt and Roger and John,
And the minutes flew fast till midnight was past
And my dollar and thirty-nine cents were all gone.
We played and we played for each hand was the last---
Oh, surely---but still it went on.

At a quarter past three,
When the deal came to me,
I thrust friendship aside and arose;
And my buddies quite weary,
With eyes red and bleary
Agreed it was time we might close.

Both Caesar and Homer have written of war;
For Homer 'twas glory,
For Caesar a story
Of strong men united and pagan defiance.
For Sherman 'twas gory;
Von Clausewitz described it as theory and science.

Oh, where in the annals of armies and conquest,
Are the words of the erudite seer that writes
Of the battle that barracks-bound soldiers
Wage over and over on weekday nights?
—*Port of Embarkation, Pfc. Irving Risner*

ENGINEER BLUES

Where the monsoons sweep and the cobras creep
And darkness falls with a thousand fears,
Where the chew is rough and the noncoms tough—
Oh, that's in bounds to the Engineers.
Where the saxes sob and the dancers bob
And the siren from darkened doorway peers,
Where the ivories click and the steaks are thick—
Oh, it's out of bounds to the Engineers.

Where the snipers lurk in the leafy murk,
Where men are bloody and sweaty smears,
Where the Zeros wing and the scorpions sting—
Oh, that's in bounds to the Engineers.

Where the MPs stalk and the hillbillies gawk
And the native soldiers leer.
Where the white wine bubbles to drown your troubles—
Oh, it's out of bounds to the Engineers.
—*India, Pfc. E.V. Andersos*

EATIN' FOOD, G.I.

"Who knows, who knows where they get the chow
That they feed in the Army"? the Doggies moan.
The beef must come from a new kind of cow
Built of fat, skin and gristle and bone
And bred and in-bred 'til the pitiful wreck
Is half of it tail and half of it neck
Supported by sticks attached to its feet
Completely and utterly stripped of its meat
So weak and anemic it's almost unable
To finish its trip to the Army table.

Where, oh where do they get the 'frank'
That makes the Doggies their appetite lose,
Which in Army feeding takes first rank
And "rank" is the word to use.
That cylinder known as the old hot dog
Which tastes like wood and feels like a log.
Now doubtless frankfurters have their uses,
But they fight like hell with the gastric juices,
With after-effects which resemble a souse
And put you into the canine house.
So please Mr. Einstein tell us how
And where they obtain the Army chow.
—*Sgt. Drew L. Ratliff*

DUTY

Our office is very quiet
In the heavy stuffiness
Of the late afternoon.
Here and there a typewriter
Slowly clicks
And, as if a million miles
Away, the telephone purrs---
But, I sit dreaming
With a silly smile in my
Heart, though my fingers
Are pounding the keys.
—*AAF, Lincoln, NE, Pfc. Samuel Naparstek*

DREAMS OF A BROOKLYN G.I.

Lazy like I lay upon my cot,
And think and think an awful lot
Of downtown Brooklyn, Paramount and Fox,
Nathan's hot dogs and bagels and lox;
Or the parking area in Prospect Park,
A stroll on the Parkway when it's dark,
The fast talk of the Brownsville boys,
And the old ladies oy, oy, oy's;
Those pants---24-inch knee and 15-inch peg,
The cop's "Keep moving and shake a leg,"
A dance at the hall in Bensonhurst,
The Black and White to quench your thirst,
A fast-moving night at a cellar club,
The Catskill Mountain MC with a cigar stub.
No more thinking but doing till we finish the Japs,
But these are the things I dream of after taps.
—*Camp Gordon, GA, Cpl. Isidore Goldstein*

DOES VICTORY DEPEND ON ME?

I am the butt of the soldier's joke,
At me the sailors their lampoons poke.
Does victory depend on me,
The limited service, bedeviled MP?

With stalwart heart, if quivering stand,
I take the situation well in hand
When a husky marine is on a spree,
The "off limits" sentinel, the sober MP.

When the carrot-fed aviator, daring and sky-eyed,
Misses his train because he is pie-eyed,
I steady his step because, you see,
That's a limited service of the grounded MP.

I guard the work of the steady man
Who works to build the best he can
The ships, the planes, the guns,---you see,
My service is limited to just MP.

Armed with a night stick, a brassard and whistle,
In rain and snow, I hope that this'll
Somehow help in the victory---
The limited service of the poor MP.

When the heroes come home with adulation,
I'll make up the army of occupation and stay on the job for victory---
The unlimited service of the poor MP.

I walk my post in a military manner.
There is little glory to tinsel my banner.
Does victory depend on me,
The limited service of the poor MP?

Please, God, when you've handed round the glory,
Find a place at the end of the thrilling story
For the contributions to victory
Of the limited service, bedeviled MP!
Yes, Victory Depends on
Me.
  —*Presidio, San Francisco, CA, Cpl. Denis McGenty*

DESPONDENT DOGFACE

Three longs years, and never a
Hun I've seen or heard or felt;
Three long years, a hitch, I've done
And never a Jap I've smelt.

I've never flopped and shook and sweat
At an MG's rattatat,
Or cut my Spam with a bayonet
And thanked dear God for that.

This life is soft as hell up here,
Though never quite as warm;
The girls are toothless far and near,
But there's teeth in every storm.

While the wild winds scream we sit and dream
Of southern palms and posies,
After a while we start to scream
And develop psychoneuroses.

I'll prick my frostbit ears and shrug
And shake my ice-caked bones
And take a slug at the next bright mug
Who says: "This is the Army, Jones."
  —*Newfoundland, Sgt. Howard E. Evans*

DEAR SANTA CLAUS

Santa, my name is GI Joe
I've been a good boy as GIs go,
For three long years, the sum of a hitch,
 I've filled an eager-beaver niche.
I've swept my bunk and shined my boots
And tossed highballs to second lieuts.
I've not goofed-off or been AWOL
Or guzzled too much alcohol,
I've never ridden the sick book, see,
Or tried to buck for a CDD.
Though top kicks made my temper quicken
I've never labeled them as chicken.
Yes, Santa, you can plainly see
I've been a first class Pfc!

But now that all the wars are won
And de-atomized is the Rising Sun,
Dear old man with checks vermillion,
Make me, for Christmas, a merry civilian!
Before the fall of Yuletide snows
Get me out of these damn clothes!
Make Dunder and Blitzen prance and caper
On the double with that Discharge Paper!
But if things should go
Snafu I'll tell you what I'm gonna do;
I'll re-enlist---(a home I've found!)
Santa, bring a around!
  —*Sheppard Field, TX, Sgt. Shelby Friedman*

COMPARISON

In the glaring day
The land is boring
And trucks are dusty mechanisms,
Though 'tis true
That high above the plane may climb
Twisting and turning,
Then falling to catch the sunrays,
Like a handful of small, bright coins
Thrown by gods.

Ah, but at night
The roads are peopled
With stubborn, coughing beasts
That probe the hillside,

Showing great white eyes
To the silence,
And against the silvered sky
Palm trees are tall women,
Their back to the wind,
Hair blowing round their faces.

The sun, I grant,
Claims the favor of fickle gods,
But darkness brings such art
That even those careful poets,
Heed the ancient song
Of the surf.
—*Saipan, Sgt. Stan Flink*

CHOW CALL

Chow call was blown.
The line soon formed.
It stretched for half a mile.
Those at the tail were full of groans,
While those in front did smile
And first in line, the first of all,
Our hero proudly stands.
He holds a battered messkit
In his outstretched, eager hands.
The chow is on, the doors flung wide,
Cooks yell, "Come eat, by heck!"
Our hero races in so fast
He damned near breaks his neck.
He grips his plate. A yearning look
Has crept into his eyes.
A cook, in pity, swears to feed
Our hero 'till he dies.
He walks away, his plate heaped high
With soup and meat and beans,
Potatoes, corn and gravy,
Rice pudding, cake and greens;
A cup of GI java.
He drinks his coffee neat.
(There is no man can drink two cups
And stay upon his feet.)
A brief three minutes' chomping,
And our hero's plate is bare.
He grabs it up, runs to the door,
Breaks through the chow line there.
Another gobble of his grub,
Another chow line run,
Our boy is soon at work on "thirds,"
Before most "firsts" are done.
The K.P.'s and the cooks depart,
And steal into the night.

But still our hero lingers on,
To have just one more bite.
And when at last he is full gorged,
And staggers through the door,
He is still game enough to try
To finish one bite more.
Full-fed and surfeited, he stands
And fills the air with groans
"I never saw such lousy chow,
I couldn't eat," he moans.
—*Pfc. James Hinson*

CHATTAHOOCHEE RIVER

Far from the Gulf where the colorful fishing boats play,
Far from the hills where the turbulent waterfall roars,
The muddy old stream inexorably measures it way
Like a blinded man, tapping the sides of its ill-defined
    shores.

Here where the brilliant *odonatous* dragonfly flutters
And waters are reeking with putrefied, redolent gasses,
Ponderous sycamore trees, in its weak-moired gutters,
Flop like dead drunks, while the river goes by like
    molasses.

Here by this spillage of massive conglomerate slime
Tourists and lovers and brow-wrinkled lecturers make
Pilgrimages; claim they see beautiful sights in this grime,
The collected refuse of an antediluvian lake.

How people ever find beauty in lusterless brown
Waters, surrounded by crab grass, is not very clear.
I think I will go to a place of great beauty in town,
Where purple lights glimmer and gobble some pretzels
and beer.
—*Ft. Benning, GA Sgt. Leonard Summers*

LINES WRITTEN DURING A SUNDAY K P

Somewhere the sun is shining,
Somewhere hearts are light---
Somewhere soldiers loll and chat,
And talk of yesternight.

But me---I sing this mournful tune
To fate, so cruel to me,
Who snatched me from my bed to spend
My Sunday on KP.

Oh, KP weekdays has its points,

Like missing drills I dread,
Or absence from a 10-mile hike,
Whence men return, half dead.

But KP Sunday? Say not so!
Forever I'll regret it.
Ah, well, no time to mope and sigh,
"Chow's on, you hounds, come and get it!"
—*Camp Gruber, OK, Cpl. Henry Foner*

LETTER TO THE PX

My dear PX: This is too much.
It's still the same old story.
Twice a week it's "Closed---Repairs"
Or "Closed for Inventory."

I do my bit---seven days a week
To help to keep 'em flying.
Get out those burghers! Open up!
And dammit, keep 'em frying!
—*Hendricks Field, FL, R.E.M.*

LETTER TO JOE

It was a year of days, like any other,
A year of nights when the hunted heart
Panted out its fear in the baying dark
And the face that recurred in dreams
Most often was a face with numerals
And somewhere secret moving hands;
Was a year of midnight snow and lights burning;
Girls, petals of them brushing our lips
Filling our hands; jukebox music
Stained with a sailor's blood;
The river white with ice, hands frozen
To riflebutts, striding voices,
The squadroom lit with snow,
And the phone in the hallway ringing ringing
Like the insistent tender bells
In a girl's crying;
Was a year like this, like any other---

The hut's lights glow like a jack-o-lantern In the swamp.
Carnivals of fireflies Swarm the palms.
And this Is the dog-howl of loneliness, I know;
But---kiss Detroit for me, Joe.
—*Philippines, S/Sgt. Troy Garrison*

"KISMET"

There are the Army men and Navy men,
In Uncle Sam's regime.
The Army men and Navy men,
Are held in high esteem,
But those Army slobs and Naval gobs
Noted for their valor,
Are apt to shy when bullets fly
With just a tinge of pallor!

There are the Army men and Navy men,
In Uncle Sam's regime,
But the only real hard fighting men
Wear khaki, blue and green.
For when cannons roar on distant shore,
'Tis known and proven fact,
Those bellhops fought till the final shot,
The Army stayed in back.

We've been told by a dogface boy,
Who wears a golden bar,
Just what we think Marines can do,
And what we think we are.
But let me task his brain and ask
That stupid dogface cuss,
"How many men in this wide world
Are quite as fine as us?"

So why shouldn't the stars if anxious to rise,
Or the moon wishing to beam,
Get permission to do from the Leatherneck crew,
The fighting, well-loved Marines?
And now, dear old looey, you shouldn't be sad,
Though ruined's your field of clover;
If your sweetie's found charms in a Leatherneck's arms,
These bellhops have taken over!
—*USMC, Alaska, E. A. Pforsich*

JUST ONE LAST FLING

Oh, I must go down to town again, for a snort of mountain dew,
And a shot of rye with a certain guy, and a dance with a girl or two.
For the whisky's kick makes a larynx thick, and I feel my frail knees shaking,
And a wan sneer on my sallow face, from the beating my ulcers are taking.

Oh, I must go down to town again, for the fragrant, tipsy life,

And to demon rum I will succumb, to free me of worldly
    strife.
In joy let me wean on some stale kerosene that is merely
    mildly disguised;
You may worry of war, while I sprawl on the floor, bliss
    fully paralyzed.
    —*Camp Gordon Johnston, Fla. S/Sgt. Franklin M. Willment*

JUST A PRIVATE

You can have your deeds of glory,
All your tasks so nobly done,
But if not for all the privates
Then this war could not be won.

Master minds may plan the battles
And strategic things to do,
Yet it's just a lowly private
Who must carry these things through.

So next time you drink to heroes
Who are known from coast to coast,
Just think of the simple private
And then drink another toast.
    —*Canada, Pvt. Hyman Lazarowitz*

JUNGLE PARADISE

Life is so sweet in the tropics,
Life is so calm and serene;
The taste of dehydrated rations,
The smell of an outdoor latrine.

The stench of a rain-soaked wool blanket,
The mud that creeps up to your knees,
The nights filled with stars and mosquitoes,
The beetles that drop from the trees.

The coconut milk so effective
(It works in the wink of an eye),
The coating of dust o'er your person
Each time a jeep passes by.

Your skin that turns yellow as sunflowers
From taking too much atabrine,
The rust that clings to your rifle,
The mold on your shoes, thick and green.

Yes, life is sweet in the tropics:
So happy, so jolly, so gay.
But describing this Garden of Eden
Is not what I came here to say.

For it's not here my heart beats contented,
Nor my soul really happily belongs.
So here's greetings from Paradise Island,
The home of the palms and sarongs.
    —*Dutch New Guinea, Cpl. George A. Harris*

JUNGLE LAMENT

Pvt. MacGrinder Fitzgerald McJeep
Moaned and groaned and tossed in his sleep.
In his cot was some sand and an ant or two;
He was covered with chiggers that stuck like glue.

He had caught a cold in the jungles damp
And from stabrine pills developed a cramp.
He was dopey from taking those thousands of pills
That the medics dispense to banish all ills.

His GI garments were covered with mold,
And the only papers were six months old.
The sun never shone and his shoes never dried,
And his waterproof tent let the rain inside.

His folding mess kit would always fold up
As he tried to juggle his tools, kit and cup,
He discovered that the beans weren't confined to the
Navy.
  And his pie never missed being garnished with gravy.

Shows were few and his gal didn't write;
When at a last she did, she said:
"Last night I weakened, now don't be enraged.
To an aircraft worker I'm now engaged."

But for all these troubles he cares not a whit;
His mind's on the homefolks doing their bit.
His father's at Lockheed, his mother's at Bell;
Three sisters at Boeing are doing quite well.

With all that money and no gas to roam,
With victory bonds they have papered their home,
And still our poor private is out on his feet,
Wondering how his home folks will eat.

The jungle has got him, 'tis sad to state,
And the moral of this I will now relate:
Forget the home folks and the gals that don't write;
Lie under a tree and watch the natives turn white.
    —*New Guinea, Cpl. Carl Shute*

JOISEY BOUNCE

We'll fight with the jerks from Joisey
To set the rising sun,
If they'll get the hell out of the Lone Star State
When'er the war is won.

Guys and gals in Texas
Like to drawl "out yonder," "you all" and "sho nuff,"
We don't think "jeeze, "youse" and "how long are you here"
Exactly up to snuff!

When it's round-up time in Texas,
And the Jap rats have met their doom,
May the sidewalks on Few York be crowded
And we'll no more hear their gloom.

'Tis a shame there isn't room for all
To live in the very best state.
Let's begin a "Joisey Bounce" campaign,
Before it is too late.

Let's tell them the Dodgers are good
And need all the support they can get.
Why should they stay in Texas,
When in Brooklyn they'd be all set?

But when they're home and look things over,
Open their bags and start to unpack,
Memories of Texas will unfold
And they will wish they were back!
—*AAFES, Childress, TX, Pvt. Robert D. Midkiff*

ICELANDIC SPRING

This barren land of wind and waste,
This broken rock spewed from the maw
Of a nauseous ocean—ash of the Atlantic,
Beaten down by precipitation,
Numbed by cold gales—
Comes to life sometimes.
Black night turns gray and shrinks
To nothingness.
Wild grass shoots up enigmatically
From volcanic dust
And spreads like moss
On a wet stone.
—*Iceland, Pfc. E.V. Anderson*

ICELAND

Post 1—0400 Hours
The black clouds vault from Asja's top
Upon the backs of winds, for some Walpurgis rite
That sets the night amoan and hurls the snow
In cruel phalanxes against the sentry box.
The frost with slow persistence gnaws with teeth of rats
While quisling sleep caresses lids with promises of dreams of home.
"To talk to no one"—not to wraiths who plunge deceitfully
The honed poniards of nostalgia deep within the breast,
"To walk my post"—but not in dreams nor fantasies
But head erect, to try to pierce the night.
To see beyond the dark to dawn, relief.
And fit this tortured moment in its niche.

Post 2—0600 Hours
The chimneys in our huts spin whorls of heat
Into a sunshine scarred by barriers of wires:
The mountains glow as with internal fires
But are cold and wear about their shoulders
Boas of clouds. Pale yellow bars of rays
Press through the sky toward Reykjavik
And fondle the camouflaged ships
Drowsing at anchor into a quiet awakening.
Wonderingly the cattle stare then moan
While the supple throats of cocks cry "reveille"
As I stand, a sentinel upon a hill
Staring across a land that is not my own.
—*Iceland T-5 Henry C. Meyer*

"HOME, HOME ON THE BASE"

Oh, give me a case, and a cool shady place
Where a sand flea can never be seen;
With a girl at my side, I will holler with pride;
"Oh, I'm so happy to be a Marine."

Home, home on the base,
Where the chasers and work-details play,
Where seldom is seen an unhappy Marine,
And the M.P.s are grouchy all day.

Oh, give me a horse for the obstacle course,
And a valet to carry my gear;
With a new pair of feet, and a cure for the heat,
I'd be happy to stay here all year.

Oh, give me some change and a big
Post Exchange Where I won't have to stand in line,

With a USO show every three days or so,
And a messhall exclusively mine.

Home, home on the base,
Where recon cars and jeep drivers play
Where we dream of all our fill of chow and sack drill,
And a bugler who's gagged every day.
  —*Pfc. G.L.*

HERE COME THE WAVES

Dressed in our Navy blues,
Here comes the WAVES,
Each heart is Navy true.
We're loyal all the way.
No job's too great a task,
We're here to serve,
Each lass is proud to be,
A member of the USN Reserve.
Heave ho! there sailor,
Everybody up at break of day,
Roll along, sing a song, though you're
Up at break of day---hey!
We'll help to win this war,
We'll do our share,
Backing our
Navy men, on land, at sea
And in the air.
Our course is charted now,
We'll never swerve,
We're very proud to be,
The women of the USN Reserve.
  —*Mary Carpenter, Ruth Hindenlang, Ethel Woechter,*
   Calista Halstead, Helen Baysor

SUPPLY SERGEANT

"I say there, supply sergeant, how do you fare?"
A growl, "I'm busy---and what do you care?"
"Oh, come now," we soothe, "don't go into a huff;
We just sort of wondered how you do your stuff.
This room you preside over---floor up to rafter
And filled with equipment we're forever after---
Is a model of neatness. The outfit is proud

Of you and your work, and their praises are loud"
A grin cracks his features. Could be that he'll say---
It could be and is---in a tone almost gay:
"I got forms, requisitions, three-twos and three-threes,
Memorandums and receipts. The work is a breeze
When Joe, my assistant, for private or sarges

Procures what they want, or a statement of charges.
I got what you want and I get what you need,
And to army procedure I pay strictest heed."

His smile is a radiant expression of one
Who is well satisfied that a good job's been done.
We talk of the weather and some other topics
Of those whom we like and of prejudiced top kicks
"Ah, yes," he resumes, "there are methods that work,
That to some men are clear and to others just murk.
At one time or another we best get supplies
When some guys don't ask questions and we don't tell lies.
  —*England M/Sgt. Larry McCabe*

SPECIALTY OF THE HOUSE

The chow at our mess is just fair,
Though mostly it's coffee and air;
But I add in just haste
There's one dish to our taste;
The sirloins are always quite rare.
  — *Fort Eustis, VA Pvt. David Altman*

SPARTANBURG STATION

O, simple for an engineer
To set the train in motion,
And simple for smoke to clear
The beams above the station.

But for the cars the women wave,
And from the platform, we;
And hard it is for them to leave
Lads of the Infantry.

And hard it is for marching men
To walk the road to camp,
Back to the agony of the pen—
And writers cramp.
  —*Camp Livingston, LA, Pvt. Edmond M. Zaslow*

SONNET FOR MY OUTFIT

This is a thick, discordant counterpoint
To oratory and the martial strain,
A marching line is weaving out of joint.
And greasy clouds are spilling fain
On rifles pointed down, on standards cased.
On sharp resentments held in muted throats

As transitory hopes become erased
By swamps and fascists wearing khaki coats.
We are the tutored mob; the infantry,
Redeemers of some words we vaguely know.
Who soon shall find the sharp philosophy:
That moment when a whistle's final blow
Shall signal the deploy, and we disperse,
Alone, and tangent to the universe.
—*Camp Claiborne, LA, Pfc. Perry Wolff*

SONG OF THE PERMANENT PFC

CO, though many a ballad I've made for you,
Rhyming my verse with artifice nice,
I never thought that the songs that I played for you
Cut any ice.

I never dreamed that my plea so hysterical
Rated me aught but a kick in the pants.
I always thought that our smile so satirical
Meant "not a chance."

I never expected a break as relating to
My line of bluff. That's the reason mayhap,
I wasn't surprised when you handed the rating to
Some other chap.
—*Loxley, AL, Pfc. Lewis Clark*

SONG OF AN EXILE FROM ALASKA

Ship me somewhere north of 56
To the land they say God doesn't know,
Where man is master of destiny
And free as the winds that blow.

For the husky dogs are howling
And it's there that I would be,
On that old Yukon River
Drifting lazy to the sea.

I'll take that road to Alaska,
Where the sunsets flare forlorn
And the little kit fox cries in the night
Up where the storms are born.

Yes, I'll hit the cold road to Alaska,
Where Borealis meets the day
And the dawn light s up the icebergs
Like diamonds in the bay.

I'm sick of wasting leather on a gritty city street,
For I hear the North a-calling and I'm getting itchy feet.
And I'm learning here in Gotham what the old-timer tells.
If you've heard the Northland calling, you won't need nothin' else.
—*Staten Island Terminal, NY, Pvt. Guy Owen*

SHINOLA O'PEAL

There once was a sergeant named John E. O'Peal;
He claimed he was Irish and walked on his heel.
He browbeat and bullied from morning till dusk
And God help the man with some metal in rust.
Now J.E. O'Peal had the esprit de corps,
Though his manners were truly as sharp as a boar;
When bright work did glisten and metal did shine
O'Peal wore a look that was almost divine.

I've seen many a sight with these old eyes of mine
And there's nothing as pretty as bright work in shine;
So from private to sergeant he jumped a short span.
He owes most of his rates to the Shinola can.

Now some people drink and many more smoke,
But I never knew John to take even a coke.
His day was complete and his attitude fine
If all buckets and buckles and brackets did shine.

Now J.E. had service---his stripes numbered three;
He had sailed all the oceans and every last sea,
Done duty in China, in Guam, and Haiti,
But, hell, was I glad when they shipped him from me.
—*Sergeant W.D. Cahill*

"SECRETS OF A SELECTEE"

I've talked to lads of every walk,
And lots of lads to me,
About the jobs that they once had,
And things they'd planned to be,
About the raise there would have been,
Had they not been inducted,
About that case of solid love
The draft had interrupted.
I've talked to lads who had no goal,
No mark wherewith to aim at,
Who thought that life and all therein
Was meant to wax profane at.
I've talked to those who never had
A home with friends and dear ones,
Conversed with those who had degrees,
And too, some mighty queer ones.

I've heard our land, our President,
Our Congress and our Houses
Discussed in terms, both pro and con;
Heard Nazis labeled louses,
But when the breeze of talk has died,
Each man, without exception
Would give his all for Glory's cause
And that's no misconception.
    —*Sgt. Gail D. Salley*

SATURDAY CQ

In solitary grandeur where he sits,
The charge of quarters in the captain's chair
Head man of all he sees about him is.
(Except that he's the only person there).

Awhile he writes and smokes and tries to sleep,
Then heeds the brazen summons of the phone,
His friends, his foes, his brothers in OD
Have gone on pass and he is all alone.

Gone is the top kick, gone the Old Man, too;
Vanished the techs and loueys; far away
In distant juke-joints privates hold wassail.
But he, the charge of quarters, has to stay.

What twist of fortune is it that decrees
The charge of quarters must a noncom be?
This is one detail that he cannot buck
Down to the private or the pfc.

The men of lower rank and stripeless sleeve
O'er whom he used to lord it through the week
Have taken off; I, too, shall catch the bus
While you, dear sergeant, lonesome vigil keep.

Oh, how you laughed when my name would appear
For garbage detail, stevedore, KP!
But now, oh Sarge, the worm of chance has turned
And you, for once, are It instead of me.
    —*Camp Callan, CA, Pfc. Raymond E. Lee*

SADISTIC OLD SERGEANT

I want three good typists
With nice finger nails.
Let's go, fellers!
Grab three mops and pails!

I want three college guys
Who speak Latin and Greek
Get a monkey wrench apiece
And fix that leak!

I want three smart guys
Who are nice and clean
Get into your fatigues
And scrub the latrine!

The rest of you guys
Who ain't so wise
And never went to any schools,
Don't hang aroun'
Here's a pass to town,
You thick-skulled, empty fools!
    —*Fort Belvoir, VA Pvt. Murray B. Schoen*

ROOKIE'S NIGHTMARE

I went down to the PX
To drink some three-point-two,
To rest my drill-weary doggies,
And cure a case of the blues.

But that old drill-field cadence
Pounded through my brain once more,
And I heard the Sarge yelling,
"Cadence---hut---hup---hep---fore!"

I pulled off my G.I. shoes,
Crawled in my bunk amid snores,
And they seemed to be in cadence,
That old "Hut---hup---hep---fore!"

Will I ever find a place,
Where quiet reigns once more.
Where's there's no damned cadence,
No "Hut---hup---hep---fore?"
    —*Paine Field, WA Pvt. H. E. Hammond*

RETURN FROM FURLOUGH

I have been gone
These three weeks,
Yet all is the same.
All unchanged.

The barracks hut is cold,
The fires are dim.
Only a slight flicker
Reminds that men sleep here.
Soon in the quiet land,
Before the dawn,

In the shivering light;
They will arise, dress.

And yawning slowly
Trudge off to the line.
Hello, Nap. Back?
How was it?

But I am creeping too,
In the darkness.
And brightly lit streets
Are only a shadow.
Dancing women,
Only a memory.
  —*Lincoln AAF, NE, Pfc. Samuel Naparstek*

REST

When day is done and the bugler blows
Taps for the night, a soldier knows
That at last has come the end of day;
His time to rest, to think and pray;
To think of his loved ones ever so far,
And to pray that he sees them after the war.

He builds his castles while at night he does rest,
Determines to give his country his best,
And once in a while, as strange as it seems,
These thoughts are carried along in his dreams.
He thinks of valiant deeds he will do,
Then at night, in his dreams, they come true!

But then at last, night turns to day!
His thoughts and dreams both fade away,
His arrogant castles about him fall.
The valiant deeds aren't there at all;
But a soldier knows that one by one,
He'll rest and dream, when day is done.
  —*Alaska, Pvt. William C. Folbe*

REAR-ECHELON DAY ROOM

Men lean over letters home,
Looking for something new to say,
Though this day was the same for them
As the day before,
And the day after that.

Outside, in the warm night air,
The generator hums, Suggesting sleep.

Men look at a snapshot
Night after night,
Or hear conversations
Dwindle into repetition;
Or the last good bar,
And always of a woman.

Men lean over letters home,
And there is nothing to say
Because they remember
That they know about tomorrow,
And the day after that.
  —*Marianas, Sgt. Stan Flink*

REALITY

As I lie here on my lonely bunk,
I hear a failing bugle call.
It leaves as softly as it came,
And now there is no sound at all.

By God, I wish that I were home,
Amid the city's roar---
The newsboy's shouts, the subways' shrieks,
The crowds in Macy's store.

And now I hear another call:
This one's not soft, but shrill.
And then I hear that familiar yell:
"Okay, fall out for drill!"
  —*England, Pvt. George Kriegsman*

RANTING ON RATINGS

The Army's inconsistency,
It never fails to baffle me,
For in the front-line Infantry,
Non-technical as it can be,
T-ratings all abound.

While in the Air Corps technical,
Where T-stripes are unethical,
Line duties only mythical.
Line ratings all are typical,
None other to be found.
  —*France, Cpl. B. J. Cate*

PX

I understand the Post Exchange
Right here inside the camp
Will sell you almost anything,
A radio or a stamp.

I guess they sell all sorts of stuff
But though I've often tried
I've never really seen the place
Except from the outside.

For every time I go around
It's just the same old story;
I can't get in because the joint
Is closed for inventory.
—*Pvt. Russel A. Ninedorf*

PSALM OF LIFE

(Officer Candidate Version)
With apologies to Longfellow,
Down the path of toil and trouble
Headed for we know not where,
We are marching at the double
Praying that we'll soon be there.
Though the way be dark and dreary,
Growing worse each passing day. . . .
Though our aching backs are weary,
We just laugh our woes away.
Many things occur to irk us,
But we lift our chins and smile.
Though our tutors drive and work us,
We are cheerful all the while.
Out of bed before the daylight;
Toiling until the set of sun.
Often does the stroke of midnight
Find us with our tasks half done.
But we'll go on to the finish
With our faces toward the stars;
Never let our hopes diminish
That we'll win those golden bars.
—*Ft. Monroe, VA 111th C.T., M/Sgt. W.F.Kennedy*

POTS AND PANS FOREVER

Of all KP duties, the lowest I've seen
Is the scrubbing of vessels for GI cuisine.
The cooks and the bakers delight, so they say,
In the soiling of pans twenty times in one day.

The scrapings are scorched, and the grease is congealed,
And the soap leaves the hands with the skin nicely peeled.
But some day each scrubber a surcease shall find
From this dank abnegation of body and mind.

Let each reeking vassal of brush and harsh soap
Balm his grease-sotted soul in retributive hope
That the cooks and the bakers, yes, mess sergeants, too,
Will in Satan's good judgment be given their due.

Old Satan's first sergeant will tell each to go
As a scullery slave to the regions below,
Where white-coated knaves of the cookery clans
Will spend eons unending on pots and on pans.
—*Luzon, Pvt. Edgar M. Young*

POST-WAR PLANNING

When the war and duration are over
And I hold my release in hand
I shall head for my home to recover
And do all the things I have planned.
I shall strip off my uniform quickly
And I'll fling myself down on a bed,
That is padded with mattresses thickly
And sleep like the dead.

Oh, fie on fools who like fishing,
And a fig for the fellows who feel
That the wildest extent of their wishing
Is a river, a rod and a reel.
And the same to those who crave dances
And scotches and women and tea;
My mind one vision entrances---
It's slumber for me.
—*Camp Shelby, MS, Sgt. Grant A. Saunders*

POST NO. 7, FIRST RELIEF

His carbine slung, the guard walks pace by pace
Along the motor pool down by the lake
Just after guard mount. Clouds above like lace
Shine in the sunset's glow. He got a break:
His guard came on a night of starting spring.
The air is mild and as the darkness falls
And colors gray, frogs croak and peepers sing.
Like sleeping elephants in circus stalls
Stand 10-wheel trucks and bulky medium tanks.
The surface of the lake reflects metallic light
And forms a background for the vehicles' ranks,
Hoarse cadence counting marches through the night.

Of course he gripes that he's on guard again;
He'd like a date with that brunette the most.
Still here is beauty which no order can
Prevent from sneaking in an Army post.
—*Fort Jackson, SC Pfc. Walter Kuttner*

TWENTY-ONE DASH ONE HUNDRED

Aye, tear its tattered pages out
Declare it obsolete,
All for the scrap drive's open snout.
Rescind, destroy, delete!
What matter that his midget tome
Was blueprint to our life,
Advisor, counsel, bridge from home
To Army? Whet the knife!

Yes, abrogate, annul, revoke;
Proclaim afar the ban.
Replace the Handbook? Heartless joke!
It fears no mortal man.

It lives, in spite of protocol,
Ingrained in all our brains;
Shot though it was against the wall,
Its spirit still remains.
—*Camp San Louis Obispo, CA, T-4 John Greenleaf*

'TWAS THE NIGHT BEFORE MERS-EL-SALAAM

Christmastime, as I remember,
Used to come in late December,
Bringing mistletoed romances
Climaxed by swank New Year's dances,
Skating rinks and wintry breezes,
Billboard ads for anti-freezes;
These are things that I remember---
Christmas time in late December.

Africa? Have you a Koran?
Is there Christmastime in Oran?
Do you think the singing cherub
Captivates the solemn Arab
When according to Mohammed,
Life begins with him---Mohammed?
Here it's true, is found the camel,
Christmas-famed and storied mammal.
But his burdens, though immense,
Do not include Yule frankincense.

So it seems our celebrations
Tempered by cold canned C rations,
Will not result in jubilee
But just a pleasant memory.
—*North Africa, Pfc. Edwin H. Roper*

TROOP MOVEMENT

These are the young, the purebread, the highly priced,
Traveling in Pullmans, watching the states roll by;
The thin, red farm lands of Georgia, the turkey buzzards
Wheeling circles against the blue Virginia sky.
Tractor and mule teams crossing the late afternoon,
Women from dusty porches waving good-byes,
Improvised peace and home and family are posed
In neat and familiar patterns before their eyes.

Green shaded swaying evening; poker and craps
Continue, the train turns westward, and singing starts.
The air grows colder, gradually night begins
And quietly tightens around them and in their hearts.
—*England Pfc. John D. Preston*

TRAINEE ON GUARD

Midway he turns upon the beat,
Thumbs taut on carbine sling,
Survey in half good humor
Barracks no enemy will blast,
Shattering quiet sleep.

Classroom, where clacking keys electric
Enjoy well deserved rest
From awkward signaling of student hands,
Passes by, shadowy
In his path.

Mess hall, whose early morning smoke
Releases reassuring odors
Redolent of the coming day's meal
Winks amiable light
In friendly greeting.

Morning's gleam dissolves the cooling night
With promise of another day,
And slow diffusions of the newly wakened sun
Bring clearly to his view
Another post, Some future shore.

Obscure and shapeless masses,
Deformed by expert hands,
Under his protective vigil
Lie ready to breathe their warming breath

Of sustenance
On bodies limp.

Rugged, drab gray instruments
Rooted in the sodden terrain
Of concealment,
Upon his instant notice
Sound their clipped bright tones,
Transforming into nervous, curt commands
The expectant air.

Huddled, sleeping figures,
Alerted to the crack and roaring
Of disaster,
On his sharp warning

Break from sleep's tight grip,
Leaping into narrow slitted
Trenches of security.

This, then, his eventual watch---
No guard in comfortable, friendly garrison,
No exercise on adolescent soldiering,
This final post---
His comrades' lives.

Midway he turns upon the beat,
Thumb sight on carbine sling,
Surveys with sober, sweeping glance
The full, clear dawn.
   —*Fort Bragg, NC Pvt. I. Freundlich*

TO THE EXILE

You interest me pal, with your wanderlust,
With your love for the frozen north,
With its women foul and husky's howl,
For what it may be worth---

Whad'da say we pitch a deal?
My word that I'll shoot square,
With terms to suit and a *klooch* to boot,
You see, I'm stationed there.

I'm not a hand to gamble my coin
Or fall for a shysters ruse,
But I'll bet my stack on a lead-pipe cinch,
When I'm damn sure not to lose.

If you're sick of the heat and the smooth concrete,
Of the pavement of sand and grit,
When the 'old boys' tell of the Yukon spell,
Well, pal, that's just tough---luck!

I gave up the heat and the good old streets
Of a burg in my home state,
And why I'm here and you are there---
Well, buddy, I guess it's fate.

So take a tip from a guy who knows,
And stick with what you've got,
Don't gripe and scoff when you're well off,
The Northland's not so hot!
   —*Alaska, Cpl. Glenn A. Lynd*

TO THE DAY OF RECKONING

'Twas the night before Sunday
Just outside the fort;
There were eight boys in khaki,
Eight men---and a quart.
They drank "chuck-a-luck" and downed the booze;
That's a soldier's pet toast to down the blues.

As they made their way homeward,
Each wearing a grin,
The rain came a-pouring---
They got soaked to the skin.
The puddles were plenty, both sides of the street,
So they walked in the road, protecting their feet.

As they passed the main outpost
Still singing with glee,
They were halted and cursed
By a lanky MP.
"Disorderly conduct---disturbing the peace":
That's what he told the chief of police.

The time: Two weeks later,
The place: Dan's café,
The eight boys in khaki
Sit drinking away.
They all drink a toast (though already plastered):
"Here's to that MP—the tall, lanky devil."

This rhyme has a moral
As you'll find in time
It's a real, true-life story
Of eight buddies of mine.
They all learned their lesson---"crime does not pay,"
But God help that MP if they meet him some day.
   —*Fort Benning, GA, Cpl. Joseph Lee*

TO A FRIEND GOING INTO THE NAVY

Manhattan is a fine town,
A legendary city
Where all the bars are wet with
Scotch And all the girls are pretty.

The ships slip out, the trains roar in.
The cabs rush up and down---
A busy place, a dizzy place,
This lovely, sinful town.

And there are pitfalls for the young:
The Times Square Lorelei,
The brimming glass, the scarlet lip,
The bright mascaraed eye.

So, if your way be virtuous
(And such it is, I'm sure)
Walk wide of Little old New York
And you'll stay chaste and pure.

But if your soul is like mine
And your thirst is, too---
Then meet me there some Friday night;
We'll see what we can do.
—*Camp Gordon, GA, T-4 Robert Murray*

THOUGHTS

I thought I heard the sergeant say,
"I need one more KP."
I thought that I had done my share,
But he still picked me.

I thought of all the times before,
I thought of plans in town,
I thought of all the guys I hate;
The sergeant won hands down.

I thought I'd tell the so and so
A place wherein to head,
But then I thought of future lists
And left my speech unsaid.
—*Municipal Airport, Memphis, TN Pvt. Herb Sheiber*

THROUGH CHANNELS

The general inspects us and everything's fine.
A soldier, no less, is each man in line;
The barracks are neat, as clean as can be;
Supply-room and mess are a wonder to see.

The general turns to the colonel and prates;
"Triple-A-One is what this outfit rates.
Please issue a three-day pass to each man
On top of a week to spend on his can."

The colonel then phones to the outfit's BC
And says, "Two-day passes for half the battery.
The rest must remain as punishment, for
I noticed a speck of dust on the floor."

The captain then to the first sergeant gasses,
"One-fourth the men get twelve-hour passes.
The others you'll detail to scrub the floor,
To polish the windows and paint the door."

The first sergeant falls the men into ranks,
With, "Okay, you bastards, this is your thanks;
The joint was filthy, as I suspected.
For the next five days you're all restricted!"
—*Camp Gruber, OK, Cpl. Jack C. Bell*

THIS IS ALASKA

This is Alaska: the towering peaks,
The frozen tundra wide,
The wolf pack's call, the eagle's flight,
The rushing of the tide.

This is Alaska: the sourdough's dream
Of the end of a rainbow's gold;
The flashing of the Boralis' lights;
The snow, the ice and the cold.

This is Alaska: the fog-bound isles,
Volcanoes' fiery breath;
The last frontier of America,
Of life and of sudden death.

This is Alaska: lonely caches,
Canyons, glaciers blue;
Land of dream and enchantment
Where sourdough's dreams come true.
—*Alaska, Pfc. Franklin Young*

THIS GI IS Z1

I feel constrained to offer a timid apology
For the accident or luck, classification or biology
That placed me in an office or a laboratory
Instead of what war correspondents, poets and
generals refer to as the field of honor (or glory).

Every time I go on pass for furlough, somebody's mother or sister or some
4F Charlie or thrice-deferred draft-board darling asks me, "How come?"
Jimmie's in India, and Laurie in England, Oscar in Africa, and Henry in Iran.
What's the lowdown, chum?
Are you dating the colonel's daughter, or are you just a personal friend of the Old Man?

Well, the fact is, I was born under a lucky star; so I was prepared for war's advent.
I was fortunate enough to lose three fingers in a shooting accident,
Or a slingshot put out my eye in boyhood, or I have healed minimal tuberculosis, or broken a kneecap in a football game,
Or infantile paralysis left me partially but incurably lame.
So this GI Is Z1.
—*Camp Shelby, MS, S/Sgt. Grant A. Sanders*

THEY ALSO SERVE

We drink foul beer in joints,
The brew fill sup with tears.
We can't get out on points,
We served but three short years.

Never saw St. Lo,
Wake or Guam or Rome. Battle Star?
Hell, no!
Our time was spent at home.

At home, in posts and forts,
In garrison and camp,
We typed and filed reports
And caught the writer's cramp.

The chicken waxed so fat
On our domestic scene,
We used a shovel-hat,
To clean it off the green.

KP and guard, and more,
We did them day and night.
Yet we've a damned low score
Because we didn't fight.

We drink foul beer in joints
The brew fills up with tears.
We won't get out on points
For years and years and years.
—*Ft. Jackson, SC, Pfc. Ben Horowitz*

THE USUAL THING

I lie between clean sheets,
I walk in well-cut grass
And eat good fruits and meat A
nd shudder at a pass.

Withdrawing into good,
I stand alone at last,
And pure beneath the sun
I count the days go past.

The big eye of the sun
Contains a red red passion---
It glares so vacantly,
A victim of irritation.

The days are very long and
The nights are spent in sadness
And the only cure I've ever found
For madness is madness.
—*Moore Gen. Hosp., Pfc. Gloria Marchisio*

THE YANKS ARE EN ROUTE

Now there's a slim and pretty girl in France,
Descended from the one of Armentiers;
And only bat-eyed hangmen watch her dance.
Hold on, and keep your smile, for we'll be there.
And there's a brave and dark eyed girl in Greece,
Who lives through hope in days of long despair,
And has no bread nor wine to make her laugh.
Hang on, and don't give up, for we'll be there.
In Holland, where the tulips are all dead,
There waits a maid with yellow hair,
Praying while her country's veins are bled.
Stay brave, and keep your faith, for we'll be there.
From Greece to Spain, from Poland to the sea, T
he girls who lost their smiles can still compare
A tyrant to a man, and wait to cheer
The flag with Stars and Stripes. And we'll be there.
—*Pvt. Arthur Emmons---10th Engrs.*

THE WAY YOU WEAR IT

When worn by a gob
On the back of his knob
It means that he thinks he's dapper.
While down on the eye
Means the tar is a guy
Who likes to believe he's a scrapper.

On the back of his dome
It means "nobody's home"
And the wearer's a boot or a rookie.

But when worn square and straight
It means in the pate
Be the wearer a vet or a rookie!
—*3rd Naval district, Author Unknown*

THE U.S. ENGINEERS

The rest may weave their laurel wreaths
From dawn to setting sun,
But without peers, the
Engineers
Are heroes, every one.
They seek the strength of hostile camps,
They mine and sap and dig.
There is no job too small for them,
Nor ever task too big.
They rush to strengthen shattered lines,
They make a midnight raid;
Or their hot guns are laid aside
For axes or a spade.
Like slaves they work the shell-torn road,
While high-explosives crash;
Or blaze their way up to the foe
In hot shrapnel splash.
They spanned the tarnished
Meuse one day
Before a leaden rain
That mowed them down like a new scythe
Mows down the ripened grain.
Their captain stood before them then
And with a will he roared,
"We're going to get that bridge across,
If it takes the whole damn' Corps!"
They leave their dead; then go their way,
Without an empty boast.
Come! Fill your glass with blood-red wine,
And pledge a long-due toast,
A toast to men with fighting hearts,
Who scorn all thought of fear,
A toast to him who stood the test;
The U.S. Engineer!
—*U.S. Marines, Marine Gunner Frank H. Rentfrow*

THE UNITED STATES MARINES

You can have all your doughboys,
You can have your sailors, too,
But I will take another,
And I'm certain he will do.

The doggies aren't too bad, and
Though the Navy's pretty keen,
You will never find the beat of
The United States Marines.
—*The Marine Recruiter Cpl. D.B. Catalano*

THE SERGEANT

I do not like the Sergeant's face.
I do not like his chatter.
And what I think about his brain
Is censorable matter.

He sits in a tent
At the end of the street
And clutters the desk
With his oversized feet.

I do not like the Sergeant's nose;
It would look better broken.
I do not like his tone of voice
When drill commands are spoken.

He walks in the rear
When we're out on the march
And never relaxes
To "Route Step, Harrch!"

I do not like the Sergeant's views
On Army Life and such,
But what I think about the Sarge
Don't seem to matter much.

He can still pull his rank
When I enter my pleas,
And I find myself stuck
With the chronic K.P.'s
—*Pvt. Joe Sims*

THE EDITOR'S LAMENT

Praise the Army Class'fication:
Fits each man to his vocation---
To the job he did before.
Clerk, with little hesitation,
Gets an HQ situation---
He makes staff or maybe more.

If he blew a tune symphonic,
To the Army he's a tonic---
Bandsman now and PFC.
If he cooked for Casey's Diner,
Nothing really could be finer---
Sergeant of the mess is he.

If he toyed with dots and dashes,
Split the ether with his flashes---
He's in Signal now---Tech 3rd.
If he worked for Clancy's Trucking,
Now for the garage he's bucking---
Making corporal, so we heard.

Butcher, baker, candlemaker,
Doctor, lawyer, merchant, faker,
Get their jobs and rank, you see.
Here's the newsman's situation:
Runs the weekly publication,
Always stays a P-V-T!
   —*Fort Niagara, NY, Fort Niagara Drum,*
    Pvt. John L. Dougherty

THE DAUNTLESS

Though some must fight the war with ships
And some with cannon's boom,
They also serve who only sit
In an orderly room.

Yes, some we say must fight with guns
Or teach weather classes,
But who dares say he fights not
Who types week-end passes?

Firm and entrenched behind a desk
There does he take his stand,
Stern defiance on his face and
A pencil in his hand.

And while o'er all the global map
The nations sway and sink,
There he will fight the murderous
Jap To his last drop of ink!
   —*Grand Rapids Training Center,*
    MI, S/Sgt. William Krasner

THE BATTLE OF PANAMA

We served, I guess, waiting there on the jungle hill in
the long days and warm long nights, waiting for maybe
bombers coming
for could-be attacks perhaps about to happen. Nothing
happened. the alerts were fake or practice, the bombers
were ours, all of them.
Days, it rained, or the sun was fierce, or the captain made
a speech; nights, the moon was full, or a guard halted and
armadillo trapped and circling a gun-pit.
We sat and waited, sour but always ready for what never
happened, soldiers with no war.
In the stale days and tepid nights,
O yes we also served. But nothing happened, ever.
   —*Puerto Rico, Sgt. Lysander Kemp*

THE AWFUL TRUTH

The kindly night doth mesmerize
Harsh truths into more gracious lies,
And, moon-bewitched, we have made passes
With sweet intent at gruesome lasses.

Yet sabled charm ignobly fails
Where GI sorcery prevails,
For squat-shaped hutments ne'er will come
To look like spire or temple dome.
Who dreams of earthly verdance must
Look elsewhere than to drill-field dust,
And it requires great mental force
To sublimate an obstacle course.

Trim as you will day's merciless lamp,
An Army camp's and Army camp.
   —*Pratt AAF, KS, Pfc. Ed Karpf*

THE ASSINGMENT OF TWINS

Has our Army so backslid
That twins are parted? God forbid.
They grew together in the womb;
Shall they be parted in the tomb?
Be theirs assignment to one station,
Be theirs a single destination:
Provided that they so desire,
And if to this their hearts aspire.

If other things are equal, then
Do not separate the men,
For one and one are always two.

Except with twins, and then it's true
That one and one are always one,
By War Department sanction.
Born at one birth and from one mother,
A twin is closer than a brother.

They suckled at the selfsame time,
To part them is almost a crime.
Dandled and diapered alike,
Shall one twin fly and one twin hike?
Shall one footslog in the Infantry,
And the other ride in the Cavalry?
If one goes to a distant border,
The other goes by special order.

Their features bear the selfsame stamp---
Then let them have a single camp.
If the twins be identical,
Their paths should always parallel.
Six of one twin to his brother
Is half a dozen of the other.
Though East be East and West be West,
The same emotions stir each breast.

The same blood pulses through each heart---
And never the twin from twin shall part.
Let twin cry to his mirror-youth
As to Naomi promised Ruth, "Whither thou goest,
I shall go By order of General Ulio;
We shall together serve the nation
By War Department dispensation."
—*Camp Shelby, MS, Sgt. Grant Sanders*

THE ARMY GOES TO TEA

"I should like to see the Captain," said the colonel to the Wac.
 "I'm sorry, sir, he isn't here; but he will soon be back."
"But come, we're going on a flight; the plane, it leaves at three."
"I'm sorry, sir," the Wac replied, "the Captain's out to tea."

The telephone it jingled, and the Wac with the voice of cheer
Said, "Colonel Doodle's office, but the Colonel isn't here."
"This is General Snipe," the answer came, "so tell me, where is he?"
"I'm sorry, sir," the Wac replied, "the Colonel's gone to tea."

"I've got to get an order through," the irate Major said.
"If we don't get some rations soon, my men will all be dead!"
Please take me to Lt. Snoot, I know my point he'll see."
"I'm sorry, sir, Lt. Snoot has just stepped out to tea."

And so it goes across the world, wherever tea they serve,
This strange civilian custom that the officers observe.

But if you're just a poor GI, you're frowned upon you see,
If you should try, at four o'clock, to stop your work for tea!
—*India, Pfc. Joan Riedinger*

TEXAS REVERIE

Now Texas is part of our great domain,
To be cherished, just like the rest,
And the soldiers raised on this great terrain
All swear by it as the best.

The reason for this is hard to be missed,
Like a dog with his precious bone;
The one place dearest to all of us
Is that wonderful place called home.

Now home is wherever we hang our hat,
Or barracks bag. I should say,
And we gripe sometimes of this and that,
With our thoughts at home far away.

But soon we'll have that ape on the run,
The one that started this row,
And when we do, believe me you,
We'll put him in hell---and how!

Now Texas might be the biggest state,
And flyin' weather the best,
But when I'm lucky and get a break,
I'll get me out of the West.

All the cactus, coyotes and sage brush,
And the scent of the orange trees---
I'll leave it to the natives,
For a cornfield ripe in the breeze.
—*Moore Field, TX, Pvt. Harold S. Moody*

TAPS

Often I heard it,
Turning the night
Into a respite
From the days fight.

Over a barracks
Silent with sleep.
Taps is a love song
Haunting and deep.

Facing the darkness,

Day at its end,
Taps is a handclasp
Sent by a friend.
—*Asheville, NC, S/Sgt. Virginia C. Smith*

TALE OF A THIRSTY GI

'Twas the night before payday
And I looked far and near,
I searched through my pockets
For the price of a beer.

But the kale was off duty,
Milled edges had quit;
There wasn't a quarter,
Not even a jit.

Forward, turn forward,
Oh time in flight;
Make it tomorrow
Just for tonight.
—*Westover Field, MA, Cpl. Andreas Helmuth*

YOU'RE ON REPORT

You're on report, that's all they say,
You're on report, day after day.
You shine your shoes, you clean your hat;
But even so, in spite of that;
"You're on report," it gets you mad!
But it's no fun, it's really sad!
They give you work detail, KP, fire watch and such;
In fact the things they make you do is just too much.
Although you try to be "on the ball,"
There'll come a day you're bound to fail,
And then you'll hear the sweet retort:
"You're on report"; "YOU'RE ON REPORT."
—*USCG Training Station, Manhattan Beach, NY,*
Alfred McNulty, S2C

WITHOUT BENEFIT OF STENCILS

Oh, I wish I had a commission
With J. Caesar's legions of old,
When the mimeograph, as we know it,
Was a story that hadn't been told.
The orders were then mostly verbal.
And they seldom took time to write;
For the bulk of an officer's duties
Lay in teaching his men how to fight.
When they fought with the sturdy Helvetians,
A man who was absent was missed,
For they hadn't put half their army
On the Detached Officers' List.
They carried their banners to Britain,
And the Britons had no cause to laugh,
But I'm told it wasn't accomplished
By the use of the mimeograph.
Now I sit in a big city office
That's furnished with tables and chairs,
And the orderly falls down exhausted
When he's dragged half my mail up the stairs.
He deposits his load in the corner
And then he is done with his chore,
While I have ten hours before me
Just reading the memos from Corps.
Now back in the days when J. Caesar
Marched from the Rhine to the Rhone,
They had to get out special orders
With a mallet and chisel on stone.
There were no carbon copies of that stuff
To bother the staff and the line.
And yet, so historians tell us,
His doughboys just got along fine.
The Senate once sent him a letter
The kind many readers recall
"Explain, by indorsement hereon, sir,
Results of campaigning in Gaul."
So he chiseled a snappy indorsement:
"I came and I saw and I won."
Put that in your pipe now and smoke it.
You pink-whiskered son-of-a-gun!
Now if I should write such an answer
And send it, through channels, to Corps,
The chances, my son, are a hundred to one
That I'd not have to write anymore:
For they'd hold a conclave on my record
And I'd be in Class B in a day,
And then they'd withdraw my commission
And stop all the rest of my pay.
Each day, as I sit in my office,
With my shoulders acquiring a stoop,
I wish that I had a commission
In J. Caesar's headquarters troop.
And yet I could die well contented
Should this be my true epitaph:
"Here lies the American Soldier
Who Abolished the Mimeograph."
—*Jefferson Barracks Hub*

WHATTA LIFE!

Give me the life of a soldier
Who lives in an open tent,
(He doesn't know what to do with dough
Because he pays no rent).
Give me the life of a soldier
Who works and plays and drills.
(He enjoys his chows, for the law allows
He need not foot the bills).
Give me the life of a soldier
Who's up at early dawn.
(His eyes are bright, for he slept all night.
Excuse me while I yawn).
Yes, give me the life of soldier
Who meet s all kinds and types
(You can give me those good ol' G.I. clothes. . . .
But, God, please add some stripes!)
—*Camp Beauregard Pelican*

WATER BUFFALO

Along the roadway, tortoise-slow he paces,
Nor cares his bland medieval eyes to turn
Upon the Army truck that past him races,
But pulls his ancient cart with unconcern.
Resentfully, he ambles past the hollow,
Now rife with soldiers, where in other years
He daily took his heaving hulk to wallow
In stinking mud up to his sacred ears.

But on a stormy night he comes cavorting,
Across the nullish, plunging through the deep
Dank grass capriciously, with joyous snorting.
Ecstatic grunts invade the alien's sleep
As, once again carousing in the rain,
He tastes the sweets of his usurped domain.
—*India, Sgt. Smith Dawless*

WASHED-OUT CADET

I cannot ever free myself of planes
Their glides and sun-winks fever me unending.
My ardor at their coming never wanes---
The ghostly drone, the golden moonpath wending,
The sizes, shapes, the speeds, the destinations,
The goggled and the leathered human creatures.
On, on to London, Naples, leafy atoll stations;
The lolling, leering guns; the magic features
Of a ship. That turret is a turtles head:
It can go in or out at will; that gunners shield
Defies an angry wither-spate of lead.
That sight could draw a bead on weevils in a field.
Now I am hounded by the wolf packs of the sky;
Their cosmic hunting haunts me, and I know no rest.
I must run with them, do not ask me why.
Look there, a plane is silvering the west.
—*Laredo AAF, TX, Pvt. Joseph Dever*

U. S. TROOP SLEEPER, M 1

This traveler of devious trails,
This mongrel of the Pullman clan,
Hermaphrodite of the roaring rails,
Conceived by war but bred by man.

On oblong wheels and springless trucks,
It heaves and rolls and jerks about:
It leaps and jumps and sways and bucks
And finally jolts your back teeth out.

You alternately fry and freeze,
And curse the dust and smoke and goo
That come in on each vagrant breeze
And makes a GI tramp of you.

You move about, if move you can,
By scaling mounds of full field packs
And crawling o'er your fellow man
Or squeezing under the rifle packs.

Oh, speed the dawn which ends this fray!
Put down that gun! Turn in that jeep!
Empty these cars and cheer the day
That sends them back to hauling sheep!
—*Fort Leonard Wood, MO S/Sgt. S. E. Whitman*

UNIFORMS AND THE MAN

The khaki is solid, but infinite variation
Will single out the soldier by his dress;
Some tilt the cap in Saturday elation;
Some wear it straight in Sunday soberness.

The sergeant passes; every dazzling button
Asserts the ancient rectitude of rank.
His graceless girth distinguishes the glutton
By generous waist and meager, flabby shank.

A sullen hunch of shoulder shows the grouch,
Forever bitter in his Army status.
The poet under his arms, with dreamy slouch,

Invokes a warlike, olive-drab afflatus.

Neutral as looking glass, the khaki norm
Betrays the man within the uniform.
—*Camp Shelby, MS, Cpl. Ephim G. Fogel*

THE RECONVERSION

When bugles sound their final notes
And bombs explode no more
And we return to what we did
Before we went to war,
The sudden shift of status
On the ladder of success
Will make some worthy gentlemen
Feel like an awful mess.

Just think of some poor captain
Minus all his silver bars
Standing up behind some counter
Selling peanuts and cigars;
And think of all the majors
When their oak leaf's far behind
And the uniform they're wearing
Is the Western Union kind.

Shed a tear for some poor colonel
If he doesn't feel himself;
Jerking sodas isn't easy
When the eagle's on the shelf.
'Tis a bitter pill to swallow,
'Tis a matter for despair;
Being messengers and clerks again's
A mighty cross to bear.

So be kind to working people
That you meet where'er you go,
For the guy who's washing dishes
May have been your old CO.
—*Fort Knox, KY, Pfc. Edward Blumenthal*

THE RANKS

The colonel has his eagles,
The captain has his bars,
The major has an oak leaf,
The general has his stars.

But if you are counting chevrons,
Then honey I am done:
The corporal has his two,
The bugler has but one.
—*Camp Wolters, TX, Bugler Pfc. Alton C. Gillespie*

THE RADIO

The radio, in days of yore,
The days before the draft,
Caused family rows and quarreling
Which almost drove me daft.

Soap op'ra swung dear Mama's vote
And Papa wanted Bing;
My sister screamed for Frankie's voice
And brother yelled for swing.

But now, up in Alaskaland,
As Uncle Sammy's guest,
I've never heard a single tiff
On where the dial should rest.

Hell no! No fight, no dial to turn;
But here's the situation;
There ain't no choice, no choice at all;
We've only got one station.
—*Alaska, Sgt. Walter Armbruster*

THE PENTAGON

The Pentagon is huge, colossal;
It houses souls warlike and docile.

Think of the buck slips, pile on pile,
Think of miles and miles of aisle.

Pencils by the thousand gross
Wielded by the bellicose . . . .

Thirty thousand agile hands,
Typing out the war's demands. . . . .

Acres of military minds
Unraveling the tape that binds. . .

Oceans of words that froth and bubble,
Turning what, please, into rubble?

The Infantry is battle's queen.
But here the battle's heard, not seen.

In war the men admire a chassis;
The only chassis here's a lassie.

Some of the Infantry is airborne;
Pentagonians are chairborne.
—*1st Decontamination Battalion, Pfc. Y. Guy Owen*

THE OUTCAST

(Appreciated only by boys who have been on board a
transport, where hand inspection is made in chow line.)

Contemptuously, they passed him by,
With coldness in their eyes,
A brother once, a leper now,
A creature to despise.

The line moved on, his shame was clear;
He stood for all to view,
The worst of sins was his this day,
And sinners get their due.

He'd come this far with all the rest,
Then---parting of the way,
"Those hands are mighty dirty, boy,
No chow for you today!"
  —*Australia, Pf. Dan Laurence*

THE NIGHT LIFE GETS ME DOWN

A young Marine was trudging
Upon a night patrol,
No moon was there to guide him
Around the swampy hole.
The briars tore his clothing.
His feet slipped on the clay
And he fell into the mud.
His buddies heard him say:
"It's not he fleas and blood-ticks
I mind when on the trail,
The heat and rain may pelt me
And yet I shall not fail.
The hardships of the boondocks,
My weary, aching feet,
The thirsty, dreary, endless miles,
Have never made me bleat.
For rugged, ragged, rock-strewn hills
And canyons, sere and brown
Are easy in the day time. It's
The night-life gets me down."
  —*Marine*

THE NEWFOUNDLAND EXPRESS

See that lonely soldier
With a bayonet by his side
He's going back to the States
To wed his promised bride;
He's fought some mighty battles
And he has done his best,
But he takes his life in his own hands now,
On the Newfoundland Express.

There's hobos in Newfie,
I just met one today;
He said that he was anxious
To be getting on his way.
The only thing that stopped him
Was he needed sleep and rest,
And he'd take no chances sleeping
On the Newfoundland Express.

Next month I get my furlough,
To St. Johns I will go.
They gave 10 days furlough time,
But I'll need more I know;
I must go through Shoal Harbor,
Which takes five days I guess,
And means I'll spend my furlough time,
On the Newfoundland Express.
When the season is winter
And snow's on the ground,
And we wait for the postman
To bring the mail around,
He says that he's sorry,
He has done his best;
The mail's in a snowdrift,
On the Newfoundland Express.

A soldier once decided
To heaven he would go;
He tied himself to the railroad track
When he heard the whistle blow.
He must have lain a long , long time
Because he starved to death,
Waiting on the railroad track,
For the Newfoundland Express.
  —*Dow Field, ME, Pvt. Sidney Deitch*

"THE MORTAR-MAN"

The mortar sat there squat and clean,
And death---it hovered close.
He didn't know just what to say,
A few words seemed verbose.
His movements had been swift and sure,
His calculations clear.
His face was set, his mouth was grim.
The hour of test was near.
"It'll work! It must" he prayed aloud.
But fear---it shook his knees.
Then steadied---calm---he looked around.
"What's your prescription please?"
—*Pfc. George P. Johnston*

THE MONDAY DEAL

Monday again and back again
To the aimless weapons---
The Underwood, the carbons
And the copies to be copied,
Re-copied and copied till the file bursts
(Will the last file burst?)
Monday again, morning reports
To be done by eight, no later---
Five EM found to be hanging by their braided hair;
Barracks enchanted, ringed by fire,
Insistent swans storm orderly room
Swearing to be long-lost KPs;
Infant found in pfc's foot locker,
Answers to no name,
Hindu caste mark
On forehead, no other clue;
First sergeant immures himself in broom closet,
Weeping incessantly, stripes discovered
Hanging from willow in company area.
How went the night? Out like a light.

Monday and here they come again---
Phantoms of the far-flung fronts,
Each with his line and length of chain;
"Hail to thee, thane and Underwood!
Woodstock thou art, and Remington!
Hail, Royal that shalt be!"

Helmet by helmet, the crowned heads of
Europe Underground, and cheek by jowl,
The sailors off Saipan reclining
A league below the reach of the Red Cross,
Untouchable by plastic surgeons,
Beyond the pigmy havens
Offered by apple stands and cotton poppies
Such sentries on patrol, who can deny
Monday is here, Sunday is here and gone?
The desk stands idling, anxious to be flown.
—*San Antonio Aviation Cadet Center, TX,
Sgt. Halsey Davis*

THE MARINES

The Marines, the Marines, those blasted Gyrenes,
Those sea-going bellhops, those brass-button queens,
Oh!
They pat their own backs, write stories in reams
All in praise of themselves—the U. S. Marines!
The Marines, the Marines, those publicity fiends,
They built all the forests, turned on all the streams.
Discontent with this earth they say Heavens scenes
Are guarded by---guess?---Right! The U.S. Marines!
The moon never beams except when the Marines
Give it permission to turn on its gleams,
And the tide never rises, the wind never screams
Unless authorized by the U. S. Marines!
The Marines, the Marines in their khakis and greens,
Their pretty blue panties, red stripe down the seams,
They thought all the thoughts, dreamed all the dreams,
Singing "The Song of Myself"---The U.S. Marines!
—*2nd Lt. Earl J. Wilson*

THE MARCH OF SNOWSHOE SAM

You've heard of the ride of Paul Revere,
The ride that Americans still hold dear.
That a great ride it was we know of course,
Yet most of the work was done by the horse.
But the trek I'll tell, of a powerful man,
Was the famous march of Snowshoe Sam.

Now this was up in the arctic snow,
Where men perspire in 40 below.
So as not to go bushed or rum-dum-dum,
They drank of 32-overproof rum,
And that my friend, if you've never tried,
Is a stuff to keep your eyeballs fried.

You may have drunk cognac, vodka or gin,
Okulehau, tequila or strong brandy-wine,
Scotch, bourbon, rye or corn from the South,
Or some drink that lifted the roof of your mouth.
Compared with this rum, for blowing your top,
They all are as mild as strawberry pop.

As the men sat there silent, in the little tin hut,
Their minds seemed to groove the same homesick rut.
They all slowly sipped the hot buttered booze,
While the radio blasted the 10 o'clock news,
When out of the speaker, like a bolt from the sky,
This terrible news smacked them all in the eye.

Two weeks from the day of this stark tragic night,
All surplus hard liquor would be sewed up tight:
The ration per month would be one quart, no more;
Pandemonium broke, they screamed, they swore;
"We'll be damned, who can live in this perpetual freeze.
Who in hell can keep warm on just beer and no shes?"

Then the sergeant spoke up to quiet the din.
"There is just one way out of the fix we are in.
It's 500 miles to where we get rum;
G-2 only knows when the next plane will come.
To try going snowshoe who'll volunteer?
Who'll get the message through?
Who has no fear?"

Every eye in the hut turned to look at one man---
The huge hulking frame they called Snowshoe Sam.
Then all seemed to shout, as if in one voice,
"For the message to Garcia, there stands our choice.
He's the only one here who could make it in time,
Over so many miles to beat the deadline."

Sam just swelled up with magnificent pride,
His expanding ribs nearly burst through his hide; "
Just fill up my pack boys, I'll be off in a wink;
The quicker I get back the sooner we drink."
While they filled up his pack he strapped on his shoes
And then started on the long trek for booze.

Three hundred hours later almost to the dot
He fell in the doorway of the place that he sought
With weathered-black face like a man straight from hell,
He moved not a muscle but lay where he fell.
Some hours later he finally came round;
The news of his great feat spread all over town.

Next day 30 quarts lay snug in his pack,
He waved them good-by and then started back.
His slow dogged pace seemed to eat up the miles,
He thought of the men who would meet him with smiles.
His burden grew heavy, his eyes seemed to dim,
His breath in his parka formed ice on his chin.

Two hundred miles later he sank with a groan,
His raw back felt broken, his legs made of stone.

He knew that unless he lightened his pack
He would never return to the iron-bound shack.
He knew they'd forgive him if he unburdened some,
So he opened a bottle and filled up on rum.

So onward he traveled, his spirits on high,
As each bottle emptied his lips breathed a sigh.
But one eye got frozen and shrank up quite small,
The other bugged out from rum alcohol.
And soon his eyes saw with so much of a bend
That he wandered in circles for days on end.

In the old iron hut days grew into weeks
Ere the men lost their gloom, the tears from their cheeks.
And weeks grew to months and months to years
But still they conjectured while sipping their beers
As to what had become of the strong mighty man,
Famed through the Army---the great Snowshoe Sam.

Somewhere in the wildness of the long polar night,
There stands alone the world's strangest sight.
For poor Sam stands frozen, his face to the stars,
His soul having flown to the northern lights' bars,
And Eskimos passing this figure so cold
All bow down to worship this odd totem pole.

Eons must pass till the great northern floes
Melt with a future sun and tropic wind blows,
And some distant race the secret will fins
Of the most famous trek since the dawn of mankind.
His tracks will burn scars on history, too,
As the world's only martyr to rum 32.
    —*Canada, Cpl. C.D. Kron*

THE MAN WITH THE SHOVEL

It was once upon a Tuesday, in the merry month of June
There was born a little boy, and in his mouth a silver spoon.
He had a thousand silken diapers and an air-conditioned crib.
His mild was brought from purebreds in a diamond –
    crusted bib.
As he grew his life was sheltered and his pants were valet
    pressed,
But he wasn't left to venture from his little golden nest.
Soon his beard proclaimed his manhood, and his father
    kicked the bucket,'
Saying, "Son, life's just a lollipop; just sit back and suck it."

So the guy became a playboy, and he had a lot of fun,
Until came the fatal when we took up our gun;
And he opened the mailbox, and he thought that he was balmy
When a little card informed him of his entrance to the Army.

Now his diamond-crusted bib has been transformed into fatigues,
And dapper little slippers are the boots of seven leagues;
He digs the deepest ditches and he scrubs the cleanest floors
And he does the private laundry back of most un-private doors.

With his jaw unhinged and open, he proclaimed, "This cannot be!
They can do this thing to others, but they can't do this to me!"
Now he's digging deeper ditches, but he's whittled down to size,
Knowing well now that it can be, and he's very Army-wise.
—*Reception Center Gazette, Fort Dix, Pvt. Bob Tourin*

THE LIGHT TURNER-ONNER

Oh, quarter me not with the barracks pest
Who gives not a thought to another's rest;
Though tired men around him sleep,
He'll rush in like a charging jeep,
And, heeding not their sweet repose,
Turn on the lights to doff his clothes.

There's just one cure for this guy's gall;
Wake him up often for a curtain call.
—*AAFSU, Englewood, CA Sgt. Shelby Friedman*

THE MAN WHO WENT TO EARLY CHOW

He figures up the shots you need
He checks on just the way you bleed
He puts in everything you owe
He knows just where you're gonna go
He watches your close order drill
He smiles at KP's fit to kill
He loves to chitchat with the guard
And he leaves camp when leaves are barred
Three vertical butt-strokes for the jerk,
That friend of all, the COMPANY CLERK.
—*Pvt. Ray Palmer*

THE LAWS OF THE SERVICE

Now these are the Laws of the Service
And ever she maketh it plain
That sergeant's or acting-jack's chevrons
Are difficult things to maintain.

Alcohol serves in the compass;
Without it the needle would cleave.
But it spinneth the head of the soldier
And washes the stripes from his sleeve.

Give heed to the voice of thy sergeant,
But keep thine own wisdom mute,
Lest he figures thee out as a wiseguy
And runneth thee up for a shoot.

Ye will find in the tome writ by Webster
That "can't" meaneth one "cannot do."
But "cant" on the tongue of a trooper
Meanth rifles are slanting askew.

Boast not of thy former employment
With its income of ninety per week.
If thou shoot off thy face in this fashion,
'Twere better thou never did speak.

Dost thou spend thy pay before payday,
Let thy head, not thy pockets revive.
Seek not the twenty-percenter
Who will lend thee four dollars for five.

Do they give thee a task disconcerting,
With crumbs of defeat on thy plate.
Remember that thirteen is often
Slapped right in the face with an eight.

Keep furbished thy gear and thy brightwork;
Look well to the tools of thy trade,
Lest the rust of neglect be discovered
In thy rifle at sunset parade.

Remember the one tainted apple.
Forget not the chain's weakened link.
But neither the one nor the other,
Else repent of thy sins in the clink.
Hark well these Laws of the Service,
Graved deep by the saber of Mars;
Conform to the mandates thus blazoned
And rise to thy place in the stars.
—*Marine Barracks, Quantico, VA, Gunner Frank H. Rentfro*

THE LIEUTENANT'S LAMENT

A lieutenant is an officer,
Or some people say.
He wears pink pants and shoulder straps
And draws commission pay.
But if you pause and ponder
You will see that they are wrong;
'Tis such a cause for wonder
That I have put into song.

The colonels live in quarters.
The privates live in tents;
By the post commander's orders
The lieutenant merely rents.
The USO gives dances
For the poor enlisted men;
The colonel's wives plan parties
Where each rooster has his hen,
The college girls
Cast their pearls
Before the crude cadets;
But the men of Mars
With single Bars,
'Tis them the world forgets;

To buy their meals they are allowed
Just sixty cents per day.
But they must mess in with the crowd
And ten bits for it pay,
And if a post commander
Does perchance, provide them quarters,
He builds them out of tarpaper
And living there is orders.
What is the rent? Oh, it is meant
To provide such quarters free---
Lieutenants merely do without
A forty dollar fee!

Oh, lieutenants they are officers,
Or so some may have thought,
They wear pink pants and shoulder straps
But really they are naught.
They must respect their betters,
And 'tis numerous they are.
Their bars are really fetters
To an eagle or a star....
Rank without authority,
Duty without power,
Service without glory,
Officer, for an hour!
       —Lieut. Donald E. Super

Section Six
Poems About War

TROOPSHIP

There is numbness, Not of dark waters
Nor of icicles flung across the night,
Each star a predestination
For each pack-bent figure.

It is a numbness born of the heart,
Growing quiet and sad
In spite of a band at the dock
Wisely playing "Deep In the Heart of Texas"
And not the false nostalgia
Of "Auld Lang Syne,"
In spite of spry Red Cross workers
Who try to warm you with a smile
And a hot cup of coffee.

You want to pause, contemplate,
But you are a soldier
And automatically march Into the ship's womb,
Pregnant with promise.
The shoreline fades,
Even as the body weariness,
When your pack slumps off,
For weariness fades into delirium,
And delirium, they say,
Is a disease of the night.
You, too, become diseased.

It is a merciful disease
Which pierces the fetid warmth
Of close-packed bodies.
It cuts a broad highway
To the land of yesterday,
The land of lilac air,
Of soft bluegrass and home.

Now the night Is lulled to sleep
By each mournful wave,
Each swishing wave
An echo of the heart.
Each wave a cry of sadness
Between two worlds.
—*China, Cpl. Charles L. Leong*

A TIME WILL COME

Shadowed though these years may seem,
Blighted though these days appear,
Time will come when we shall dream
Of the joys of yesteryear.

In that time, yesteryear will be
The one we gripe about today;
For we shall look behind and see
A highly polished far-away.

A yawling baby on our knee
And two or three on the floor
Will make us think how quietly
Buddies came through the barracks door.

Our relatives who read the news
Before they flush the thing they sit on
Will give us all the deep-sea blues
And curse the luck we've hit on.

When told that mother-in-law of course is
Installed at home and means to stay,
We'll dream about the unharmed forces
That we were part of---oh, bright day!

And when the Ides of March come around
And income taxes must be paid,
We'll envy lucky men who found
Homes in the Army, men who stayed.

Oh, these and many other trifles
That will plague us when we're free
Make us dream of using rifles
To shoot some folks with—two or three.
  —*Alexandria AAF, LA, S/Sgt. Russell Speirs*

A TANKMAN AT THE GATES

A tankman at the Pearly Gates
Was faced by Old St. Pete,
And told to go on down below,
Because he was not neat.
Says he, "I'm dirty all the time,
I live in grease and murk;
I don't sit at an office desk,
I do the dirty work.
I don't march up and down a post
In uniforms so neat,
Nor strap a pack upon my back,
Nor blister up my feet.
I know what it is to bathe
And shave, most every day,
A bath tub or a sink inside
A tank is in the way.
Now if I were artillery
I'd primp up every night,
And look like Esquire all the time,
But never know a fight.
Or if I were a Q. M. lad,
With uniforms so snappy,
I'd catch most everybody's eye,
And make the girls so happy!
But being just a tankman
I'm used to dirt and stuff;
Now may I enter thru the Gates?
I've lived thru Hell enough.
Yes, being just a tankman
I'm not much used to waitin';
Now may I live in Heaven, Sir,
Or must I call on Satan?"
  —*Sergeant John V. Sullivan Company A 191st Tank Battalion*

ALERT

The beams of light, like giant scissors, snip the sky to
 shreds, See!
Two have met and cross above the chapel on the hill!
Now satisfied, they flicker out and stars fall back into
 place---
The threat is gone, but nerves are tight; alert, the land is
 still.

Oh the fingers of light are out tonight
Probing the fringe of mist,
And the outpost lines under jungle vines
Are waiting with mailed fist.

Hark! The beat of giant feet across the star strewn floor!
The million-candled fingers leap and point where wings
 are barred;
But now the word dit-dits between, and friend is greeting
 friend;
The beams flick off; again, the land is taut, alert,
 prepared.

Oh, the pencils of light are eager to write
A one-way ticket to Hell.
Dream on, my sweet, in your distant retreat
Dream on, we are watching well.
  —*14th Inf. New Orleans, Lieut. Robert G. Rashid*

AIRBASE

Not runways, these are concrete
Arms stretching out to engulf
The countryside with spitting,
Hustling steel-sheathed avengers

They daily hurl from their bosom.
This base cannot die, for we
In our right have given it life.
—*Lincoln AAF, NE, Pfc. Samuel Naparstek*

A GUNNER'S DREAM

I wish I were a pilot,
And you along with me,
But if we all were pilots,
Where would the Air Force be?

It takes guts to be a gunner,
To sit out in the tail,
When the Messerschmitts are coming
And the slugs begin to wail.

The pilot's just a chauffer,
It's his job to fly the plane,
But it's we who do the fighting
Though we may not get the fame.

If we all must be gunners
Then let us make this bet;
That we'll be the best damned gunners
Who have left this station yet.

Author Unknown Submitted by:
—*Sgt. Edward F. Casey Lowry Field, CO*

A FIGHTERS LAMENT

I am sitting here and thinking
Of the things I left behind;
And I'd like to put in writing
What is running through my mind.
We have dug a million ditches
And have cleared 10 miles of ground.
We have drunk our beer and whiskey
In every honky-tonk in town.
But there is one consolation,
Gather round while I tell:
"When we die we'll go to Heaven,
For we have done our stretch in Hell."

We have built a million kitchens,
For the cooks to burn our beans;
We have stood a million guard mounts,
And we have cleaned the camp latrines,
We have washed a million mess kits,
And peeled a million spuds,

And killed a million snakes and ants
That have tried to steal our grub.
When our work on earth is ended,
Then our friends on earth will tell:
"When they died they went to Heaven,
For they've done their stretch in Hell."

When the final taps have sounded,
When we lay aside life's cares,
When we stand our last inspection
Of those shining golden stairs,
The angels will welcome us,
Their golden harps will play;
And we will draw a million canteen checks
And spend them in a day.
It is there we will hear St. Peter
Tell us loudly with a yell:
"Take a seat, you boys from the desert,
For you've done your stretch in Hell."

This poem came to YANK the same day from:
—*Sgt. Clyde Hogur, Panama, and Pvt,*
Paul F. Chenoweth, India

A CHRISTMAS POEM

This is a Christmas of memories and promises
Memories of snow and lighted trees and laughter around a fire
And promises of snow and trees and laughter to come,
To come home to.

This is a Christmas of regrets and longings
Regrets for things we left behind
As intangible as the whisper of wind around the corner of the house
Or the smell of pine and sweet cider
Regrets as sharp as a last kiss
Or a good-by at the station Longings for the girls.
Faces eager under the soft frame of hair Lips half parted,
Clear eyes looking into yours.

This is Christmas of war and novelty.
The lights on your tree are a display of shells
Bursting in a patterned pyramid over Leyte
The presents strewn beneath the tree are moments,
Moments of rest and a bath and rationed beer.

There is no stocking hanging by the chimney
That stands alone with the house about it shattered
On the edge of France.
Just the chimney to remind you how you went out late
Christmas Eve…….
You'd said before you thought Christmas stockings were corny

But that evening you noticed a look in the kid's eye
And put on your coat and went looking for an open
store,
Bought gadgets, candy, and a horn
And back at home stuffed them into the stocking…..
Hung it silently on the chimney
That might be that skeleton chimney in France.

This is a Christmas all in the heart
The day-room tent has an imitation of a tree
And the chaplain and the Social Service officer
Drummed up a carol-singing group last night
And it was fine that they did, but it wasn't Christmas.
It was only an arrow pointing to Christmas inside you,
The Christmas that you could keep only with yourself,
A waiting, hoping Christmas.

This is a Christmas of memories and promises,
Memories of snow and the wreath in the window
And Santa Claus on the corner,
His face a little dirty, Ringing his bell,
And relatives coming to dinner.

Memories around you with the strange palms of the Pacific,
Dug into the side of a hill in Italy with memories.

These memories
And promises of Christmas to come.
  —*Sgt. Al Hine*

KEEP DEATH PURE

Yes, ground the *Vulgar Virgin*
And clip *Lord Cesspool's* wings,
For death's a holy terror,
And bombs are moral things.
More sober names, they tell us,
That will not raise a brow,
Must grace our fighting aircraft
And deck the bomber's prow.

No more will death and fury
Be carried without stint
By bombers lewdly labeled
With names unfit to print.
It's not the heavy bomb-load
And not the mighty wing
That counts, officials tell us---
The monicker's the thing!
  —*Camp Shelby, MS, S/Sgt. Grant A. Sanders*

ON RAVEL'S CONCERTO FOR THE LEFT HAND

Made
for a man who lost his playing arm in war
to compensate for what's a shell's steel fragment tore was
what he made it for---
the keys set smashing
all with the five left fingers bashing into the board and rushing
armies of sound against the crowding arms of armlessness crushing
the inarticulate but muscled mass
of silence back into a twenty-minute soundwalled pass

Ravel did well
made for a one-armed man a one-armed thing that stands
with music made for two sound hands
we are all left-handed
wrenched from act and sounding
by multiple slash and a jagged wounding---
we need left-handed things---this we admit if we are can-
did--- we have but half or less than half
what we once had---but that's enough to play with if we
get left-handed stuff

given concertos for the left hand
we can fill with bold and competent sound
this shelled land though we're left handed
  —*San Francisco, CA, Sgt. James Steel Smith*

ONE SOLDIER'S CREED

There is no music left in me,
But weariness that knows no sleep;
A constant vigil I must keep
Until war's end.
There was a home, a walk, a lawn,
A girl I loved, games, dreams and books,
High hopes and laughter, quiet nooks
I do not feel
That I could live if they were not
Eternal, and forever things
That tyrants, demagogues and kings
Dare never touch.
If there are madmen who would try
To take these from me---if fury brings
Them, let them come.
There is not room beneath the sky,
There is not room in all the world
Where freedom's banners fly unfurled
If they should come.
  —*Hunter Field, GA, Pfc. Dudley Shoemaker*

ON BEAUTY DURING WARTIME

Write Beauty out.
Write it in mile-high words
Upon the plane-racked sky.
Scrawl it in crude wounds upon the heart.
Rivet it against the snarl of angry lead
That tunnels through the chattering air
In graceful arcs of death.
Play it up big but plenty.
Startle midnight with the noon glow
Of advertizing flares and tracer blurbs.
Paint it, with blood for media, on the grass.
Sing it, holler it out loud
Above the orgiastic brawl of drunken guns.
Etch it on the kiln-crazed surface of the mind
With acid-bitten lines of deep despair.
Do it, brother, do it now
Write Beauty on your heart.

For otherwise
It isn't and will never be.
—India, Cpl. John R. Cook

ODE TO NEW GUINEA

As a soldier in the service
I was feeling rather nervous
When they told us very likely
We were soon to meet the foe.
Soon the vicious rumors started
And our course was ofttimes charted.
Though we hardly had departed
From the camp we all loved so:
Only then we loved it so.

Eighteen days of blue Pacific,
Then an island loomed specific
And that night we slipped our anchor
Just inside the harbor's door.
There were MPs to direct us
And a general to inspect us
With some dump trucks to collect us
As we leaped upon the shore'
Made a beachhead on the shore!

Soon our fighting spirit failed us
As we left the ship that sailed us
And we bounced through muddy jungles
To our new mysterious home.
Liquid sunshine was the weather
As we huddled all together
Wondering if and when or whether
We had rather not succumb,
Wishing that we could succumb.

Ah, New Guinea, how I love thee
And those wet clouds right above thee
And the dust that tried to blind us
When the sun came shinning through:
There will be no want or famine
Long as Uncle Sam has salmon.
Bully beef in us he's crammin'
Powered eggs and ration stew;
Atabrine and cabbage , too!

How my draft board must be sweating
When they see their own names getting
Near the ones that are replacing
Casualty lists that grow.

Over here in dear New Guinea;
I got very thin and skinny
And the doctor wept so when he
Told me I'd soon have to go.
Told me home I'd have to go!

How my eyes were burning, smarting,
As I saw the ship was starting.
Taking me far from the island
I had learned to call my home.
Soon my stomach was offending,
Turning over and unbending.
And the food I ate was ending In the blue
Pacific foam: Feeding fishes in the foam.

Now those days are gone forever,
Mem'ries time can never sever
And the thought of them now moves me
Till I cannot stay the tears.
As I sit at home and ponder
On that South Sea island's wonder
I can hear its story thunder
Still among my souvenirs,
Haunting me down through the years.
—Bruns General Hospital, NM, S/Sgt
Robert C. Ellenwood

ODE TO MY FOXHOLE

When three quick shots are sounded
And the Nips are overhead,
I wouldn't trade my foxhole
For a pin-up girl in bed.

Ever see Frankie Sinkwich
Streaking downfield for the goal?
Well, he'd look like a turtle
When I'm headed for my hole.

A bomb might have my number
When the Zeros take their toll;
But if they ever get me,
Bud, They must get me in my hole.
—*New Guinea, Sgt. Max Scherer*

ODE TO AN INFANTRYMAN

Oh the poets chant
Of the armed gallant
Who boldly rode to war,
Encased in mail
From head to tail,
A mobile hardware store.

But did this guy
Armed 'cap a pie'
E'er trudge the dusty track,
With sixty pounds,
And eighty rounds,
And an M-1 on his back?

Did he rant and rail
As he hit the trail
When his shirt was dark with sweat,
To the sergeant's roar,
"Hep, two, three, four,
Ten miles to cover yet"?

Did he ever curse,
Blaspheme, and worse
At a canteen that's gone dry,
When the hike's half done
And a molten sun
Burns in a brazen sky?

Did he stagger in
With a dusty grin
That changed to a snarl and sneer,
While the guy with the bar,
Who had come by car,
Said, "You'll pitch your pup-tent here"?

Did he vent his ire
As he strung barbed wire
From pillar to post to tree,
Did he howl with hate
When the mess was late,
And gripe when he got K.P.?

Yes, poets write
Of the gallant knight
And his deeds, in history,
But never a pen
Tells of the men
You'll find in the infantry.
For though we yell,
And holler like hell,
Get this, we're on the ball.
Despite what we say
We like it this way,
We're Infantrymen, that's all.
—*Tech./S Howard Kirtland*

NO NAME JIVE

Artillery shells explode in the sky
Like giant hyacinths, while bursting rays
Of sunlight pounded through a staggered maze
Of regiments of crimson clouds.
The eye Perceived barbed-wire fences strung nearby
Where purple-red intestines hung for days
Like brilliant streamers of Hawaiian leis
Hung out like Monday morning's wash to dry.
In such a manner ultra modern, new
And very finely polished poets sing
Descriptions of amazing World War Two.
Their stanzas have a most exciting ring.
And if their stuff is colorful, then who
Can say that war is not a pretty thing?
—*Fort Benning, GA, Sgt. Leonard Summers*

NO GLORY OURS

No glory ours
Who head this native shore and fill these scenes.
We walk the cities' streets, and so it seems
We are apart.

No place have we
In which to serve, save labors commonplace,
Dull tasks which gall the spirit, lacking grace.

A man must fight
To know of war; it is not learned
On sheltered earth; fame is earned
On foreign shore.

Yet for the whim of fortune's wheel
We, too, might now be facing steel
So judge us not, nor rancor feel.
Our turn will come.
  —*Adams Field, AR, S/Sgt. Charles Grogan*

NOCTURNE

When soldiers sleep
There is not the quiet suburban street,
The arched trees
And quick footsteps, Brisk,
Echoing,
Then the key in the latch.
And distant wheels on tracks,
As if in the clouds,
Rhythmic, Lulling,
Then the cool white slumber.
There is not the blind on the window,
The shadows across the ceiling,
Molded by imagination,
Darkening, Fading,
Then forgotten.

When soldiers sleep,
There is an awakening of naked nerves,
That pluck at the tendons of twitching muscles,
Restless.
Worn.
There is the mumbling of hidden day words,
Articulate in the night,
Plaintive, Incoherent.
There is the match struck for a late cigarette,
Giving the mosquito net a fantastic solidarity,
As though cloth were imprisoning.

When a soldier sleeps,
There, is the lurking of death
And the need for rest,
That is more than time,
As all the world spins Into one bright spark,
Both ember and flame, In the fretful wind
When a soldier sleeps.
  —*Marianas, T-5 Stan Flink*

NIGHTTIME IN A FOXHOLE

When it's nighttime in a foxhole,
Dark the shadow shapes that form
To deceive the watcher, waiting,
Waiting for the man-made storm.

Watching, waiting in the darkness
Straining each and every sense.
Madness lurks o'er every shoulder.
Nerves are taut and muscles tense.
What is that now creeping inward:
Creeping, crawling shape so gray?
Breathe a prayer, brother watcher.
It is morning, it is day.
  —*Aleutians, Pvt. Carl Ennis*

NIGHT SKY

The winter sun
Haunted all day by cloud
Slips wearily into the low hill.
An eager moon, in gray struggle with the dusk,
Catches the cobwebs of twilight
And sweeps them off the early stars.

Soon pewter light spilling from overhead
Is scribbled with twisting smoke,
Scrambling from the flues of a score of tents.
Tents all in line mimic the soldiers who call them home;
Their roofs rise sharply to hooded points
On green pyramids.

Subtly the sky like some electric sense
Picks up a moving speck, a muffled hum
That all day long betrayed the presence of war birds in flight.
Though sharp and clear, the night sky
Has no flood of full, extravagant brilliance,
The arrowed light of precision.
Men who can scan the night sky must see
And decide in the time of a distant star's blink
Whether the speck that slivers along the sky,
The hum that echoes in the heavens,
Is friend Or foe.

Thus suddenly mighty shoots of light
Flower from man-made roots planted in vast perimeter.
Stalking the unknown, they examine it in miles-long beam.
Convinced of safety in the sight,
They slash back into the roots that gave them birth,
Searing the night sky with a brilliant path of retreat.

Grown weary with such nightly stagings
Of a grim play it now knows well,
The moon drops casually into its schedule of setting.
And lets the dark curtain of the night sky
Safekeep for the rest.
  —*Britain T-3, Leslie A. Goldman*

NIGHTFALL

The last gold shadow from the hill
Lies on the quiet corn.
Along the deepening rim of night
This starry darkness borne Invites the world and all its folk
To rest until the morn.

But, oh, the sons of men, we pray
With words we will not keep.
And sow in cruel discontent
The whirlwind that we reap,
While countless wrecked tomorrows race
Through our unquieted sleep.

How orderly the mountains march
Into the setting sun,
How are the myriad faces turned
From battles sorely won,
Too well aware of each new day,
The wars are never done.
 —*New Guinea, Pvt. Littleton Todd*

MY PRE-PEARL HARBOR RIBBON

I trim my chest with yellow, lest
My friends should not remember
I got my gun in Forty-one,
Sometime before December.

Through awful peace, through
Lend and Lease I stood up like a man
And won the war a year before
The goddam thing began.
 —*TCOCS, New Orleans, LA, O/C Charles P. Graves*

MY ONLY PLEA

"Still laugh," said I, "when I'm away,
And gather all the flowers of May;
Still keep my room, the pictures all,
That I have loved upon the wall;
For I shall want them every one
That moment that the war was won.

Still play the records, dance and sing,
And spread no fears by sorrowing;
Be happy, every time you can,
For victory, work and pray and plan,
For I shall want you looking well
When we have fired the final shell.

Still bake the pies, as it might be,
That I were coming home to tea;
Still plant the garden, roundabout,
Still grub the sturdy thistles out;
And stake the blue delphinium,
As if the war had never come.

For if this struggle shall be long,
At home there must be mirth, and song;
Since these are what we fight to keep,
So hide away, when you must weep;
And be brave at home, as we
Who fight in sky, on land and sea.
 —*Sergeant George L. Davidson, Headquarters Company, 116th Infantry*

MOTOR TRANSPORT SERVICE, IRAN, 1943

Walled cities sleep along the trading road,
The golden road that time has turned to steel.
Khaki and olive-drab in tractors wheel
Where caravans once eased their precious load.

It was frankincense and gold and fruits of Tartary
And fair-skinned women for the Khan's amusement
That went these ways when Polo was a boy,
Camels and horses, patient little donkeys,
All plodded by, laden with priceless wealth,
Between the towns they slept beside the road
In spreading tents with carven ivory poles,
Shielded from wind and sun by latticed screens
Adorned with dragons, flowers and painted birds.

Now dusty trucks with strange outlandish names
Like Studebaker, International,
Reel past, trailers a-swing, loaded with cans
And motor parts and ugly metal shapes.
But this is war beyond these merchant's knowledge,
Putting the conquests of their Khans in shadow.
This war needs sinews, gut of steel and carbon
For those men northward who patrol the skies
And ravaged earth in men-remote machines.

Dust and exhaust fumes mingle, part, reveal
The convoy rolling past the frightened sheep,
While by the road great crumbling cities sleep
And dream of gold that time has turned to steel.
 —*Iran, Cpl. Joey Sims*

MISGIVINGS ON GOOD FRIDAY
(For Certain People)

The hope of the world is hard to kill.
Hard to keep buried, hard to guard.
Seal it up with what rock you will—
When you've stoned it, hanged it, stabbed it hard,
And trooped to its agony high on a hill,
Seen it die with your own two eyes,
Seen for yourself its burial.
Still,
Never be sure it will not arise
Go to the small folk, dry their tears.
Smile at their doubt, overlook their lies
And walk the earth for a million years.
—*Greenland, Cpl John A. Dunn*

MICE OF MORESBY

Rats of old USA, or merely Moresby Mice,
We've had our full of fighting, and of hardships once or twice.
We have hugged for cover, with the bombers overhead;
We have seen the bombs exploding, heard the swish of
    falling lead;
We have dived into the trenches, with our last remaining breath,
Just a fraction of a second ahead of fire, din and death;
We have toiled and we have sweated, in humid tropic heat,
And we've longed for many comforts and fresh food we
    could eat;
But we'll gnaw our way to freedom, and we'll nibble at
    the scum
Till we drive them back to Nippon or hell where they belong.
And when they've learned their lesson, then maybe these
Foreign Lice Will remember Pearl Harbor and New
    Guinea's Fighting Mice.
—*Australia, Pvt. Matthew Spiller*

MAYTAG CHARLIE

Douglas, Vought-Sikorsky, Bell,
All make planes that sound so well;
But the Japanese, strange as it seems
Make planes that sound like washing machines.

On an island in the Coral Sea
That we took from the Japanese,
From it comes a story of
A guy called Maytag Charlie.

Ever night about 10:15
The air-raid siren used to scream.
Up would go the searchlight's beam
And in flew Maytag Charlie.

Now this guy Charlie flew so high
That he could never score a hit,
And then one night we set a trap
And sure enough, Charlie bit.

He saw the lights and came down low;
The antiaircraft guns let go
You could hear the blast in Tokyo,
And down came Maytag Charlie.
—*Guadalcanal, Pvt. Frank Ellis*

MAN OF THE YEAR

And I will walk through the night unseen, un- heard---
walk through dark avenues where shadows dark and fade;
And I will be followed by many more walking
---walking through crumbling cities, past many a gutted
    church and smashed façade.
Stumbling through mangled fields and shredded trees,
wrapped in heavy mist, grope the for- gotten and the broken.
Sing the wind and the rain, tell our lonely tale in the
night, write on the scarred and tor- tured earth our token,
For we are the earth, we are the sand of Tarawa, the rich
loam of Sorrento and the red clay of Tunisia.
We felt the cool spray on coral reefs and the hot sun of
Africa's wadies, and we saw the spires of Rome come nearer.
And yet once more this earth, this loam shall feel the
plowman's hand and wheat shall rise,
And once more the builder shall touch his brick and steel,
and cities shall reach the skies;
And we the shadows, who walked in the night through
dark avenues broken, and forgotten, shall rise, too.
We shall enrich the wheat and our souls shall strengthen
the spires and we shall encourage the true,
And we shall leave the dark mangled fields as silently as
we came, past gutted churches and reddened rivers.
And where we walked the sun shall bathe many towns
and fresh green fields, and we will
live forever.
—*Columbia AAB, SC, Pvt. Davis H. Markoe*

GREETINGS

I find it hard my time to bide,
Oh, would I couldst be at thy side!
I'd kick thee in the teeth, my pet,
And spit thee on my bayonet.

Oh, how I wish that I could go
Across the sea to Tokyo
And hoist thee, son of Heaven, high
Upon a gibbet toward the sky.
—*Camp Maxey, TX, Pvt. Vick Jester*

GHOST HOTEL

There , like a monstrous apparition, she remains,
A great, gray, lifeless thing against the skies.
Splendid Regina, she no longer reigns,
Shattered and sightless are her thousand eyes.
Her upper chambers, where the shells tore through,
Smell yet of scorching, like the bloody pyres
They were. Their ruins wear a ghastly hue
Made by the fading light as the sun retires.
Around her lacerated casements moan
The winter winds and sweep her drapes aside,
Chilling her once snug passageways, now lone,
Forbidding haunts, where memories reside.
Charming and gay she was; and when all men
Break through chaotic night, she'll live again.
—*France, T-4 Herbert J. Risley*

FOOT SOLDIER

Any field a road for me,
Son of hard-boiled Infantry;
Darkness and unknown wooded path,
Gully and stream and Nature's wrath
Level out---to me a floor,
Mountain pass---a simple door.
All these things are sought for me,
Son of hard-boiled Infantry.
—*Fort Sill, OK, Pvt. Adolph Schusterman*

FIRST LOVE (REMEMBERING SPAIN)

Again I am summoned to the eternal field
green with the blood still fresh at the roots of flowers.
green through the dust-rimmed memory of faces that
moved among the trees there for the last time
before the final shock, the glazed eye, the hasty mound.

But why are my thoughts in another country?
Why do I always return to the sunken road through
corroded hills, with the Moorish castle's shadow casting
ruins over my shoulder
and the black-smocked man approaching, his hands laden
with grapes?

I am eager to enter it, eager to end it. Perhaps this one
will be the last one.
And men afterward will study our arms in museums
and nod their heads, and frown, and name the inadequate
dates
And stumble with infant tongues over the strange place-
names.

But my heart is forever captive of that other war
that taught me first the meaning of arms and of com-
radeship
and always I think of my friend who amid the apparition
of bombs saw on the lyric lake the single perfect swan.
—*CA, Pvt. Edwin Rolfe*

FIGHTING MEN

Oh, war is grim and war is bold, and many the tales they tell,
Of Pickett's charge at Gettysburg, through flaming pits of hell,
Of Little Big Horn and Custer's stand, and wild the bugles blow
To the forlorn sweep of the Light Brigade, and the men
    of the Alamo.

But when you write of fighting men, to history's scroll add on---
How the naked Igorotes rode the tanks at old Bataan.
Write not of dashing heroes, spurred and booted cap-a-pie;
But of simple men, of heathen men, men unafraid to die;
They seek not an armored shield to magnify their deeds,
But clamored up with warrior shouts and rode their iron steeds;
There face to face they met the foe, no quarter gave nor sought;
The only men that ever tamed a rolling Juggernaut.

Aye, war is grim, and war is bold, and heathen Gods are strange,
And Christian prophets ever strive their ancient ways to change;
But when the roar of battle sounds, all men find equal place.
For color is a pewter stamp high courage knows no race.
So when you speak of mighty deeds, remember to add on---
How the naked Igorotes rode the tanks at old Bataan.
—*Avn/C M. Lyle, Windsock, Lindberg Field*

ENGINE OF DESTRUCTION

Aboard a Flying Fortress!
What luck to catch a hitchhike ride like this
And, suspended in the plastic nose,
Like a goldfish in a bowl,
To leave the earthbound travelers far below
Waiting on the chilly curbs
And standing in the jam-packed aisles of trains and busses.

Old Seventy-Six, creeping behind five other planes

That roll off one by one, mutters to himself,
Pauses, tense-sinewed for a moment,
Then like a lion roars defiance to the sky, his realm,
And hurtles down the stretch to spring into the air
O'er, scraggy treetops snatching ineffectually
As he sheaths his claws.

O god, I haven't eyes enough to seize a fraction
Of the beauty that encircles and envelops me!
The perfect summer day with the sun
Slanting through the hazeless air
Bringing life and color to the outspread world below.
Winter-worn yet green, a carpet patterned by the hedge-
    divided fields
And undulating to a raveled margin at the shore.
The sea, restless yet deliberate, ever changing yet the same,
Nibbling at the curving wafer of the beach,
Steel-blue today except where sparkling
With the silver powder of the sunlight,
Looking like foaming suds and bubbling with unhurried
    yet explosive power;
To the right a shower cloud,
A soiled and formless mass, like melting snow upon a stump,
Sprinkling down a pool of gray upon the surface.

By the time I looked if front again
Another cloud had cast a somber cloak upon the sea of glory;
But in the center, like old Excalibur upthrust from the lake,
Burned a white-hot bar of light
That seemed to sear my very eyeballs.
It was gradually extinguished as the cloud-framed skylight closed
And above the plane's unheeded roar
I could imagine that I heard the hiss.
Five minutes served to put the pattern in reverse;
For now appeared a headline of the farther shore,
A coal-black battle-ax that boldly cut
Across the shimmer of the westering sun.

Over land again the crazy quilt of green and brown,
Unreal and lifeless save for the beetles that were cars,
Dotted with toy houses and lightninged with streams
That for a moment mirrored back the silver of the sun,
Unrolled beneath my feet so swiftly
That it did not seem a minute
Till *Old Seventy-Six* was banking and then skiing smoothly
Down the hill of air into the waiting runway.

My spirits still somewhere far aloft,
Left behind in the realm of Shelley's
Western Wind and Skylark, I stepped to earth---
Stepped from the most efficient engine of destruction
Yet devised by man in ten thousand years of war.
    —*Britain, Sgt. George Fredrick Stork*

CPL. DOYLE IS TO AFRICA COME!

Oh, sound the trumpet and beat the drum!
Cpl. Doyle is to Africa come!
To Africa come in enormous force
To alter the global battle's course.
Already the dastard foeman fly;
We'll all be home the Fourth of July.

Oh, clash the cymbals, sound the tabor!
For Cpl. Doyle, his gun and saber,
His tanks and artillery (self propelled),
With which the enemy shall be quelled.
Already in dread the Nazi blenches;
By Christmas we'll be out of the trenches.

Oh, smite the zither, rattle the goard!
Cpl. Doyle's in *Afrique du Nord*!
Now for a speedy end to the war;
Summon a hearse for the Afrika Korps,
For here comes the guy the enemy fears---
The paragon of the Engineers.
So smite the zither, rattle the goard!
Cpl. Doyle's in *Afrique du Nord*!
    —*North Africa, Cpl. John J. Doyle*

CONVOY

The trucks move
Over the convolutions of the land,
Militarizing the valleys,
Rubbering up the hills;
Spaced like the teeth on a gear
They roll with their cargo.

Under the canvas and the ribs
Of the machines,
Tight on the wooden benches,
Rifles held at vertical,
Are the men.
Battlers with a woman or an idea
Or a maneuver whirling
In the cell structures of their brains,
Aching for the lightning of battle
And the hard reward of peace.
Khaki-wrapped, metal-topped;
Strength on the highway.
    —*Fort Devens, MA, Pvt. Norman Sak*

CITIZEN-ARMY

We are not professional soldiers.
Bullets were strange to us a year ago.

We were the farmer---the teacher
We were the clerk---the businessman
We were the actor---the mechanic

Yes, we were the citizens of last year---
Now we are the citizen- army.

Since leaving peace and our loved ones---
We have been taught:
to sleep as the warrior---
to eat as the soldier---
to march as the fighter.

We build bridges---we students
We repair bombers---we artists
We shoot well, we butchers, we plumbers,
We of the citizen-army.
—*Lowry Field, CO, Pvt. Harold Feigenbaum*

CATHEDRAL SQUARE

No leaves on the trees,
But shadows pattern
The square dark blotches.

The sun has turned
The stones white
And the blood black:
Shrapnel twists
The trees and the dead
Into agonizing postures.

Here are the stains
Of a Sicilian summer:
Here is the death
Of Fascism
—*New Guinea, Sgt. George Kauffman*

CAN WE GO BACK?

A soldier back from the lines, far-staring, dirty, worn thin,
Sat musing of war in the islands and what it can do to men.

His outfit had been in the thing too long, too long for men to stay
In the jungle's hell of mud and heat, where three hours mean decay.

In the hills where machine guns sputter and mortar bursts spread wide,
He'd fought till his arms hung useless, and something within him had died.

Kill or be killed is the way it goes---it's always him or me;
There's no other way to live up there; it's the way things have to be.

Keep down the fear that gnaws inside when a sniper's shot hits near,
Damn a man you can't even see, and hit where a man breaks clear.

For fear a man can't live with; it's blind madness that makes him go
Into the face of fire and hell. The Lord must have made it so.

We ask no mercy and give none, and a rifle's butt of steel
Will knock out teeth so easy. . . God! we've lost our power to feel.

We shoot when danger's right on us and shoot when a man's asleep.
Who gives a damn how we kill 'em---as long as death will keep?

They made all of us killers, and we've laughed at the sight of blood.
I wonder if ever we'll know again the sweetness of a white rose bud?

Can we go back to the polite old ways? Can we change to a civvy suit,
And smile and be tender and thoughtful. . . .after eating forbidden fruit?

Can we ever be refined and decent, like most of had been?
War in the islands is ugly, and it does strange things to men.
—*Guadalcanal, Sgt. Mack Morriss*

LITANY FOR HOMESICK MEN

A litany for all men homesick:
For all men crying sick
In all camps over all America
And too far away across the waters
For even the furloughs we yearn about,
In a circle under one dim bulb
In the barracks.

A litany for all men:
Those who dream at night of home
Before battle-dawn and the bombers rising;
And those with too much time to think
Here in the humdrum barracks,
Training finished and waiting for shipment,
With MPs at the gates; and those
Behind electric wires with the jaded guards.
Japanese or German, hoping to shoot
When they cross the dead line.

A litany of all our longings,
Walled in overweight khaki
Or turreted in the nauseous tanks
Bolted down for the break-through.

A litany of yearnings:
For the towns we came from,
Joe's place on the corner
And beer and chili and
Cincinnati Dutch accents;
For the sickish ozone of the
6 o'clock rush In the subway; or the Polish cry
Of the El conductor in Chicago; for the thick steaks
Of a little restaurant in DuBois, Pennsylvania;
Or the sleepy streets of Georgetown, Kentucky,
Walking into stone-walled blue-grass meadows;
For Memphis and the great bluff on the Mississippi
And the high woods of the Arkansas shore
After sunset.

A litany for all homes we lived in:
For tall apartments in Yonkers with zig-zagged
Fire escapes, and round and rich with the Yiddish voices;
For the cabin in Kentucky cove, puncheon-floored
And with a Spanish rifle won from another war
Gracing the mantelpiece; for the tall-gabled
Brick villa in the wide-lawned suburb.

For my own home, small weathered white cottage
On a quiet street in Bloomington, Indiana,
And a robin nesting under the front-porch eaves,
And a rabbit in the garden thinking it is his right
To lop my tomato plants, and a great black table
With a line of my books on it, and Peggy my wife
To walk with on the back lawn among limestone walls
With twilight coming on.
A litany for all of us:
O words that bring back our homes for a space
And give us a quiet place for worship,
And peace in our hearts, after the cursing camp.
Home will always be with us, whether or not
We ever see it again, a picture in our brain,
Colors and odors and sounds half remembered.

When hate of an unseen enemy cannot hold us,
This homesick litany will lead us into battle;
For the homes we lived in once long ago
Are strength on the march and a steady grip
On the killing tools and a tried hand
On the poised trench mortar.
—*New Guinea, Cpl. Hargis Westerfield*

LINES

I do not know how many there are
Who have been touched by your magic
Here in this little town.
Perhaps they are few who carry it,
This flame-tipped, soul-felt, tender thing;
Perhaps they are many.
I do not know.
I know the juke box blares in Cedarville
And it's Saturday night
And perhaps there in the USO
A pfc is remembering your smile.
I do not know but that tonight
In a blacked-out, soot-covered sleeping car,
Cramped by barracks bags piled high,
A frightened lonely boy is whispering your name.
And somewhere there's a man-made hell
And through the bloodied muck
A soldier cradles his rifle close
Almost the way he held you when you danced
And he was a gay good American boy.
Then suddenly he pitches forward, lies still
And the eyes are glassy that but a moment before
Were filled with you and happy things.
We are many of the same mien---
The boy from Council Bluffs,
The boy from Texas,
The boy from Memphis
And I---
And we are only passing through.
I do not know

How many locked the memory of you in their hearts.
I did.
But, where I will carry it
I do not know.
— *Camp Sibert, AL, Pfc. John J. Ryan*

LIMITED SERVICE

The Fortunes of War…
Are bitter ones and
Those with the most
To lose pay the
Highest price……
Battlefields are
Littered with jeweled
Movements of thousands
Of fine men while
Many a broken
Dollar watch
Sits at a desk….
— *Jacksonville, FL, M/Sgt. Sherwood Stokes*

LIGHTINGS IN THE SKY

Oh, Hedy Lamar is a beautiful gal
And Madeline Carroll is too.
But you'll find if you query a different theory
Amongst any bomber crew
For the loveliest thing of which they could sing
(This side of the Heaven's Gates)
Is no blonde or brunette of the Hollywood set
But an escort of P-38s.

Wordsworth, Shelly, and Keats ran a dozen dead beats
Describing the views from the hills,
Of the valleys in May when the winds gently sway
An army of high daffodils. Wordsworth, the wild flowers,
Shelly And you the myrtle, friend Keats,
Just give me a bunch of American Beauties— An escort
of P-38s.
— *North Africa, T/Sgt. R. H. Bryson*

LAMENT FOR SOME AMERICAN WOMEN

We have no issues to face,
No great decisions to make,
No life and death dice to cast,
No burning hope and in a sense,
No goal but to live
Until the war is past.

And when it's done, we will not know.
In the same ignorance we will go
Down the same roads, riding musty-
Smelling buses, lying stiff and patient
In the summer sun, blushing
In the well-preserved shame at the same joke
And in the end
Weeping softly for the days lost,
The work not done.
— *Moore Gen. Hosp., NC, Pfc. Gloria Marchisio*

KILL OR BE KILLED

Brass knuckles and knives are your new tools;
Skip the Marquis of Queensbury rules.

Gouge out his eye and kick in his knee,
Knife him from behind when he can't see,
Bludgeon his head and go for his groin,
Honorable ancestor let him join.

Slap the enemy down in the dust,
Using the butt stroke and the short thrust;
Kill with bare hands and let nothing delay
His timely end. Hooray for foul play!

Stamp and crush him with your hobnailed boot;
Bite and kick him. Hell, when do we shoot?
— *Shreveport, LA, Sgt. Benjamin Borax*

JOHNNY DOUGHBOY

He's six feet three and he's five feet four
He's as slim as a slat and wide as a door
He wears a twelve shoe, and a cap marked #7
He hails from Fort Benning,
Swift, Deven.

He talks like Georgia, and his "H'ya all?"
Has a Vermont twang and an Iowa drawl
He's silent and gabby, melancholy and merry
He hails from Forts Schuyler,
Livingston and Perry.

He's a farmer, a clerk, a miner and a broker
He kept a country store, and sailed as a stoker
He's backwards and he's shy; he's a wit and a wag
He hails from Forts Slocum,
Claiborne and Bragg.
He's Yankee and he's Polish; he's Spanish, German,
French

His home is in the barracks, a foxhole and a trench
He can shoot a squirrel's eye out at a hundred yards or more.
He hails from Forts
Riley, Gordon, and Orr.

He's poluglot, a melting pot; a mixture of race and creed
With a job to be done and a war to be won
And hail to the East, North, South and West
Give Johnny Doughboy the weapons
and he'll do the rest.
  —Fort Belvoir, VA, Pvt. Murray B. Schoen

IMPROVISATIONS FOR A SOUTHERN NIGHT

The native's myth, as lavish as the night,
Tracks down the centuries of his half-light,
Naming the moving people of the wind
By logics that his waking cannot find.
Lacking a legend, let me improvise:

There was a lady in the moon's round house
Loved by the Sun, who, bound to other skies,
Wooed her as Sultans would, or Khans, or Shahs,
With couriers and gifts, till her jewel box
Groaned with his trinkets---and her locks.
(She had a woman's instinct for the real.)

Nightly she took his signal and his gift
Reflecting love and light, till on the wheel
Of chiming orbits came at last---the rift;
She looked too long on Mercury or Mars,
He felt his heavenly oats, and hot with pride,
Came, bristled, threatened, flailed her hair and hide,
And flung aside her jewel box, scattering wide
The shattered shining trinkets of the stars
Lavished forever on the Southern night
When the Sun sulks down, and the lady of the light
Speaks to the native children on the sand
Beside the white man's swath burned on the land.

Well, it will do or it will have to do.
I listen, drowned in surf sound, and recall
Our angers shall outshine us after all;
We have no other prodigy left us now,
And we are planted on a coral walk
Between two surfs, above and below;
The first extravagantly hurled on rock,
The other droning where the bombers go
Hurling their sound at cloud, themselves at space
In the enormous rift of moon and sun
And threading red light, green light on the face
Of a legend improvised by gun and gun.

And as the sun might love his arrogance,
Or moon her light, her darkness, and her loss;
I weaken toward the engines of our madness
And almost think we scatter stars across
The ukase of our bombfall down the air.

.......Until I need your light and your despair
Across the metal crackle of the rain
To satisfy a human night again.
  —Marianas, S/Sgt. John Ciardi

I WILL TURN HOME

I will turn home again some day,
Putting my back on all these things
Of war and blood:
Of pain and mud;
Of aching hunger and of maddening stings.
I will go back along the way
I came, until I stand once more
Beneath home skies,
And see sunrise
Upon the beloved shore.

I will turn home again when war
Is past and honor's call is quiet.
Till then my face
Is set in place
To one established goal in freedom's fight.
I will turn home at last once more,
Knowing that a true soldier's rest,
Once earned, is sweet;
His peace complete
Who gave until the last his best.
  —New Guinea, Sgt. R. A. Larsen

IRISH NEUTRALITY

I'm gullible, trusting, extremely naïve,
And yet I simply cannot believe
What nature disproves and history belies;
It isn't the way or likes of those guys
To sit calmly by and a battle to scorn.
A neutral Irishman has yet to be born.
  —Herbert Smart Airport, GA, Cpl. Nathaniel Rogovoy

IN TIME OF WAR

In time of war a man finds out about himself.
Or does he?
If he doesn't want to fight, he's surely a coward.
Or is he?
His greatest energies are called upon to do their best.
Or are they?
His civil life is put behind him.
Or is it?
He can prove he's got the stuff to do a big job.
Or can he?
He will learn to take orders without question.
Or will he?
He discovers that his comrades should be treated as his brothers.
Or should they?
He gets used to answering calls of nature in multi-populated latrines.
Or does he?
He might take up religion after being an atheist for years.
Or might he?
He learns to eat slum and beans and like it.
Or does he?
His ideals become great as his aim is noble.
Or do they?
Under stress of war his latent abilities are brought to light.
Or are they?
He begins to drink, gamble and fight at the slightest provocation.
Or does he?
He makes most of all the companionship of women. He sure does.
—*USCG Base, San Juan, Puerto Rico, B. J. Talkin S2c*

SUPPLICATION

Let me not fear the battle's roar,
Or dangers flying overhead,
Nor weaken me at sight of gore,
But strengthen me, Oh Lord, instead.

Though bullets whine right past my ears,
I pray to take it all in stride;
Lift up my head and banish fears,
I've faith, for right is on my side.

If He is just, as we have learned,
And merciful and true and kind,
He'll walk beside and steady me,
Encouraged, I'll find peace of mind;

Though I be fallen in the fight,
I'll rise again, as rise I must
To march always beneath His light,
For my God, I put my trust.
—*TCAB, Charleston, SC, Pvt. Alfred Baskind*

SUNDAY MORNING IN ALABAMA

The narrow white-sand road lures me on
Downhill through open fields of waving grasses,
Waist high,
And comes to an abrupt ending at the forest's edge.
No space for road,
No tempting path to follow;
Only a giant water oak,
An ancient bearded prophet,
Swathed in Spanish moss
Waves an eerie greeting;
The musical notes of water
Slipping over a rocky ledge
Green with velvet moss,
While down below
Dead brown leaves float aimlessly
In the quiet pool.

The cushioned comfort of leaf mould underfoot
Makes the ascent of the hill ahead
A silent one.
The glossy green-leather leaves of magnolia,
Evenly spaced like dummy trees in store windows,
Reflect the sun like a rajah's emeralds.
The lacy fingers of the sweet gum
Pierce the blue,
Framing a spot of open sky
Where a turkey buzzard dips and circles in effortless ease.
In the dappled brush across the creek a blue jay flashes.
A shaft of filtered sunlight breaks suddenly
Through the ever-present needled pines
As through a cathedral window.
Nature reigns supreme.

Suddenly and without warning
The far-off sound of guns is heard.
A faint humming like a thousand bees in flight
Swells into a crescendo
And overhead a giant man-made bird skims the treetops,
Its body and wings like beaten silver.
The arrival and departures are simultaneous.
In its roaring wake
Every bird in every tree Cries in protest.
Once more this corner of paradise

Returns to its Sabbath stillness,
I turn and slowly make my way to the white sand road
Which leads to a green-roofed white frame barracks,
My present home.
—*Camp Shelby, MS, Pfc. Gene Wierbach*

SOUVENIR

I walked beside a silent stream
Flowing green between the trees,
By ferns and broad-leafed tropic plants,
And festooned vines, stirred by a breeze.

And looked into its cooling depth,
Saw sands as white as crystal salt,
Drank of its peace and heavy scent---
Yet stumbled on a glaring fault,
That shouted ugliness from out the growth
Along the bank. A twisted, half- burned wing
Of crusted metal with a scarred red sun
Drawn on it. A misplaced, worthless, foreign thing,
A fallen bird, that died here. In its craw
An apish, slant-eyed face, stained with old blood,
And crazily askew on stiffened shoulders.

Obliterating vines and saw-tooth grass
Sent tendrils out to hide the open tomb,
And cleansing mould and fungus were at work.

And then I watched a sweating soldier come
And rip the metal with a broken-edge blade.
He sliced the red sun painted on the wing,
To make a bracelet for a far-off maid.
Dutch New Guinea, Cpl. George Harris

SONNET TO A STATESMAN

When that which lies before us is behind
And days and nights of restless waiting end,
Shall we in bitter recognition find
No worthy use of all we freely lend?
What years might hold for us to put aside;
To other days belongs the planned career,
Shall we who now comprise a country's pride
Find lost as well so much our lives make dear?
The simple truths are those for which we fight,
The freedoms men have won and known as good
No sophistry that colors wrong and right
Enlists our arms against our brotherhood.
What value battles won in foreign lands
If freedom here elude our reaching hands?
—*Casper AAB, WY, S/Sgt. Raymond Harris*

SONNET FOR VETERANS

Ask not that you be given special gifts,
Or treated in an extra-special way;
Although today a grateful nation lifts
One voice in thanks, you soon may see the day
When gratitude is spent; the very men
Who thank the loudest now may then forget
The blood you spilled. If so---I warn again---
Expect no mention of a special debt. Instead of asking
to be kept in mind
For payment of a very special kind,
Ask only for those things that all men ought
To have---the very things for which you fought;
A decent job, a busy world at peace;
And ask that free men's progress never cease.
—*Kirtland Field, NM, S/Sgt Morton Brooks*

SONG OF THE SOLOMONS

On Guadalcanal the days are fair,
No discord troubles the dulcet air
Till the raucous shout pervades the night:
"Hey, you---turn out that flaming light!"

Condition red and condition green,
Just strike a match in the tropic scene;
A chorus appalled howls in the night:
"Hey, you---turn out that flaming light!"

If you drive a jeep you'd better park
When the lights fade out to purple dark,
Or you'll hear the song of the tropic night:
"Hey, you---turn out that flaming light!"

Safe in his hut the squadron's major
Will light his lamp, and it's a wager
You'll hear the scream from out of the night:
"Hey, you---turn out that flaming light!"

You'd better turn out that flaming light
When you hear them howl in the silly night,
For a slappy guard or a tough marine
Will shoot it out with a mean machine.

Reluctant dragons safe home in bed
Will spring into action from the dead,
When a thrifty wife says low in the night:
"Hey, you---turn out that flaming light!"
—*Guadalcanal, Cpl. R.A. Beard*

SOAP AND WATER

You might think this nonsense and so much palaver
Till you've gone for a month and not even seen lather.
I think someone said that a bath is a bath
When a man's in a tub and can both sing and laugh,
With no one to watch him or tell him to hurry
And soapsuds are flitting about in a flurry.
I've bathed in canteen cups and helmets and cans,
I've gone for three weeks without washing my hands,
But I think if I ever get out of this war
I'll live in a bathtub for time evermore.

Just give me a tub that is porcelain-lined,
With nice tile floors, and I'll soon be reclined
The full length of that lovely containment of water
And neither my wife nor my son or daughter,
Through threat or enticement, shall lure from his lair
The father they love. They can pull out their hair,
They can rave, they can rant, they can scream, they can roar:
But I'll smile and remember this bathtub war,
And I'll lie midst the wonderful soapsuds, I think,
Till my skin and my soul are a rose-petal pink.
—France, Cpl. John E. Abel Jr.

SEPARATION CENTER, EM

Look elsewhere for the big operators,
The spinners of stratagem,
The weavers of plans and tactics.
Look elsewhere for the lads with glitter in their garments
And swagger in their walk.
Here strode those who did not blueprint victory,
They won victory;
The guy who lobbed grenades on Okinawa,
The driver of the Red Ball Express,
The rifleman who absorbed shrapnel beside the swift Volturno.
Your future is erected upon firmer ground that dreams
Because the strong back
And the enlisted mind,
Have saved your civilization.
—Washington, D.C., Cpl. Martin S. Day

SAKI MISSED ME

(Apologies to Leigh Hunt and Jennie)
Saki missed me on patrol,
Peeking from the tree he hid in!
Clerk who checks the morning roll,
Kindly note I ain't been did in!

Mark me AWOL, eat me out,
Say I'm ailing when you list me,
Say I'm late, but never doubt:
Saki missed me!
—New Caledonia, S/Sgt. Ira J. Wallach

RUSSIAN SNOW

A frosty courier shall sweep
From seas congealed in ice, and blow
Across the steppes a tryst to keep;
O Year, bring on the Russian snow.

As Soviet heroes rally flanks
At Stalingrad to stem the flow
Of onward battering Nazi tanks,
Oh Year, bring on the Russian snow.

Thus tactfully the blistering cold
Will check, repel the lethal foe;
Ascent of Star again behold.
Oh Year, bring on the Russian snow.
—Camp Forrest, TN, Pvt. Charles E. Woodruff

REFUGEES

A footstep in the night,
Faltering yet strangely stubborn,
The leather moves, slips on a stone,
Rises, falls and moves again.

Postlude of a fury spent,
The ragged bodies sway and lurch,
The hollow glazed eyes stare
With fixed intensity at the road ahead.

Slowly---God, How slowly---
They leave the floodlit stage of war,
While out beyond the lengthening shadow
Fades quietly into night.
—Germany, Pfc. J.T. Waterhouse

REAR GUARD

Back from the swamp, he ran rear-guard,
This rookie fresh from the States. Proudly
He straightened up at the order, scraped muddy hands
On his sweaty jacket; his first dangerous job;
Dropped to the lonely rear, that last man
The sniper's long-bolted rifle soonest

Strikes into the mud; (red crackle, like a cap
Sparked on a stone, and hard-boiled
American's Long dying groan). Rifle ready to swing
To shoulder, he halted, scanning the dim trail
Through brush and water, the black mosquito
Hells of the sago swamp. On higher ground,
The long brown slot lay straight and bare
Up to the curve by the vine-wrestled trunks
Of giant trees. In the slumberous, insect-sleepy,
Long jungle afternoon, red face blazing.
He ran off the patrol, slipped on the roots,
Swung over the logs, fought free of the vines,
Fell prone in the mud, hour by hour,
Too proud to pray for relief;
A little guy with a lot of guts
Doubling knee-deep in mud, with hardly a glance
At the new-made corpse in the curve of the trail;
A little guy with a lot of guts
Waiting a long clean standing shot
Down the green tunnel of the sunlit trail.
—*Philippines, Sgt. Hargis Westerfield*

RAIN AND POKER

Rain cracking hard on barracks roofs made
New lakes stretch out on springtime jade,
Like children reciting, the bubbles spoke
For scarcely a moment before they broke.
Perhaps they forgot their simple lines
When the monster in the Gulf wind whines
To touch off San Antonio town.
Were these the flares to designate
Some target or seeds that hibernate?
This Gulf wind raiding overhead
With bellied bomb-bays and thunder tread
Couldn't chase the planes that lunge
Intently through this opaque sponge.
And while all springtime turned up its collar,
Card players said, "The limit's a dollar."
—*San Antonio AAF, Texas A/C Norman Gelber*

PROPHECY

Hard by the sea the storm-locked flyers wait.
In sleepless sleep they toss and dream.
Each man the keeper of another's fate.
Some distance off the beach, beyond the breaking sea,
A lone ship burns and each man seems to say:
"It might be you, it could be me!"
Soon as the storm subsides, swift as hungry gulls
They will go out to where the wolf pack rides,
And peace will come to those who wait---
World-wide and quiet, beautiful as girls
And homey as some pasture gate.
—*Tinker Field, OK, Pfc. John C. Rogers*

PRAYER, 1944

God, let us have some peace to live,
Carved out from all the time
You have in store; Just some centuries that
You could give
Without disturbing
Your Forevermore.
You've got it pretty soft, God:
Your sky Is silent as the heart of night should be,
With an occasional meteor going by
To shake the edges of Eternity.
It's a little different, God, down here;
The bitter curse of war is everywhere,
With blood and flame, sorrow mixed with fear,
And Death, instead of Angels, rides the air.

We only ask that You will understand
And drop some quiet mercy from Your hand.
—*Camp Lee, VA, T-4 Myron W. Fisher*

POST-WAR PLANNING

The time came for the shouting, beautiful children to come down from the trackless hills
Onto the plain, where they could see the people and the cities, and the war.

They came unpained into the strange sun of the flatlands which chilled them at dusk
When the enemy bombers threw swift shadows across plains of grain. The hills were not safe.
But there were no safe plains. the shouting, beautiful children
slept in a hangar, shinning in the moonlight with whorls of stars.
The lean chucking pilots covered them with coats.

These great men, their blood ex- cited at the movement of pistons, fierce anger in their eyes,
Remained with the children until the flight.
When that evening came a little boy ran to one of them and clutched him and cried beside the thunder of motors.
The pilot said: "Son stand straightly. The evening is small to the sky.

Stand with your shoulders parallel to clouds, going every where.
There lies our strength, our joy forever."
—*Fort Monmouth, NJ, Cpl. Saul Gottlieb*

TO THE FIGHTING MAN

I want to walk by the side of the man who has suffered and seen and knows,
Who has measured his place on the battle line, and given and taken blows.
Who has never whined when the scheme went wrong nor scoffed at the failing plan,
But taken his dose with a heart of trust and the faith of a gentleman,
Who has parried and struck and sought and given and scarred with a thousand spears,
Can lift his head to the stars of heaven and isn't ashamed of his tears.
I want to grasp the hand of the man who has been through it all and seen,

Who has walked in the night with an unseen dread and stuck to the world machine,
Who has beaten his breast to the winds of dawn and thirsted and starved and felt
The sting and the bite of the bitter blasts that the mouths of the foul have dealt,
Who was tempted and fell and rose again, and has gone on trusty and true,
With God supreme in his heart and courage burning anew.
—*Alaska, Pfc. Charles W. Bodley*

TO PFC. DANIEL WALDRON

who bemoaned spending his 21st birthday on
CQ at the Brooklyn Army Base
(PX." Yank, October 5, 1945)

I sit here on this rugged rock
Despair has filled my soul
Closer comes the awful shock
Of Christmas in this hole.

No folks nor friends can hear me grieve
So distant is this place
CQ I'd love, on New Year's Eve
At Brooklyn Army Base.
—*Iwo Jima, Pfc. Arthur Adler*

TRILOGY FOR AN INFANTRY GUIDON

I

It is good to follow the blue guidon.
Remember this before the mist settles down:
It is good to the long-legged ranks, the lazy guidon
Aslant on the staff, the columns of khaki: fours
Stamping the cadence, keeping the intervals marking the turns.
Remember this before the mist settles down.
You are back in the ranks where a man belongs.
Before the mist of fatigue, muddy marchings,
The cringing to caddish superiors. Remember this:
Mortify the flesh, the flabby office muscles
Man must do penance for an epic privilege,
For the honor of crossing wide waters: commando raiders
Hurled against blazing beachheads: so keep your cadences in column:
Jealously guard your intervals, learn discipline.
Accept the mist of fatigue, sleeplessness, dirt, hunger, pains.
In these days, only man in the ranks has the right to be.

II

Sometimes in the middle of a tired morning,
Sleepily tramping in time behind the drooping guidon,
We dream of home: a lazy small town
South of the Ohio, the noon rush in Times Square,
Orange groves by Pasadena: white shirts,
Maybe somebody calling us "Mister" again,
A quiet morning of lecturing to classes,
Our homes in the evening.
But dreams are no good: the guidon flaunts
Blue with the rifles crossed; a greater dream
The fighting man's dream: breaking through the passes
Over against Bavaria, or catching a heavy tank
Notched in the battle sights. Over the dark waters
There is a greater dream for the fighting man;
An old dream made real.

III

My body groans against the blue guidon
High on the staff over stalwart shoulders
Pulling me up the long road. The rifle
Cramps the stiff forearm. The mist of fatigue,
Sleeplessness clouds my bright dream of battle
The racked things, shoulders wrenched by the pack
Make ne forget ancestral traditions of battle,
God's silent order into the ranks.
The blue guidon coils, a snake on the staff.
Streams in the breeze from the west, hisses.
Coward's body expendable on an African beachhead,

Pulped in a Guadalcanal jungle, broken where god wills---
What you endure is trivial to the hell you train for:
The crawling on your guts, blasting away Digging in under fire.
Face the fact of your flesh To be blasted, scorched, paralyzed, ripped from
The broken bones. Coward's body
A man's soul has started you east On a long, hard road!
—*New Guinea, Cpl. Hargis Westerfield*

T N T FOR TOKYO

Up! Up! My lads, the moon is fair,
We've work to do in upper air.
Cargo, tonight, as you must know,
Is T.N.T. for Tokyo.

Avenge Pearl Harbor and Bataan?
Hell Yes! We'll do that---every man.
And time is near when we will sow
Our righteous wrath on Tokyo.

We'll comb the land, the clouds, the seas
Until we find the Japanese.
And when we do we'll fix them so
They'll not return to Tokyo.

So gather, Eagles, in your might,
A battle brood that's fit to fight,
Equipped with men and planes to go,
We'll blast the Hell out of Tokyo.
—*Lt. Col. N.R. Cooper*

TITO

First came the planes. A flock of vultures:
The corpses meticulously staked
Well in advance; cadavers picked
That still were breathing; ancient cultures
Marked for methodic murder, raked
With bombs and bullets while the shutters clicked.

Then came the tanks. A crawling pest;
A herd of locusts, belching steel and death;
A plague of insects waste and ruin unbridled,
A clanking monster with a studded chest,
Vomiting murder, stopped with leaden breath,
Took careful aim, while its bowls idled.

Then came the men. A gang of thieves,
Of hoodlums, fed and drilled and proud;
A band of cutthroats, damned and cursed;
A stinking storm that drove dry leaves
And shattered bodies in a rising cloud
Of terror, planned for and rehearsed.

Then came the miracle. A naked hand,
Muscled with hatred, fist of fury, blunted
The scavenger jaws of the fascist beast, broke
From the fangs the weapons, manned
The guns with women. Children hunted
The insane hunters and a leader spoke.

Hot pride and prowess, anger, hurt persist
But above all their highest art,
Their deepest wisdom; unity, defended
With stubborn patience both by priest
And Communist; shepherd and lumberjack; the start
Toward a world secure and a nightmare ended.
—*Fort Lewis, WA Pvt. Rudy Bass*

THOUGHT FROM A BOMBER

Which cynical god
In the arrangement of things
Placed this woman
Squatting on a hillside
Near where the ox flings
Moist clouds
From an impatient hoof

And gave her
The inscrutable passion
For silent
Unfeeling stoicism
That moves her to fashion
A tool from
Pieces of blasted roof

"Neath which once
She lived and weaned the child
That today raises
An innocent face
To squint curiously at the wild
Silver bird, once deadly
And is now so aloof?

Did this god
Know that from the sky
Men would look
Down at primitive toil
And have time to wonder why
The past lived on
Despite the future's proof?
—*Saipan Sgt. Stan Flink*

THE BEAUTIFUL RUINS

Do not be proud that you destroy the cities.
Remember gardens shimmering in the sun.
Doorways in shadow and the peaceful duties
Of women there, If this is to be done,
Let it be done without the shame of pride.
That in an hour to come our unbelieving
Sons, judging us, must say: "The cities died;
Our fathers did this; but they did it grieving."
For with the cities die the guiltless dreams
Of the brave, the innocent unwary,
Who long ago, pausing by unnamed streams,
Began to build the tall and visionary
Cities that were to be their children's shroud.
Destroying them at last, do not be proud.
—*Britain, S Sgt. Charles E. Butler*

YOU READING THIS VERSE

You sitting there by the vines and cleaning your rifle,
You leaning there on the rail to watch the gray
Convoy of anxious ships, you feeling the awful
Cold at your throat but standing quietly by
The stove in the pilot's room;
O let us remember
The things we hated, the things we sickened of,
That we may build a world of better timber
When we go back among the things we love.

The beaches beckon, and the landing barge
Must scrape the sands again; patrols must creep
Upon the hidden sniper; planes must surge
Over the last tall mountain till they sweep Past cities going down in granite thunder. But hold to this, O break this promise never;
That younger eyes shall wake on things of wonder, That younger hearts shall sing in peace forever.
—*Waycross AAF, GA, Sgt. James E. Warren Jr.*

WHY WE FIGHT

It is the fashion nowadays, it seems,
With men who have more time than us for dreams,
To raise great hue and cry on what we do
About the soldiers when our work is through;
To string together many words that show
Just how our scheme of living is to go;
To wrack their brains, work fancy overtime;
To legislate our futures, line by line.
They seek to please by promises of gold
And by this catch the votes---that trick is old
As Caesar. Can't they ever learn
It's not for small favors we may earn
We fight? It's that we may go home.
We'll do all right; just let our lives alone.
—*Alaska, Pfc. R. E. Lee*

WALTER WINCHELL'S PREDICTION

Walter Winchell says the war will end in just six weeks.
He must be drinking a certain lotion from the way he
speaks. Six weeks? It takes longer for laundry to be returned.
A letter won't clear channels in that time, as you've
learned. Six weeks? After a furlough list had reached your name,
It takes the adjutant longer just to sign the same. Six
weeks? A cold sends you to the infirmary, And it takes
more time before they set you free.
Six weeks? Why just to vote while overseas our Yanks
Will spend that time in filling questionnaires and blanks.
Six weeks? Here is a fact that must impress:
It even takes longer to go through OCS.

I feel like the old maid of whom it has been said, She had
no hope but nightly peeked under her bed.
I don't believe he's right; don't see how anyone could,
But I've got my fingers crossed, and I'm knocking on wood.
—*Herbert Smart Airport, GA, Sgt. Nathaniel Rogovoy*

UNRELATED QUATRAINS

War has always periodically appeared
In spite of being incessantly jeered;
Perhaps if mankind would take it to heart
War would manifest its gratitude and part.

When I have fears that I may cease to be
Before my pen has gleaned my teeming brain,
I leisurely dispose of a pint or two of
Scotch And in no time am I feeling great again.

Under the greenwood tree
Who loves to lie with me
And kill time in a manner
That's the rage January to December.
—*Puerto Rico, Pvt. Louis Fisher*

THE LEGION OF THE UNCOUTH

The pages of the magazines back home
That feature stuff of war---the march of men,
The awesome crawl of tanks, the flight of planes---
Have shown a tiresome lot of "glamor Yanks,"
With trousers razor-creased and shirts that still
Retain the sheen of new-spun factory cloth;
With ties adjusted right, and shoes, the gleam
Of which will blind. Too much of new-blown rank
With chevrons bright and neatly sewn on sleeves
Of sarge or corp; and when I view those lads,
So sartorially complete and nice, I think
Of Hollywood, with extras dressed to fit
A part in some stage scene, instead of soldiers
Girt for deadly, bloody, filthy war.

From the Stevens in Chicago town,
To our sun-blistered, bug-infested post,
Is a far, unholy cry---and the difference
Much the same as that which lies between
My lady's boudoir and a stable stall;
For here we boys are not—oh, really not
The photogenic type! Our hair grows long,
We seldom shave; Svengali would be proud
To flaunt the beards that some of us have grown.
Our pants are frayed and bleached and baggy-kneed;
We wear no shirts---and as for ties,---say, tell
Us, please---what is a tie? And it's a certain sign
You're "tropo," if you start to shine your shoes!

We're a motley, rugged, crumby lot,
No subjects for a Sunday supplement;
But somehow, I don't think a man of us,
Down deep within his heart, would trade his place
With fortune's darlings in the Stevens lounge.
We're "in" the thing, you see---not quite as much
But something like---our buddies at Bataan,
Corregidor, the Solomons, and Wake;
And because we walk in shabbiness---unkempt,
Ungroomed---and live with pests, and breathe red dust
And thirst and bake in searing heat, and drown
In tropic rains---like them---we're fiercely proud.
Let others have the dress parade, the show,
The full-page spread in magazines. We like
Our role---the real, the earnest, cussin' sweatin'
Dirty, ugly role of men at war!
　　　　—*Australia, S/Sgt. Thomas P. Ashlock*

THE FREIGHTER

Slowly the freighter splits the green motion
With rhythmic ease. The bow turns eastward
Where the misty chemistry of the ocean
Spreads over the hulk and bobbing driftwood.

Below sky in agony, where the cirrus
Is near, bombers tread heavily on space;
Toward war, where fascists learn to fear us,
This freighter goes---while I get sun on my face.
　　　　—*AAB, Miami Beach, FL Pvt. Norman Gelber*

THE FOXHOLE

Leaning at night on the edge of a foxhole,
Left fingers locked in a grenade ring,
And the deadly drip-drip of the rainy jungle
Around him, then a man learned to live.
Sensing dark forces around him,
And what he is fighting for,
Battling his tired body
To fight for him, staring at the void
From the edge of a foxhole,
Then a man learns to live.

Roused for a graveyard watch by my buddy,
Suddenly bolt awake, I helmeted myself
And gripped the grenade again. My clips
Were all counted, my rifle slept handy,
Sheathed in the sand, the bayonet upright.
Fighting my falling eyelids, the fear
That fires at the flutter of bird's wings,
That makes the tired eyeballs turn in the sockets,
I have cajoled my tired body, held it
By dreams of the world I had once:

Walking the avenues of the university,
White collar open; walking at night boldly above the
ground to a movie,
I stopped for a double-decker ham and cheese
On toast, and coffee , black under glass,
Or tasted the peppery chili, thick peach pie,
At a Greek restaurant, or chewed juicy chicken,
The pulley bone cullied by my wife, or green lettuce
I grew in the garden. I never enjoyed
Better eating; for what I had once,
I have always---no longing that tears the body apart.

When I fought the sleep back long enough
For honor, I squeezed the shoulder
Of my sleeping buddy; instantly he took helmet,

Turned to his guard---this American, Lithuanian,
Catholic, American of an alien state.
Brothers against the bestial dark, and secure
In my faith in God and my friend, I curled
In the warm wet sand and I thanked God
More truly than ever before for the half-death
Of sleep---the strength against full death.

With the first white of dawn, he gripped me.
Together we rose to the rifles and waited.
Maybe the Japs would come then; the
Banzai-ing death rush, our right to travel
Ten thousand miles of blue water
to break evil. But the dawn
Turned flaring yellow. Delivered from fear,
We lighted our cigarettes off one match;
No mother's cake tasted better---
Heat, and sweet tobacco,
And death still a long way off.

Leaning at night on the edge of a foxhole,
Left fingers locked in a grenade ring,
There a man learns to live.
  —*New Guinea, Cpl. Hargis Westerfill*

THE FOXHOLE

It was a dark foxhole, dirty and wet and slimy. Saki had left our foxhole,
Saki had to leave it;
But Saki was back, high above the clouds. The drone of planes was faint.
The drone grew even louder,
The drone swelled to a sickening roar; Saki was dropping his bombs.
We sweated and hoped and said: "Now is the time to pray,"
But we didn't pray. Then the roar stopped.
We were quiet; we waited and listened; Saki was leaving, Saki was gone.
We crawled out of our foxhole, We looked around and saw death Gruesome and black everywhere,
Then we looked at our foxhole, dirty and wet as slimy, It was a wonderful foxhole,
It was a beautiful foxhole.
  —*South Pacific, Pfc. Arthur Vaupel*

THE FOREIGNER

They welcomed Hayden back from the war, and fed
Him horn-pout chowder, muffins, and berry pies.
"He hasn't changed a bit," the village said---
But there was the look of Asia in his eyes.
They fussed, and petted him; they wept again.
Telling the neighbors horrors he had known;
"Two years he lived among those naked men
Who worship hideous idols carved from stone!"

He remembered the Chinese coolie, Long Nee Lum,
Who fought in the Burmese jungles by his side,
The Kachin scouts, and the headsman at Nhpum,
And other dark-skinned brothers who had died.
How could he make these good folk understand
That this, his Maine, was now the alien land?
  —*AGF, Washington, D.C., Sgt. Smith Dawless*

THE FIGHTING SEABEES

We work like hell, we fight like hell
And always come back for more:
The Navy's advance base engineers
On many a foreign shore.

On half the lousy islands
From here to Timbuctu,
You'll find a hive of Seabees---
One hell of a fighting crew.

The admiral just dropped around
To chat the other night,
He said, "Now boys, I know you work
But you've also been trained to fight.

"So if there's any trouble, don't stop
To put on your jeans;
Just drop your tools, grab up your guns
And protect those poor marines."
  —*Camp Peary, Williamsburg, VA, Author Unknown*

THE FIGHTING 24th

Listen my children, I'll tell you a story
Of a tough bunch of Negros who fight for
Old Glory. It was a lecture one February morn
That the captain hinted we weren't there for long.
When we left the barracks and moved to the wood
The Army grapevine started operating good.
We moved to a new location
Which proved to be our port of embarkation.
I was on the first ship to leave the shore
Maybe never to see the States any more.
For 21 days we sailed the Pacific blue---
A long time on the water, I'm telling you.
Early one morning we sighted land;
The leader decided to strike up the band.
We unloaded our equipment with the utmost of haste
Amused by the natives, red cloth around waist.
We couldn't interpret the native language
So we tried to teach them a little English.
After exploring the island for many days
We became more familiar with the native ways.
Winning this war is going to be hard
But the Fighting 24th will do its part.
Not for love and glory, but for the good of men
To make this world a better place "for all races to live in."
  —*South Pacific, Pvt. Thomas M. Swift*

Section Seven
Poems about Death

BATTALION OF THE DEAD

The bugle never more will blow
Across this camping ground.
And men for welcome mail from home
Will never crowd around.
It's silent now; no guns are heard;
The war for them has fled.
And now they are immortal;
The battalion of the dead.

And each of these mute crosses
Is a symbol, stark and white,
Of hopes, of plans and treasured dreams,
Which now have taken flight;
Out to the blue horizon stretch
The rows in solemn state,
And join the shafts of sunlight
Stretching up to heavens gate.

They died because they knew that man
Was destined to be free,
And freedom's price is often death,
Met far beyond the sea.
So there they lie; as heaven paints,
With comic bars of red,
That silent final camp of
The battalion of the dead.
  —*France, Cpl. O. Arthur Hertell*

AT ANZIO

I saw him die.
I saw the life blood ebb away,
The healthy cheeks a deathly pallor take,
And o'er those virile limbs
The final palsy spread; I saw him die.

But hold! I see him live
In kindred spirits past, the young and clean,
In age-long battle with the form obscene
Of hate and fear and greed
And shackled man and fettered mind.
His victory is not far behind.
I see him live.
  —*British Forces in Italy, Pfc. Frederick Dinswood*

A QUIET SUNDAY AFTERNOON

Filing slowly out the mess hall,
Russell, Dennett, Hector, and I
Remarked the imminent clouds
Ina threatening sky.
"What's on the air today?"
Lalo's '*Symphonie Espagnole*'."
So to our hut we went
And there we lay,
Each in his own way "sent,"
Relishing the flavor
Of each demisemiquaver.

Then Dennett said, "I have some wine,
Warm, but good; it's sherry,"
And filled their cups and mine.
Again he filled to summon merry
Thoughts more suited to a time
Of peace. And on our cots
We lay like happy sots,
Drunk with wine of quietude
And Muse's song. Nectar brewed
By Bacchus ne'er was so sublime.
Images came unbidden
Stirred by the warm wine
Which smelled of springtime.
Thoughts came, half-hidden,
Each to his brother tangent,
Fleeting and lambent
O'er the mind of a dreamer At rest.

Warm wine spilled
In the springtime on
Iwo Jima,
Spilled in the springtime of life,
Might make the barren rocky ground
Of Iwo
Yield a bloom as precious and as deathless
As the seed.
What will grow?
A lovely flower
Nourished best
By wine spilled
In hot blazing strife?
Or will the plant grow
Nurtured best
By vinegar chilled
In the Ardennes Forest?

The concert ended and we rose,
Stretched and yawned and uttered protest
"Gainst the ending of repose
Serene and sweet and unmolested.
We talked a while and sped the time
Until the whistle sounded chow again.
At the table quips and banter
Spiced the food and added laughter.
Someone raised the question,
"Why Is an onion called a scallion?"
Russell made him quick reply
"Because a horse is called a stallion."
And I wondered if on Iwo
A troop is a battalion.

The first drops of rain
Fell from the evening sky
And brought a sadness and a hope
The men had not died in vain.
—*Camp Joseph T. Robinson, ARK, T-4 Charles Wolfman*

A MEMORY'S AN ESOTERIC THING

A memory's an esoteric thing.
You could not make a stranger understand
The value of a melody you sing,
Its tune a spider's web, a thinning strand
Between remembered time and time called now.
A huge smooth rock in icy lights of stars
Allows you memory it will allow
No others. Old thought burns and often chars
With bitter black the edges of the mind,
But more often it holds time in its flight,
An anchor to the hurrying feet of life.
Each man remembers something that will bind
The past and present strongly, until spite
And death shall sever them with a quick knife.
—*Laurinburg-Maxton AAB, NC, Sgt. Philip R. Benjamin*

FOR CERTAIN FLYERS

(Senior officers officers at Port Darwin listening over the radio communications systems to pilots cursing the Japs as they fought them, decided that the flow of profanity was too much. Henceforth only flyers who had shot down one enemy plane could swear at the Japs, and then could use only one word, "bastard."---Newsweek.)

Though you saw Louis shot out of the skies,
And Texas spiral down to crash and burn,
And Cooper, who had knocked them off like flies,
Lose half a wing and dive to death in turn;
Though you saw Thompson swinging in his chute,
Riddled with holes before he hit the ground;
Though Green was tortured and cut up to boot---

That is, if his corpse was found,
You must not curse your enemy, not even
When he is in your sights just as you squeeze
The trigger to send one more Son of Heaven
To hell forever for his infamies.
But for each Japanese that you have mastered
You may permit yourself a single "bastard!"
—*Camp Shelby, MS, Sgt. Grant A. Sanders*

RETURN TO BATAAN

They dream now, in that peace the valiant gain,
And there is no more weariness or pain
Or fury or despair. They heard you say
You would be back again; God will it soon
That you shall walk the old accustomed way
You knew so well, beneath the tropic moon
When the lights glitter down the beaches far
And the soft voices of the tides complain
Against the sands that once were gulched by war
And know death's footprints; you will walk alone:
Remembering. They shall hear you pass that night,
And many a sleep will in that hour break,
Many a whisper from eternity
Shall flow through all Bataan that you are there.
They shall be proud that night, and everywhere
Around you there will be
A voiceless paean of the proud dead young
As full of triumph as war ever sung.
—*Fort Jackson, SC, Cpl. Edward A. Martin*

UNKNOWN SOLDIER

I ventured where no other trod,
And there upon some alien sod
Still virgin midst that man-made hell,
Weary in body and soul, I fell.

The pain I felt, it mattered not,
My thoughts were with that lonely spot
Serene and still; oh God, to rest
My heavy head upon its breast.

I died, but did they bury me
Where I forever wished to be,
Alone beneath that grassy plain
Unknown except by worm and rain?

They came and took me far away,
But what they took was only clay;
My soul forever shall abide
On a foreign plain in the countryside.
—*State College, NM, Pvt. Ira Jackson*

ON THE DEATH OF A FRIEND IN THE WAR

I need to be well drunk and rid of all care
Others may sleep but I must not be sleeping
For even in sleeping still the dreams are there
And the weeping

Today the sunlight glistens on his hair
But the bloated face is not of him nor the eyes
Nor the way the air is heavy with dead-man's stink
Where he lies

I will look at he naked legs of girls as I drink
There comes a silence after many glasses
And for a while I will not have to think
But the silence passes.
—*Austria, Sgt. David Perkins*

NOCTURNE 2

The world is filled with dying light,
The streets are shadow-filled,
The busy town is hushed at night,
The working hands are stilled.

The stars slink out of their gloomy dens,
A silent watch to keep;
From somewhere comes the sound of guns,
My mother will not sleep.
—*Camp Wheeler, GA, Pfc. Jerome Hoffman*

NO CASUALTIES

Let the cold rain fall on the faces
Of the corpses in the trail's curves
Where the outguard's first shots flung them.
(Squeeze the trigger; shoot again at the brush;
Be certain; take no chances with suicide
Grenades gripped under the armpits.)
Let the cold rain seep again through muddy fatigues
Of the singing soldiers sprawled on the supply truck
Where the trail meets the new American road.
Let the Americans sing and joke how they killed
Texan and Pole and Spaniard, Assiniboin and Swede.
(Scar-faced Texan with officer's
Blade and the slitted blue eyes, sing!)
Let us sing; we still live; crawled the brush
And kept silent and watched all night
In the black jungle. Forgive us our pride,
Our loud laughter, Lord, at the thud
When a Japanese warrior hurtled dead.
Lord, forgive us our laughter; we still live.
—*Philippines, Cpl. Hargis Westerfield*

NIGHT BOMBING

Metal wings along the night
For St. Joe's birds are stretched in flight
Cologne for Coventry,
Ruhr for Dover:
And when the holocaust is over,
When the walls are flat and bare,
Stark will be the ruins
Of another Saint-Nazaire.

Sound in the darkness, high and faint,
Sirens in darkness, making complaint,
Long-fingered lights probing in the black,
And the rocket glow of arching flak.

Hamburg for Warsaw, Tunis fro Dunkirk;
And when the gods have played their quirk,
When their laughter fades away,
Still will be the shadows
Of the graves around Cambrai.
—*AAB, Topeka, KS, Pvt. S.N. Wernick*

NEXT OF KIN

She will do many things in years to be
That she has done in all the years that were,
And love and laughter will return to her
And she will half forget. But suddenly
Across her peace will come on strange winds blown.
(Sometimes in music as the music ends,
Sometimes in sunsets or good-byes of friends)
A chilling ghost that she has never known.

It is that moment when his engine stammered,
Flamed over Rome and screeched to the ground;
When he first heard the sickening Channel sound;
Or splashed his life into the Saipan mud;
Or when, while all the battle howled and hammered
Upon Attu, he thought he saw her face
And cried to her across the frozen grass
But lost her in the silence and the blood.
—*WRTU, Waycross, GA, Sgt. James E. Warren Jr.*

GENERAL MONTGOMERY

I like this man's face.
I like the laughter wrinkles from his eyes.
I like the larger nose,
A good handle to his face, Like Lincoln
I like the firm upper lip,
The firm mouth,
The resolute chin,
The generous ears,
The deep-set eyes,
The long deep lines on cheek.
Not a smooth visage, to say the least;
Not suave, nor urbane, nor
Buddha-like in calm;
But seared and marked,
And yet alight in some strange way
By a spirit born of pain,
Of defeat, disillusionment
And long effort when hope was gone
And fortitude was all.

A face human and homely,
Strong and humble
Exacting and kind.

A face of victory,
But not of triumph personal,
For he is matched with Death.
—*India, S/Sgt. Hugh M. Lindsey*

GAS

This is the odor of our blood,
The fragrance of our breath that burns the nostrils of
our foes;
This is death.

Dimensional and infinite,
This lightness bears a weight
To crush their breasts and well defines
The circumference of our hate.

There is a hand upon this mist
Beneath the yellow sky,
And who shall lift their eyes to us---
They shall die.
—*634d CA (AA), Seattle, WA,
Cpl. Lester Ewing*

ENGINEER OCS

Here lies the bones
Of Lt. Jones,
A graduate of this institution,
Who in his first fight
Thought he was right
In using a school solution.
—*Pvt. Anon.*

ELEGY FOR AN AMERICAN

The time to mourn is short that best becomes
The military dead. We lift and fold the flag,
Lay bare the coffin with written tag,
And march away. Behind, four others wait
To lift the box, the heaviest of loads.
The anesthetic afternoon benumbs,
Sickens our senses, forces back our talk.
We know that others on tomorrow's roads
Will fall, ourselves perhaps, the man beside,
Over the world they threatened, all who walk;
And could we mark the grave of him who died
We would write this beneath his name and date:

Epitaph

Under this wooden cross there lies
A Christian killed in battle. You who read
Remember that this stranger died in pain,
And passing here, if you can lift your eyes
Upon a peace kept by the human creed,
Know that one soldier has not died in vain.
—*New Guinea, Pfc. Karl J. Shapiro*

DUST ON MY SHOES

There is brown dust on my shoes,
It fills the weather cracks---
American dust raised by restless feet.

My friend had shoes much the same,
But the waves washed away the dust that night,
They washed the sands that trickled through
His loose fingers.

My friend once said he loved the soil,
The harvest growth.
Even in death his hands sunk beneath the sand
As if he were holding it,
For when they found him
It trickled through his fingers
And carried his blood to the sea.

I think my friend must have felt the sand
And smiled when he thought of home soil:
I think my friend thought of harvesttime
That last moment,
And wondered when he would see the crop
Or cut the earth with a singing plow.

I shall remember my friend
And the men who wait for harvesttime,
Who yearn for home soil.
I shall not clean my shoes this night,
They are covered with brown dust
That fills the weather cracks---
American dust raised by restless feet.
—*Camp Butner, NC, T-3 Stan Flink*

DIRGE

The night wept, and the trees:
And on the hill
Appeared a ghostly cross that bore no name.
The earth spoke,
"Rest in peace."
"I will, I will,"
Came from the heart, frozen in smoldering flames.

The night watched and then the trees:
Upon the cross
They saw a lonely name inscribed with tears.
The earth spoke,
"Rest in peace."
And silent moss
Lent to a breathless form of dearth of years.

The night slept, and the trees:
Lost on the hill
Appeared a withered flower and a thorn.
"I will, I will."
And only desolation greets the morn.
—*New Guinea, T-5 Harry Eckstein*

La HAVRE, 1945

Cigarette pour papa,
Cigarette pour papa......

Gone the savage Gallic fire
Of barbed wit and Latin love,
Gone the whistle, gone the jaunt,
Gone the tart in this gaunt shell
Of city crucified.

Here the docks that once gave birth
To flaunting queens of sea,
Point gnarled and broken strands of steel
With passive accusation to the sky.

Ah, gravestone for a continent;
Ah, marker for ten million shattered lives!
Look ye well and ken, Here the sword of Mars was

sharpened,
Here the sword of Death was forged.
—*France, Pfc. J. T. Waterhouse*

JAP COINS

He held them in his hand.
He fingered them smiling, then he said,
"Jap coins. Tinny things. Three of them.
A pal sent them. Great guy. Name's Red.
These are from Guadalcanal.
See---here's the letter.
Look at those three things---tinny things,
Ain't they? Ours are a whole lot better."

Yeh, tinny. I held them.
Light ----like aluminum or tin, I suppose,.
Fujiyama on the back with the Rising Sun above,
And what it said, God only knows.

I looked at them; three coins---tinny things;
An epitaph for one more Jap now dead.
—*Fort Taylor, FL, 1st Sgt. Luman S. Nutter*

JAPANESE GARDEN

Come walk with me in the garden of the dead

Ushiyama tended them well, and watered them with gunpowder, made them fertile with rich mines and TNT and multiple cannon and ten thousand rifles bloom as flowers.

Ushiyama was fond of details, exquisite sense of placement and effect And all was sweet for pleasure of the Emperor.

This, Ushiyama is Imperial garden now;

What lily-beds the skulls and yellow gentians the old unburied bones, what sacred odor of disintegrating flesh, what ample alters for glad offering in kind divinity are tanks shattered midst the garden's carnage.

Naha's rubble, all so delicate
and Itoman, sequestered, provided bed of roses red with blood and piles of roof-slate.

Hill 89. its coral caverns wrought huge and fanciful,
to be visited only with a flame-thrower or satchel-charge.
How dear you made us pay for all your garden, Ushiyama--- us, proud and fair, and golden-haired,
with eyes to match the purest sky.

Starlight is the guardian of these graves And always the odor, always the savagery, dust of morning and men fresh interred, winding up from Nozato's tombs again.

And always sound and fury of ships guns,
battle-planes deployed and swinging in from missions,
high bright pinpoints of green light in the infinite night;
Midnight holocausts of flak, and flash and fire of bombs.
And always the gentle fall and beat of rain.
Tenderly we walk death's ways
On our own graves no flowers but mud, no peace but
furor of artillery.

Starlight is the guardian of these graves,
the tender of this garden, of this island of the dead.
—*Okinawa, S. Sgt. A.G. Karpen*

IN MEMORY OF A PRESIDENT

In the first hour of grief, when the attack of spring
had flung the children on the streets, and torn the trees, a
majesty came out of doors, to shroud the sky.
Companions mourning, carry night into your house, possess it utterly before the crest of dawn;
it holds our tears and common love for him who died.

The sleepers feel his history, the mothers fear their watch
will never end, over his mighty grave, over a land that
breeds its black solemnity.

We take his dreams into our heads, and bend like priests
and poverty before his heart---the greatest man
and soldier, lost in darkness and the hollow streets.

Now dawn lays flowers, and the lagging sun brings out
our loss and burns our hiding eyes. The watch is done---
because his grave is now his own---and we are free.

All freedom in our blood, and births and funerals, for
which he died, torn by our loves and honored in our
fears. We were his faith and led his gallantry.
He holds us by the terms of spring. Through him the
dead will lie in grass, in roots of rain that follow on
across the acrid cities and the bloody sands.

Come out into the street, where all the children run in
violence and discovery and share the world;
stand in the sun beside his grave, and know the land.
—*Sgt. John Hay*

IN MEMORIUM

(Freeman Nimhouser, killed in action)

From pen to rifle
It was a long way
From Greenwich
Village to New Guinea
Yet it was the same.

Mourn for the dead who died in vain.
But not for him.

When the poems gave out,
When it wasn't enough
To sing of freedom,
He fought for what he wrote for.
He died for what he lived for.

Mourn for the dead who died in vain,
But fight for him.
   —*ASTP, Atlanta, GA, Pvt John S. Brown*

HE CAN WAIT

I walked with Death, and he steps along In rhythm with
my every stride;
And when I pause to rest
He kneels in mud beside me, Matching breath for breath.
I crouch with him; Together we flatten bodies
Against the yielding ground.
His eyes turn with mine to the sky And his ears hear the
echo, as do I,
Of bombs that dig their noses into men, Rooting the
earth like hungry swine…. And they ask me to be patient.
Only Death smiles…….for he can wait.
   —*Phillipines, Pfc. Joseph Paul*

SUNDAY AT SANANANDA

This is the Huggins perimeter.

As you are standing, Gona's ahead of you,
The green desert of Papua and Dutch New Guinea
Beyond it: beyond the Halmahera Sea, the islands of Molucca
And the far-off places of the Moros and the temple worshipers.

To your left are the Owen Stanleys---
The spiral column of the Papuan tortoise:
And behind you the mightiest of the oceans,
Though from here is it only a breath and a sigh.
To your right, a scant mile up this devious, bucolic trail,

Around many a bend , through the haunted, primordial tangle,
Past dugout and slit trench, by ford across tropical rivers,
Through mud to your thighs, and the murmuring clouds
  of mosquitoes,

Through *kunai* and sun…oh, when you get there
You'll know…you'll not mistake it, this hell hole:
The bloody black sands, the brown tainted sea water---
This Point Sanananda…

Don't mind the skeletons.
We haven't had time to remove them:
And while we sit here with hands limply folded,
We haven't the heart.

No, it isn't the heat or the dampness;
And it certainly isn't sickness, at least not physical sickness---
Though they may come later, the retching, the spewing.
They had it, these grandsons of Heaven,

These stench-making ex-patriots lately of Honshu:
From the slums of Kyoto, from gay Nagasaki,
These pallid-complexioned mother's sons from the rice paddies,
From fermenting Formosa and the smokes of Fujisan…

They had the sickness, and not wholly the fevers,
Through the swamp miasmata weren't the least of it.
And so here's what is left of them…hell, I don't wonder
Your face grows a bit green…it's not a sweet atmosphere

Here with the cadavers.
But after you've slept with them…
There's Charlie the brainless one; and Henry the Horror.
He was clever at sniping, but my cobber resented him

And even the tree-boys are shy at machine guns!
That beautiful specimen under the quarter-ton
Will have to grow features or else his ancestors
Might fail to remember him among the chrysanthemums

In the honorable Heaven of Japanese heroes…
But these are the harmless ones. If you wait until nightfall
You won't be misled by the quiet out yonder;
They're clever, resourceful, and they're not half of it….

The jungle draws in on you, the sound of the wild things
Keep your heart in your gullet, and I'd not advise you
To sleep with both eyes closed, for fear you might yield
  to it---
To sleep--- for above all, give the go-by to nightmares.
You see, there's the nightmares, and the start-up in cold sweat,
The scream that you can't suppress though the darkness
is listening:

And the terror remembered, of the sudden reversal
When these foul. bloody messes that lie her so motionless

Became boys from Brooklyn or Terre Haute or Omaha,
And you recognize all of them and hear the low crying
Just before the death rattle, since none of them wants to die.
And the shadowy shapes glide around in the midst of them,

And the glinting of bayonets and the steaming red rivers
Of warm blood gushing soundlessly…
You're pale…you're pulling out…back to the cities?
Glamorous cities up and down the land.

Well don't let me detain you
With ranting and preaching.
That's just our habit here.
Your blood turns to wormwood.

Though here it is Sunday
We forget the days. Just tell you newspaper
That the boys are still pushing, the Japs still pocketed.
You'd better tone down a bit—don't tell; them too much of it---

Of the corpses and skeletons, the stink and the filthiness
On Point Sanananda.
—*New Guinea, T-5 Don E. Rohrig*

SONNET FOR R.K. JULY 20, 1943

You did not die Hollywood's planned death
For warriors who fight in frightful skies:
No final truth revealed in your last breath,
Nor visions as the winds spilled from your eyes.

You broke in bits—God knows where you fell;
The raucous motors veiled your final moan,
Or you screamed the mute sea cannot tell---
It is pain enough to die alone.

Midsummer's sun can light but half a world;
You are lost in ocean's shuttling black
Too long; our memory has furled
Your name, and we must think to turn it back
We forget; we are as we were before;
Forgetting, we kill you a little more.
—*Lehigh University, PA, Pfc. Perry Wolff*

SONNET

If in the dreadful and imperiled ways
Which lead men to achievement and to peace,
I shall seek shelter in the withered leas,
Stretching beyond the content of my days.

Let them not plead with a finality,
Invoke the mercy of eternity,
But offer for the hulk which stays
Three faded roses and an ancient vase.
These shall be my remembrance: blooms which die.
Three withered remnants of a fertile plot,
A shattered memory of sunlit days
Let these adorn with an unmuttered sigh,
Perhaps a grave, perhaps a tortured cot:
Three faded roses and an ancient vase.
—*Australia, Pvt. Harry A. Eckstein*

SONG OF THE EMPTY MAN

I am the empty man who died an empty death,
Not on the seas, clutched by sinuous tentacles of depth,
Not on high rocks, bruising against the granite,
Not in forests on a couch of pine.

With mud and dirt cutting my breath, My dying phrases anticlimaxed oratory,
Frustrated and denied, I turned and bent Beneath the weight of loathsome slime, Saw the last dot of blue erased by black And felt the rasp of gravel in my throat.

Nor did I perish at the battle's height
In time of glory, famous deeds, heroic circumstances.
Much more prosaically, grotesquely too---
Amusing and grotesque I almost laughed Before my tongue was blocked and I was dead.

It was so long ago, I can hardly remember;
The time was morning and the month November; The day, strangely enough, was the eleventh.
I am the empty man who died who died an empty death.
—*Newfoundland, Pvt. Lauriat Lane Jr.*

PORT OF EMBARKATION

One would never think,
Hearing the scratchy victrola
And the laughter,
That these men are soon to go.
(The bent cigarette butt tufted with black ash
At the bottom of the can,
The pattern of the plywood wall
Around the torn poster
And the sensitive face across the table,
Lips moving as he writes,
Eyes pausing to follow the fly on the magazine,
Eyes suddenly showing unfinished griefs.)

One would never think
They are to go far from this room.
(The row of light bulbs,
The coke bottles,
The sound of an American city nearby
And, beyond the darkness, the ocean.)

One would never think
That some of them may not return.
(The handprint on the window,
The waterproof wristwatch,
The boy with the small, pale hands
Tapping his fingers on the chair.)

One would never think
Of such things
Or feel the ugly shudder
If one were alone with only the beating of one's heart,
If one did not hear them laughing.
—*Overseas, T-4 Stan Flink*

TO J's WIFE

He was the man you loved and my good friend
For all his faults; and now you ask
Why he should come to this quick, bitter end
While other live. Well, I will ask:
Why did we love him? What is it we miss?
You know the average human, it is said,
As salt and fertilizer, minerals and dross,
Is barely worth a dollar when he's dead.
Yes, you protest he was something more.
Imponderables? That's , better; if you choose
We'll leave the facts and figures---They're a bore---
And let us speak of one imponderable
That men call honor.
Now What of those men who lose?

Here is one:
He might have lived a while, mainly, without air (some men do), died for no purpose
And alone, afraid, with not a friend to claim
In all the world, and not a man
Remembering to pause and bless his name.
He fell in France.
Here is another:
Give this one his virtues; he was kind,
Put a girl through college, never broke the laws,
Built a home---a nice one; and it comes to mind
That once he gave some money to a worthy cause.

Bedridden at the last and quite a bore,
But withal, to his credit, you could find

Among surviving kin at least a score
Who grieved---and wondered what was left behind.
No, I mistook; that was another,
Different sort of man. this one died at Salerno.
I rather doubt you ever knew the other
But you remember *that* affair, I know.

Their silken parachutes are shrouds enough;
For these three hundred paratroops who jumped to death. They might have died prosaically enough;
Not in the full measure of devotion quite
But from some hurried driver or a careless cook,
Ruptured blood vessels in a fit of petty spite,
A crusing microbe or a homeless germ,

A faulty scaffold or a rusty hook…
Thus might we have fallen who went down
The glory road and somewhere on a strip of foreign hell
Faced to spitting guns into the last,
Clutching a grimy photograph of you,
Saying your name as he fell……

Some deaths mark a gain and not a loss.
He died before his time and far from home,
But do you think the sinner on the cross
Had better lived to die alone?
—*New Guinea, Sgt. Jack Campbell*

TO AN UNKNOWN SOLDIER, KILLED IN ACTION

He takes his last look at the stars tonight, Alone, here, on the outskirts of the earth. He thinks now of the mystery of birth,
Of the tangent between shadow and light, Of how to struggle is not to fight,
Of how in darkness there is little mirth, Of how in effort there is little worth.
And yet he knows there is a wrong and right. He takes his last look and prepares to die.
Death will come silent when he does not know, When his fingers burn and his head is high.
A wind will blow through him like a driven snow. He will say no prayer, he will ask not why,
Yet he will smile when it is time to go.
—*Fort Monmouth, NJ, Pvt. Robert W. Taylor*

THE FIGHTING YEOMAN

The yeoman boy to the war is gone,
In the ranks of desks you'll find him,
With pen in hand and clips beside,
And a blonde who's there to guide him,
"Down with Adolf," the warrior said
As he boldly checked a file;
"That goes for Hirohito, too,"
And leered at leg-filled lisle.
Then came the bill and came the girls
To take our hero's place,
And out to sea went the yeoman bold
With a sick smile on his face.
The bos'n piped his shrilling tune,
The deck broke into life;
And while the sailors manned the guns,
The yeoman geared for strife.
He checked the files, he checked the forms;
The office it was clean.
He even checked the muster roll
And found it "on the beam."
Then came a crash of dynamite,
Amid ships it exploded.
The poor ship cracked---a fearful sight---
With sea, soon overloaded.
And then with hope all gone awry,
the walls of dying,
A feeble voice was heard to cry,
"Tell mom I went down filing."
— *The Pelican U.S. Naval Station, New Orleans, LA*

THE DEAD

Pray do not weep for those who lie so still
In shallow trenches; pity's not for such
This valley where they fell is that much
Greener, those flowers on that crest of hill
Are tinted deep and lovelier where they bled.
Yes, pity those who make the coward's choice,
Who heed the hob-nailed boot and guttural voice,
Who calculate the odds, and live in dread.
But when you think of valiant men who choose
To fight, take courage, high resolve and pride
That they were your kind; march with firm bold stride.
With tearless eyes look up, as one who knows
That mankind must, to gain fields rich and bright,
First take, at any cost, the rugged height.
— *Italy, Pvt. Isadore Rubin*

THE BALLAD OF POOR JACK SALT

This is a tale that was told me
One night in a strange English town
While I stood in queue for a bus that was due,
And the wet English rain drizzled down;

Jack Salt was his name, Arizona he hailed from,
The Infantry claimed him. A mortar man, he
Enlisted at 18. the towns he had mailed from
Encircled the globe, were diverse as could be.
For nearly three years Jack Salt followed the mortar
To many ports, over many a sea.
But it troubled him little, Jack ne'er wanted quarter,
Twas always the same thing he'd tell us: "You see,
This place is no worse than the next place they'll send us,
No better'n the last, so I say what the hell?
Next station we ship to ain't going to befriend us.
It won't be Arizona, I won't suit me well!"

That's the way he was. Jack took the Aleutians
In full stride. The South Seas could not put a sag
In his grin, for wherever Jack did his ablutions
Would do till the day he could pack up his bag
And make for the States, where he'd lead to the alter
His love, Arizona, and make her his wife.

Last Christmas, still moving, Jack shipped past
Gibraltar On a tub bound for Britain, and still full of life.
When she docked it was raining and right from that
minute Jack changed. He was never the same man again.
"England!" he'd snarl, "I hate everything in it!
For pete's sake, I can't live much longer in rain!"
And he didn't. One night it cleared up for an hour
After six days of rain----then it started to pour
Harder than ever, Jack, looking more sour
Than we'd ever seen him, stood there in the door.

Staring out at it, he stood there for hours.
We sat playing poker; at length we turned in.
None of was sleeping, discussing the powers
Of rain and the weeks we all had been churned in
English mud. It was sometime past midnight we missed
him. I flashlit the doorway and there Jack revolved
On his heels, just outside, while the drenching rain kissed him
On his wild, upturned face!

And then
Jack Salt
dissolved

No Jack Salt sung out the next morning at roll call,
(The rain was still falling) and none of us tried

To tell the weird story (they marked him down AWOL;
They carry him thus yet). They'd have said that we lied.
But I found his dog tags on the spot where he'd melted,
Twelve shillings in change and Jack's battered green pen,
full of water, no doubt from the rain that had pelted
Its owner. We'll never see Jack Salt again!

And that was the tale that was told me
One night in a strange English town
While I stood in a queue for a bus that was due,
And the wet English rain drizzled down.
 —*Britain, Pvt. Dan W. Harrington*

TAKE YOUR THOUGHTS TO THE CHAPLAIN

Take your thought to the chaplain;
He's the one you want to see.
Take your troubles to the chaplain;
Why bring them all to me?

So you want a 10-day furlough?
Well, here's some advice for you;
Take your request to the chaplain
And see what he can do.

Getting up too early in the morning?
Working too hard all day?
Why don't you go and see the chaplain
And see what he has to say?

Why can't you stay out every night?
Brother, don't look at me so cross,
Stop in and see the chaplain;
After all, he's the one who's the boss.

And Buddy, the one thing to remember
When you're about to die,
Is be sure and see the chaplain
To say a last goodbye.
 —*Camp Gordon, GA, Pvt. Wilbur Hoover*

WORD TO THE WISE

The P-38 is a smooth little crate
That will go through chased by the devil.
It will do loop-the-loops, alone or in groups,
And it rides like a dream on the level.
But the P-38 is a plane that I hate;
Its tail is, I must say, askew.
If you're caught in a slump and are called on to jump,
Here's what P-38s do to you;

They chop you to pieces up there where the fleece is
(You are cut quite in two when you bail);
The reason for this is, the same as with kisses,
You can't jump two pieces of tail.
So pilots beware when you take to the air
And through the bright blue blithely sail;
You can handle its rudder unlike any other,
But you can't jump two pieces of tail.
 —*Britain, Cpl. Murray Hill*

WE ARE YOUNG MEN

We are young men; we love the youth of spring.
The warm, sweet April wind might be a choir,
Singing of other April loves (the sting
Of memory made soft with new desire).
In spring, when promises become a net
To catch the words we spoke for speaking's sake,
It seems to us we almost could forget
That death's the only promise we may make.

We are young men, and love's a young man's food,
And moonlight makes two shadows sharp and small
When lovers breathe more magic into night.
But bombers need the moonlight for their mood:
A mood untender when their half-tons fall
And sing of love's destruction in their flight.
 —*Maxton AAB, NC, Sgt. Philip R. Benjamin*

VICTIM OF WAR

Drape your crepe and bow your head---
A yen of men is dead.
Born the day that man first married,
Now in potters field 'tis buried.

This yen: To spend at least one night
Each week "out with the boys,"
The groom, its friend; the bride, its foe---
She didn't often let us go.

But we got out---well, now and then---
By "working late" or sneak;
Ah! poker chips and glasses brimmed,
That one blest night each week.

Out with the boys was fun back then,
Once a week---all right;
But, holy cripes, it's sickening Like this:
All day! All night!

Yep, GI Joe has had his fill
Of male associations.
He's ready for a ceaseless swill
Of female situations.

So when your khaki-clad returns,
Milady, rest in peace;
That yen of men to roam from home
Is in its grave, deceased.
—*Alaska, Cpl. Walter A. Armbruster*

THE REASONS

Resting at sunset, feet in a rut
By the roadside; champing the half-cooked
Hash that unskilled cooks hurl in our kits
In slabs; resting with soft sunset lights
Over the wave of woods dark green
In shadows, emerald under slanting rays,
Peaceful falling shadows (already half asleep),
Ruminating the reasons why men love
A soldier's life. Beauty striking at the heart
At sunset after the long bitter struggle
Over stony trails in pack harness;
The passive acceptance of hardships
(The cool grin at unforeseen orders);
Labor in the muddy gun emplacement;
The ominous port of embarkation
And the sector of trapped jungle,
Fanged Japanese under the dead logs;
Passive acceptance of hardships
(The cool, calculating grin)---how many
Lives for a hundred yards of fever and swamp?
This is why men love a soldier's life,
Sudden beauty by a strange road,
Passive acceptance (sly grin at hardships).
And high above all, the holy right
To hurl mean flesh at death, to dare
Infinity, the small fears forgotten.
This is why men love a soldier's life.
—*New Guinea, Cpl. Hargis Westerfield*

THE OVERMEN

Where are the supermen
Whose veins were ducts
For blood more red
Than common kind?

Where are the supermen,
The blond giants

The bodies beautiful,
Tremendous, powerful?

Where are the superminds,
The men of Kultur,
The intellects more refined
Than common kind?

Prophets of power, of terror,
Overknights of an overrace:
They've made beautiful bodies,
Uncommon bodies,
In a common earth.
—*IRTC, Camp Walters, TX, Pvt. Herbert H. Brin*

THE MOURNERS' BENCH

The mourners' bench is full, and still they come
From neighboring homes or from some foreign shore.
The mourners' bench is full, and still it seems
There's always room for more.

What matters now the language that they speak?
What shape of nose, what gods, what hue of skin?
For by the rule of Death's democracy
All dead are friends, all fallen kin.

Here weeps a Russian mother for her son
Who died upon the charge that made
A widow of the *hausfrau* next to her,
And who can say these debts are paid?

Now listen to a Shinto prayer that pleads
For one who sniped ere Buna's ring was breached;
The while in Brooklyn silent candles burn
For him whose heart that sniper's bullet reached.

While in Berlin a new small grave assures
A child's peace from a Fortress-haunted sky;
And back in London one more woman learns
To count no more the bombers as they fly.

So goes the tale; from every land they came,
For sorrow's congregation knows no ban.
The mourner's bench is full; its crowded ranks
Decry man's inhumanity to man.
—*Alaska, Pvt. Raymond E. Lee*

THE HEROES

A soldier said: 'There is a mourner's bench'
where our mothers sit and share their sorrow
For our dead with German mothers---
A wailing wall, with Death a bond---
And little does it matter on which side one fell.

It's true there was a time for mourning.
The sky was red. they burned the books,
The temples fell. Old men in prayer shawls
Were dragged and hung with sings: *'I am a jew."*
But no one cried. they taught their sons
To spit into a gagged man's face
Because he knew such words as "Freedom"
Or "Christ" or "Labor Unity" or "Liberty."

But yet no tears. The guns that held Cassino
Were seroed at Madrid. " Sieg Heil," "Heil Hitler"
(Read "Theft" and "Rape" and "Murder")
Drowned out in the cries in
Holland, Poland, Czechoslovakia, France. The Zeros
That stunned Perl Harbor took their teat flights
At Kholchingol. the grinning death
That jumped ashore on Luzon was rehearsed
With putrid splendor at Shanghai and Nanking.
And still no tears. The loving *Hausfrau*
Received a bundle; there were small shoes, a coat,
Blood-spattered, fur lined, warm.
Dear wife: Here are some things for Fritzchen.
But pigs don't cry. They grunt and swallow children.

Now Hans is dead. And Franz and Fritz.
And wreaths are hung, and now the cries and tears
And wailing. but the tears are cold;
They will not make the grass grow, and the pain
Is hollow and a wasted seed.
Are dead men heroes just because they died?
Are rats like warriors if they bare their teeth?

Let them die quickly and be buried quickly,
Unwilling graves in a sickened earth. But we
Shall waste no breath, no pity on them.
We shall finish What they begot and save our love,
Our heart for all who help us drain
Our world-land from this stench and filth.
Let those who learn to follow them be welcome.
—*Camp Reynolds, PA, Pvt. Rudy Bass*

THE GHOST OF GONA

Look close in the trembling mimosa. Take care as you skirt the shell craters;
The thatch roofs are not stable; they still quake from the rain of fire.
Shun the twisted coconut roots, the deserted pill boxes
Gazing asea past the Hoinicote horizon, past the ghost-ship of Gona,
Past time and past space---the unwinking eyes of the dead ones.

Go down by the sea and you'll meet them---
On the black lava sand, in the vine-choked backwater.
They aren't night prowlers especially; their term is beyond limitation.
They don't want to lie down, they don't want to be dead.
Their abasement will never allow it.

Their company is sloe-eyed and ragged, either squatting beneath the flame crotons
In the sun-beaten, rank mission gardens or high in the skeleton palm trees.
Behind the canna hedge, shrieking in scarlet and yellow,
Comes a long, weary sigh---it may be the wind or the water---
But, whatever it is, of a sudden you're sweating,
Though the breezes are fresh off the sea of the Solomons
And the ghostship of Gona is there on the coral.

Go down by the sea, where the femurs and pelvises
Roll up in the guilty surf, where skulls wail in the window,
Where encroaching breakers deny the cadavers
The dignity of camouflage, of guard from the blowflies.
Dip your feet in the water, the brown, tepid water---
You'll get no refreshment, you'll not see the normal blue
As you do in less troubled seas.

And there's another thing---don't look behind you.
The past isn't nourishing, and the lost ones of Gona
Chafe the chains of their loneliness.
In silence they follow you,
Aflame with their jealousy, indignant that you're still alive.
If their hands get too clutching, it their breath is too fetid
It's because they're the bitter dead---their death was an ugly death.

Tread light through the marigolds, bypass the white passion vine;
The poison of disaster has alike tainted all of it.
The blood of the mission folk feeds the troglodyte scorpions.

Yet here in the sunlight the blue ipomoeas
Nod delicate funnels, the flamboyant fuchsias
Wait for the caretakers.

But the mission is mute. There is none here to care.
Let them weep here at night under Alpha Centurian.
Le them rage in the morning in the hot, sun drenched silences,
Where even the kura bird shuns the bomb blasted horror strip;
Let them cringe where the mission stood, where the white cross outglitters
That other cross in the Milky Way, where their eyes hunt the Dipper.
It is all much the same to them, either here or abroad, at night.
While the waves lap the evil beach, the swamp frogs croak wearily.
They're wretched, unhappy, tired, disillusioned.
They wouldn't have much to say, were there words adequate,
Except "Take care, you living ones! Keep away from our sepulcher!
We're here for the stretch of it, the worms give us welcome!
The shades of the Samurai have broken our hari knives!
The ancestors deny us a bivouac in heaven
While our bodies' putrescence enriches a foreign soil!"
Then the mission is mute. There is none to care.
—*Southwest Pacific, Sgt. Don E. Rohrig*

Section Eight
Philosophical Poems

TIME IS AHEAD OF THE HEART

The low clouds race the moon…. A strange night,
For there is not the movement of the merest leaf
Yet to betray their silent course.
Time is ahead of the heart.

The moon takes hurried glances
Through the clouds
Whene'er they pause for breath.
Poised now,
It seems as some gigantic pendulum,
Ignores the transient notes
And holds its thunder for tomorrow.

The years become as hours,
And some of us will soon be frantic
At the narrowed circle
Which today's stern pace becomes;
And music, melody and prayer are lost
As we have only time to taste the fruit and froth.

But throw your every strength against the circle,
Leap the clouds,
Anchor in the moon
Your deep kinetic courage.
If the symphony is lost,
At least retain the chord within your soul
That what we lose will be passing days,
And what we save against tomorrow's fantasy and fear,
The heart.
   —*India, Cpl. Ward McCabe*

THE WAVE

At the beach a lonely wave broke;
It murmured, roared, then grew into a sigh
And broke upon my feet.
I watched it spend itself and then recede
Into another silence.

Somewhere within that wave I found a thought
And saw an image of another world:
I felt the silence, overhead the song
Of yet another wave that spoke and broke
And now is silent.

"Where did you start?" I asked;
Whispering still,
It touched my thigh and held me fast
In slithery embrace.

"Where will you go?"
And silence spoke the beach,
Silence the water,
Silence my heart.

And now the wave has gone to break again;
Someone has touched it, someone lent it life;
Now wandering alone,
Immersed in seas,
Will find another stone, another thigh,
Yet, touching, will remain,
And, touching, live.
—*New Guinea, T/S Harry Eckstein*

THANK GOD WE DON'T NEED YOUR SON

You say your son can't stand the Army
And that the going is too tough for him.
Do you think he is any better
Than some other mother's Tom or Tim?

You raised your son like a girl;
"He never smokes or drinks" is your brag.
Well, if all our boys were like that
What do you think would become of our flag?

You say let the roughnecks do the fighting;
They are used to the beans and the stew.
Well I'm glad to be classed with the roughnecks
Who would fight for the Red, White and Blue.

You said his girl just couldn't stand it
To send him away with the rest.
Do you think for a minute she'd enjoy
To feel a Jap's breath on her breast?

We go to drill in bad weather
And come in with a smile on our face,
While your darling son sits in the parlor
And lets another man fight in his place.

Maybe we do drink, smoke and gamble,
But we fight as our forefathers did,
So go warm the milk for his bottle.
Thank God we don't need your kid.
—*Fort George Wright, WA, Pvt.
Stanley Sheckman*

THE INNOCENTS

They call us mechanics
With a high I.Q.
But we really don't know
A bolt from a screw.
We march like farmers
And eat like a horse.
We're the pride and joy
Of the Army Air Force.
—*Goldsboro Air Base, NC, Raymond A. Crabtree*

THE HEAVENS LAUGHED LAST NIGHT

The heavens laughed last night
And rained their cosmic laughter on the earth. The moon
smiled through her somber veil.
And stars grew bright and tittered in girlish mirth.

Like a long-pent song, Titanic laughter overran
The universe and filled the heart of every living thing---
But not the heart of man.
—*Hondo Army Air Field, TX, Pvt. Bronis Tubelis*

SONG FOR A BABY WITH COLIC

It seems the lady was with child, and now the child is with
the mother, their conversation was with touch, but now
they talk to one another.

Roll the baby on your shoulder while she grows a minute
older

You once ran; I thought
that you would cease your jaunty running but now you
step, as mothers ought holding the work of nine months
cunning.

Roll the infant on your shoulder while she grows two
minutes older.
—*San Francisco, CA, Sgt. James Steel Smith*

LINES ON READING A RECORD ALBUM

When I'm discharged I'll build a house In which to play
Die Fleddermous.
I'll also rent a haunted manse
For listening to Macabre Danse.
And in a radio-wired drashky
I'll lull myself with Pete Tschailowsky.

Or, in my little walk-up flat,
Lend an ear to the Three Cornered Hat.
My taste for music, how it parches
On nothing but eternal marches.
The overture to R. and J.
Will help to while my time away;
And, in the kitchen, I'll make salads
To the strains of Dust Bowl Ballads.
After dinner, or before,
Will come Beethoven's Lenore.
I'll substitute for doorbell's ring
The guts of Goodman's Triple Sing.
Music that has power to charm me
Comes from t'other side of Army.
Mornings, Moten's South will wake me,
Rhythm out of sleep tp shake me.
And Gnowwienne when lights turn low
Will bring me slumber soft and slow.
In between I'll run the gamut
Form jive as hot as tough can slam it
To sweetly sloppy marmalade
Of Schubert's sickening Serenade.
I like coffee, I like tea,
I'll get music when I'm free.
—*Pvt. A. M. Bush*

ODE TO A TROUBLED FRIEND

My friend, I feel that you exaggerate
When you would have us think that perverse fate
Retains such interest in your rise and fall.

For you are not the first nor yet the last
To sit in anguish on this bouncing ball
We call the earth, and curse the past
And equally condemn the future.
You Are unoriginal and sometimes trite.

You wear your troubles like a suit clothes
Well tailored but perhaps a little loud,
Planned to attract the attention of the crowd.
—*Newfoundland, Pvt. Lauriat Lane*

WINTER AFTERNOON

All day tattered clouds blow past
In the sharp north wind, limbs of trees
Etched black on the sky rattle together,
Cold gathers its scattered forces, the
Leaden water quiets itself for a
Long calm time; then the heavens mix
Thicker, hover low over distant hills
And soon gently swaying down comes
The first frail flake of snow.
—*Fort Lawton, WA, Pfc. Lowell Richards*

TURN THE KEY IN THE LOCK

Turn the key in the lock
You are home again, you are home.
You are home for the night.
You have time, now, to burn.
For sleep and the hope you need
It is a long time still
Before the summer light
Gathers along the sill
And the window goes white.
Perhaps there is time for the will,
And the good heart to learn
What peace can be, that is not strange.
All that you do is driven change.
Get you to bed, now. Get to bed.

You have enough to do
Before the driving night goes thin;
Fold up the paper, then,
Turn out the lights; and leave
The letter on the desk, unread;
And get some sleep.
The dream If it should come again,
May wake you, like a scream;
Like the good citizen
You are, you know what this would seem.
The heart may not believe
That happiness and terror, bright
And real, are somehow true. Goodnight.
Goodnight, goodnight. Sleep, if you can.
—*AAFBU, St. Louis, MO, Sgt. Samuel French Morse*

IMPRESSION OF THE RAIN

Upon the silent windowpane,
Released from bonds, oblivion bound, Resound, resound
The milling drops of rain.

Interned and segregated from the clouds, The heralding murmurs sweep
In crude, transparent shrouds, Asleep, asleep.

He, instance-bound, adheres
To milling fury and the warning tone, Alone, alone,
The sheltered and his tears.
—*New Guinea, T-5 Harry Eckstein*

INDIAN CREEK

As verdant as the forest of Lorraine
Is Indian Creek. And in the mystery
Of depth, beyond reflections cast by palms,
I can find a wealth of green to cool my mind---
Abundant shade to fog my thoughts and close
My eyelids and my heart to all but peace
And cleanliness. The yellow morning sun,
Exciting on the swollen creek, is like
A winking neon sign that flickers on
And off each tiny wave, and makes the whole
A living canvas by Van Gogh. There is
No war, there is no gun that has a right
To shatter, even for an instant, this;
The beauty that is now part of me.
—*ASAFBU, Miami, FL, Pfc. Catherine Murray*

GREENLAND

As daylight falls and winter night begins
The snowy mountains seem like frozen ghosts
Which stand in watchful waiting packed in rows
Above the frozen fjords and icebound coasts.

The arctic day fades fast but leaves
A band of light still on the western peaks
To form a wavy yellow carpet where
Aurora steps upon the stage and speaks
In tongues of light, in filmy veils and banners
Which she waves across the night.
—*Greenland, S/Sgt. Basil R. Andrews*

NEW ENGLAND SPRING

I have a longing for New England rain,
Insistent at my window pane,
Washing my body and my soul,
Leaving me fragrant, white and whole.

Softly, sadly its bird wings touch
The windows that I love so much,
Far in New England, far away,
The thin rain wakes each sodden day.

It taps and croons and whistles shrilly
In far New England, wan and hilly,
It bathes your body and your soul,
Leaves you fragrant, white and whole.
—*Luke Field, AZ, Pvt. Joseph Dever*

ONE AMERICAN SPEAKS

I do not know you, England; I have never Walked
through your narrow streets at night until I stood silently
beside the river
Where the scholar gypsy wanders still.

I have not seen your white cliffs, chalk walls Against the
irreverent world, nor do I know How on the Cornish
coast the red sun falls Into the sea you won so long ago.

It is a strange love, for an unseen lover, Praying to gods I
have not felt or known;
The sharp rocks of Dover where the white gulls hover,
Or Shakespeare, walking through the woods alone.
—*Newfoundland Pfc. Lauriat Lane Jr. June 15, 1945*

SEA GULLS

I looked out past the place where tugboats lay Besides the
spiritless and silent docks
To where a few forlorn and jagged rocks Raised mist-
encircled heads above the gray And moody waters of the
tranquil bay,
And where the lurking gulls in guilty flight Lingered as
though they waited for the night To lift their stiffened
wings and speed away. But even when the night has come
and gone The lonely, guilty gulls will still be there, De-
scending to the water one by one
With blade-thin wings that cut the misty air, Still guarding
with their souls the dark unknown And furtive secret of
their old despair.
—*Camp MacKall, N.C. Pvt. Jacob Korg November 26,1943*

ARMY CHAPEL

The doors stand open for the files of men
Whose step is lighter at the Sunday dawn.
These are the ones who yesterday had been
All fierce and heavy with their weapons on.
They are the grimmest worshippers of all
Who come to sing the quiet songs today,
Who have the strident marches to recall
And who have knelt to fire, but not to pray.
Just what the troubled heart will call its own
And will remember from this steepled place,
If fully felt, but not precisely known,
And written only on the soldier's face.
It is a search for rightness, little more---
The strangest, strongest weapon of war.
—*Camp Crowder, MO, Pvt. Darrell Bartee*

IF I COULD BUT CLIMB

If I could but climb tonight the vault of sky,
With stars as stepping stones to reach on high,
And from that vault could view the earth in life,
Then all the flame, the death, the bloody strife
Would come like a hazy dream, minute, too small
To sear the brain; and the streaks of stars that fall
Might light the remote edges between God and man.
If I could but climb tonight this blue-black span.
   —*Camp Cooke, CA, Pfc. S.W. Carbone*

Section Nine
Featured Poets

Carlyle A. Oberle

MY HEART

My heart is like a flower seed
In a jar upon a gardener's shelf,
It is so useless a thing alone by itself
Yet it will keep when autumn and its winter come;
And then perhaps in spring
Some gentle hand will take it down
From its sad corner of the shelf
And plant it in the blessed ground;
And it will drink the sweetness of the rain
And feel the warmth of the sun.
—*India, Sgt. Carlyle A. Oberle*

WHEN WE WHO LAUGH

When we who laugh through life
And but once
Or twice shed a tear For sorrow's sake,
And hundred shed For love,
Tally life When all its years have sped;
Shall we find we have fared better that the rest
Who day by day
Burden themselves with fears of
Tomorrows yet unborn
And live in yesterdays?
Have we not built at least of marble
A little stronghold of our gladness,
While they have built of shifting sands?
Can we not say our days have tallied best,
That we have only laughed
Or only loved?
—*India, Sgt. Carlyle A. Oberle*

PEOPLE

People:
You have to like everyone of them
No matter what they are;
You have to like them
When you are one of them;
And you have to believe in them
No matter what they do.
For believing in people
Is like believing in God.
—*India, Sgt. Carlyle A. Oberle*

TOMORROW

Tomorrow may be the most important day of all.
Tomorrow may be the day
To change a hundred thousand lives.
Tomorrow---
The word we all have said a hundred thousand times!
It is a word of faith.
We cling to it.
Yes, we must believe in tomorrow,
In the tomorrow hid behind
Perhaps a dozen years,
And when it comes It shall be glorious.
   —*India, Sgt. Carlyle A. Oberle*

HAPPINESS

Great is the price for happiness:
Yet would I pay the price
A dozen times. I would not once
Consider any cost too great,
For I have tasted happiness
Course through my veins
And stimulate each nerve.
Yet must I flinch before the payment
Of the price: yet I must tremble
Underneath its burden-weight.
I would for freedom's sake
Cheat in its payment where I might;
The evil in my mind would have it so.
But I am seen by eyes
That ever see me as I am. How can I
Cheat and not forever lose the right
To purchase happiness?
There is a light in which I see
The price of happiness is not too great! For me—
Unless I play the coward's part.
And that shall never be!
   —*India, Sgt. Carlyle A. Oberle*

A LEAF

I am a leaf among a world of leaves.
What tempest blows? I shall be lifted
On its winds and borne in which direction
Hurls the storm and blast of fury unsuppressed.

I am no fragile leaf a storm can break,
A fury can destroy;
I shall outlive the wind that feels
That it can chant my destined course.

I am a strong green leaf that soon shall soar
Amid a time and space wherin
I then may choose to wander
On to live my life according to the schemes of dreams.
   —*India, Sgt. Carlyle Oberle*

BE NOT IMPATIENT

Be not impatient, oh my heart,
Wish not for one hour's happiness at cost
Of all the future years.
This day of sunlight, this fair summer day
Shall reproduce itself throughout the many summers
That shall follow on successive years when this one fades.
Yes, there shall be more than a thousand days of happiness
If we have patience in sufficiency to wait for them;
Though there be spendthrift some
Who heap the treasures of their lives in one huge enterprise
That lasts a year, and thereinafter
Live in barren poverty of life,
Let not the brief high luster of their false-gemmed joy
Be blinded to our sense,
Else we may lose more than the coming years
In one brief day.
   —*India, Sgt. Carlyle A. Oberle*

THE DAY

The day! The day!
Think of the wonder of the day!
Think not about this lonely heart, my mind.
There are fair thoughts for meditation,
And there are fair sights to see.
This moment must be lived! We must not die
Because today is not the same as yesterday;
Each day is fair in its own way.
Laugh now, smile now, now plan, and go about
Your business with a light, free spirit, glad
That when tomorrow opens out the door
Upon tomorrow's garden path
That leads to life and love anew,
There shall be smiles still couching on your lips
And laughter that's not lost its ring;
Sing now that you will not forget the words of song!
   —*India, Sgt. Carlyle A. Oberle*

THE SEED

Blessed hand that plants a seed into the earth.
And many hands have wearied through a day,
And many backs have bended
In pain
The seeds that drank the rain
The leaves which breathe by millions on one breath,
The limbs and branches centuries have dealt no death,
The yearly harvest on its way---
Know how blessed is a hand that plants a seed into the sod.
Blessed be the heart that feels the growing pain
Of the little seed into the glowing grain.
Blessed be the hand that works along with God.
—*India, Sgt. Carlyle A. Oberle*

THE WORK OF THE SEASONS

At my feet my eyes behold the fruits the year has brought,
The work which nature through four seasons wrought,
And first till last on each one I have sought
Death, how it hangs upon the old, upon the new yet naught
There is a sorrow only age can learn,
It is a ferment only time can turn;
The raisin grape, and yet the sprightly fern,
The newborn's cry, the old folks nod
A balance in the hands of God.
—*India, Sgt. Carlyle Oberle*

Keith Campbell

BALLAD OF BRAVERY

When mastodons of feint and slug
Stand toe to toe to kiss and hug
With brotherly caress and wile,
Then knock each other for a mile,
I put myself within their shoes
To notarize the course I'd choose If some
Goliath, rippling muscle,
Should challenge me to padded tussle.

I've thought the situation out
From opening bell to final clout,
From bloody nose to winded lung
And buckling knees to swollen tongue,
And I have reached the calm decision
That I'd be subject to derision
Since I'm 1-A among the flukes
Who have no option on the dukes.
—*AAFTAC, Orlando, FL, Pvt. Keith Campbell*

BUNA BEACH

Perhaps they struggled with geography
When they were boys, lisping the sinewy names
Of far-off lands they never hoped to see,
With thoughts intent upon outdoor games;
The wild hallos and shouts of after school,
A rag-tailed kite against a gray March sky,
And boyish laughter ringing "April fool!"
When someone took their bait.

Well here they lie,
Three lads on Buna Beach, grotesquely laid
In the informal pose of sudden death;
While we, who live secure because they paid
In currency compounded of their breath,
Would hesitate and ponder on a scheme
To bargain interest to preserve their dream.
—*AAFTAC, Orlando, FL, Pfc. Keith B. Campbell*

ON MISSING A NORTHERN CHRISTMAS

My thoughts are jewels, for they are of the past—
The untried years, the time of youth's content
When life was laden with astonishment
And each year brought more wonders than the last.

And then the fall of idols: legends gone
Upon the breath of time; the myth unveiled
And Santa Claus, the patron saint, assailed
As parent fraud upon a holy dawn.

Yet they are treasures still: the holly wreath,
With berries red as vermeil, archway hung;
The tinseled tree with precious gifts beneath;
Clear frosted air; These I shall recall
If hope should fail me at old year's fall.
—*AAFTAC, Orlando, FL, Sgt. Keith B. Campbell*

FLORIDA, 1944

There lies the town, a mile away.
Framed like a Turner's "Venice," dimly seen
In colors that have blended with the bay,
Shining and silent in its bluish green.
A sea gull swoops, then coasts on lazy wing;
Sand flies and gnats whirl madly in the sun;
A patient spider at the tent pole's ring
Broods on the emptiness of web long spun.
So, too, the little world I call my soul---
Drowsy with patience for a garland thrown---
Given a portion but denied the whole,
Given a fraction but denied the one.
For only a gift of laurelled words could thrill
My thoughts, now motionless in air and still.
—*AAFTAC, Orlando, FL, Sgt. Keith B. Campbell*

TO ONE I DO NOT LIKE

If Hell should yawn and mine should be a share
In the vast gulf, bathed in its fiery sea
Of everlasting torment, I could bear
All that, knowing that you were there---
That would be heaven for me.

But if, dear sir, I walked on streets of gold,
Then one day heard a tinkling silvery bell,
And turned to watch a pearly gate unfold,
Letting you in from out the cold---
Why, sir, that would be Hell!
—*AAFTAC, Orlando, FL, Sgt. Keith B. Campbell*

SIDELINE QUARTERBACKS

I lift my fingers,
I extend my thumb
At those who beat
The martial drum.

From the apparent safety
Of a room
Quite alien to a
Martial doom.
—*AAFTAC, Orlando, FL Sgt. Keith B. Campbell*

ADVICE TO A FRIEND

Be as you are, always.
Reserve no note
For commonplaces,
In your own tongue, from your own throat
Always the word that races
Stronger, subtler and more meaningful
Than staid iambics and measured rhyming
Tom-tomming on the page with age-old chimings.
—*AAFTAC, Orlando, FL, Sgt. Keith B. Campbell*

THE BRIDGE

There was this bridge across the Rhine; some steel
In the form of girders, linking shore to shore
In ordinary fashion, as men feel
Most bridges do, since no bridge should do more;
Yet there was something---probably the grim
View of Teutonic towers at each end---
That echoed back to history's darkest whim;
A structure with an omen to portend.
What slender hinge of destiny, this span
That will stretch out forever through the dark
Which man created for his fellow man;
The Nazi night; pierced by one tremendous spark
That gathered fury, bursting into flame
To cauterize the wounds of Nazi shame!
—*AAFTAC, Orlando, FL, Sgt. Keith B. Campbell*

LAST WORD

The thieving tricks of all enduring time
Have ground this weary heart of mine to dust
And stopped the flow of many a silvery rime
That lipward sped in urge to tuneful lust.
For I have cherished things and watched them go

From me, victims of that unerring swing---
And clasped by darkness, by one swath laid low
Far from the sun, far from the eternal spring.

Pilferer of all that I have loved, this day
Have I to bitter wild rebellion swung.
And I shall battle, I shall not sway;
With my last breath I'll see the last lamp hung
And muscled, snarling, as a wolf at bay,
Go down in darkness with no song unsung.
—*AAFTAC. Orlando, FL, Sgt. Keith B. Campbell*

ENEMY COMMUNIQUE

From the little I know
Of all I read
It's a super-ego
Gone to seed.
—*AAFTAC, Orlando, FL, Sgt. Keith B. Campbell*

John Readey

ODE TO THE MEDICS

They give me shots for tetanus;
For typhoid, I get three.
The yellow fever is excuse
For one more hole in me.

They stick the needle in me dry;
They stick it in me wet.
They punch me full of holes, it seems,
At every chance they get.

Typhus, measles, housemaid's knee,
There's shots for ev'ry thing;
Fallen arches, leprosy;
Boy, those shots do sting.

Sometimes those vampires stick me good
Right in a vein on me,
And then they take a pint of blood
And smile with fiendish glee.

Oh, I haven't been in battle, yet;
In war I haven't starred.
But if you saw the holes in me,
You'd swear I'm battle scarred.
—*Camp Stoneman, CA, Cpl. John Readey*

THE PRIVATE'S PRIVACY

He sleeps with 60 other men.
No matter how you jive it,
I cannot understand at all
Why they should call him private.

They also call him *doughboy* too,
Though why, I do not know,
For I'm aware as well as you---
A soldier has no dough.

Chorus:
Where do they get the names for them?
I don't know why it's so;
A private has no privacy,
A doughboy has no dough!
—*Camp Stoneman, CA, Cpl. John Readey*

G.I. VOICE OF EXPERIENCE

Now, listen all you Romeos,
No matter whence you came,
You have half-baked lovers look alike
To certain type of dame,
You dopes are worth some dough today
To gal who gets your hand,
For fifty bucks* a month ain't hay,
With chance of ten more grand.**

Just 'cause the dames all look at you
And give you lots of house,
Don't think that you're the
Gable type Or even Mickey Mouse.
A few things that I have to say,
I hope you'll understand;
For fifty bucks a month ain't hay
With chances for ten more grand,
There's dames out here who'll marry me
Or any dumb G.I.
They know that this is P. of E.***
And soon they'll say, Good-by.
The lottery begins the day
The dope leaves U.S. land,
For fifty bucks a month ain't hay
With chances for ten more grand.

Now, when a dizzy dame attempts
Your heart and dough to cop;
Remember what I'm telling you
And then, perhaps, you'll stop
Before you throw your dough away
To buy a wedding band;
For fifty buck a month ain't hay,
With chances for ten more grand.

*   Class A Allotment for G.I.'s wife, dope!
**   Gov. Insurance, mugg. If he ain't got that much,
      the little woman will talk him into it.
***   Port of Embarkation (as if you didn't know that).
            —*Cpl. John Readey, Camp Stoneman, CA, Cpl. John Readey*

THE SOLDIER'S LAMENT

We wait in line to go to mess,
We wait in line to shave,
We wait in line for cigarettes,
No matter how we rave!

We wait in line to comb our hair,
We wait in line for beer,
We wait in line to pay our fare,
To get away from here.

We wait in line to get some gum
Or something else to buy,
We wait in line at USO,
We wait in line at Y.

We wait in line to get a pass,
We wait in line for pay,
We even wait in line at night,
When time to hit the hay.

Oh, if I die in battle an'
God claims this soul of mine,
I wonder if to get above
I'll have to wait in line.
            —*Camp Stoneham, CA, Cpl. John Readey*

GUARD DUTY

If night time's draped in darkness and
There's not a trace of light,
Or be it clear and brilliant with
A full moon shinning bright;
If ev'rything is going wrong
Or ev'ry things all right,
A man ne'er feel quite so alone
As when on guard at night.

All living things have gone to sleep
And all the world is dead;
I lift my eyes and gaze above,
He, too, it seems has fled;
It seems that I' the only soul
Within Creator's sight.
A man ne'er feels quite so alone
As when on guard at night.

I pull my great coat tighter and
It shields me from the air,
But chill of loneliness will bite
No matter what you wear;
When morning comes and sun appears,
As God looks down, and moves aside
The loneliness of night.
            —*Camp Stoneman, CA, Cpl. John Readey*

LATRINE RUMORS

United Press is pretty good,
And AP's all right too.
I find no fault with INS;
All bring the news to you.

The G.I.s have a system, though,
That's simple and serene;
No wires, no telephones need they,
For rumors of latrine.

Mow, rumors emanate from there
As fast and thick as flies;
They tell you when you'll move and where,
And prove the facts are lies.

The rumor's hot; here comes a flash:
"We're going overseas!"
Another flash: "Our outfit is
To all become MPs."

"Our captain will be tried in court,
And furloughs all will get;
First sergeant will be transferred soon
To Burma or Tibet."

This system that the dogface has
Tells ev'rything that's new;
It's very good, except the "facts"
It gives are never true!
—*Camp Stoneman, CA, Cpl. John Readey*

OH, COSMOLINE, MY COSMOLINE

Oh, Cosmoline, thou didst protect
My friend, my trusty rifle.
Thy deed is done; thou served me well;
Why dost thou stay and trifle?

Oh, Cosmoline, my fickle heart
No more has love for thee.
Why must thou bring me pain and make
This life hard for me?

Thou dept my M1 free;
For this my thanks I speak.
But now a trace of thee to me
Means KP for a week.
—*New Guinea, Sgt. John Readey*

GI JOKER

Of all Army pests
The most reprehensible
Compared to the rest
The least indispensable
Is the practical joke.

Putting corn meal in bed
Of man, unsuspecting,
He enjoys instead
Of old coin collecting
Or perhaps playing poker:

To burn him is not
Incomprehensible.
In fact, to me, it
Sounds so darn sensible
I'll furnish the stoker.
—*New Guinea, Sgt. John Readey*

THE CADENCE BLUES

Oh, listen to the gripers sound
In voices piped and tinny;
Their bitching trails the world around,
From Iceland to New Guinea.
They gripe about the terrible heat;
Bemoan the lack of beer;
But me, I like it overseas
Where nevermore I hear
That terrible chant, the sergeant's roar
Hut---two---three---four.

Sometimes the tropics drive men mad,
The heat, the toil, the strife,
And though the fever's pretty bad,
Still I enjoy the life,
Where never a cadence count invades
The quiet, peaceful shore,
No more to hear, no nevermore
Hut---two---three---four.
—*New Guinea, Sgt. John Readey*

ADDRESS UNKNOWN

A guy I knew was want to say:
"If on a bomb's your name,
No matter what you do, my boys,
It'll get you just the same."

Whene'er the bombers flew o'erhead
And to our holes we went,
This wise guy scoffed and never moved,
Just stayed inside his tent.

One night we scurried to our holes---
I'm still alive to tell---
The wise guy stayed within his tent
And he was blown to hell.

His name was not upon this shell
I afterward did learn,
For it was marked like all the rest:
"To whom it may concern."
  —*New Guinea, Sgt. John Readey*

FURLOUGH FOIBLES

Barmaids who say your jokes are funny
Probably are after your money.
Gals who invite you to their apartment
May be looking for an allotment.
Gals who like brandy
Are always handy.
And those who drink gin
Most often give in.
With women platonic
GIs are laconic.
On furlough get married
Return looking harried.
  —*New Guinea, Sgt. John Readey*

Irving Caress

IN ANSWER TO "GENEALOGICAL
REFLECTION" IN SEPT, 23 YANK

Do Mps have a mother?
A reader yearns to learn,
And we Mps would fair reply,
In cadences that burn.

We all of us have mothers,
Kind souls with hair of gray,
And when we're out on duty
They often kneel to pray.

They pray their sons will manage
They orders to obey
And not swing out on privates
Who sneer and run away.

They pray their sons will bravely
Bear their bitter cup
And remember when on furlough
Not to beat their mothers up.

Now there's a new MP in training,
A human kind of guy;
He'll help you out of trouble
With ne'er an oath or sigh.

He'll help you solve your problems,
You'll love him, honestly.
And all the while the poor guy yearns
To be in Infantry.
  —*Fort Ontario, NY, Pvt. Irving Caress*

BEER AND SEX

The soldiers in the Army,
All he-men and the wrecks,
They do a lot of talking
About beer and also sex.

Now, it's my observation,
In spite of all they boast of,
That between beer and women,
Beer is what they get the most of.
  —*New England Sgt. Irving Caress*

WAR IS HELL

I was torpedoed on the sea,
I've been in combat, too.
I went through hell on desert sands
And fought my way through jungle lands
Where shot and shrapnel flew.

Yet when the peace has come at last
And ended all our pains,
I'll settle in some quiet spot
To heal the aches and wounds I got
On busses and on trains.
—*New England, Sgt. Irving Caress*

REPLACEMENT POOL

Abandon all hope ye who enter here
Existence now is minus every cheer.
Where you'll go and what you'll do and see
Will be determined by a lottery.
Your number's in and when it's up you'll go.
Where to? And when?
Wouldn't you like to know?
Don't try a rumor diet, or start grieving.
When you begin to like it, you'll be leaving.
—*Somewhere in New England, Sgt. Irving Caress*

GI's YOUNG AND OLD

Oh, the soldier who is younger
Always seems to have a hunger
For places that he never should have been in.
He should really have his whirl in
A place where feet are twirlin'
And not seek low-down dives to drink his gin in.

But the soldier who is older
Seems to be a little bolder
When romance is what he's bent on winnin',
He eschews the name-band dance halls
And selects the juke-box beer stalls
As the hunting ground to find his sin in.

Now, nobody should quarrel
If this ditty has a moral:
A soldier takes his fun where he can find it.
If he's old and 18 "makes" him---
Or he's young and 40 "takes" him---
It's OK by me as long as he don't mind it.
—*Somewhere In New England, Sgt. Irving Caress*

MARRIAGE OVERSEAS

If you've got marriage on the mind
And want to get it done,
Make sure that you're familiar with
File TS two-nine-one.

You've got to get permission, it's
Your CO who says "Yes";
And his authority is in
A file that is marked TS.
—*Trinidad, Sgt. Irving Caress*

IT'S NOT THE HEAT

I don't mind the heat of the tropics.
I find I'm not bothered at all.
But what irks me in body and spirit
Are the things that are small—and crawl.

I slip into bed in the darkness,
After shedding my shirt and pants.
I think I'm alone, set for slumber.
But the bed is crawling with ants.

I open the lid on my locker
Every morn when the dawn approaches.
My shirts and socks are a haven
For a slew of scurrying roaches.

I squirt bug repellent about me.
On the bed, below and above it.
The repellent is apt to rout me.
But the insects thrive on and love it.

Someday when I'm home from the jungle
And these tropical days I recall,
I know what will cling to my mem'ry
Are the things that are small—and crawl.
—*Trinidad, Sgt Irving Caress*

BONUS

You can give us all a bonus
Or keep trying to disown us;
That's something for the folks to calculate.
I don't envy you the task,
But what I would like to ask
Is how much you'll pay a guy who lost his mate?

There's a medal and citation
For each service to the nation

By fighting men who go through war's worst hells.
I think Congress should declare one.
Yes and let each GI wear one
Who found his girl friend married to someone else.

It's quite easy to determine
The effects of steel and vermin
On servicemen whose task was so immense.
But someone must be aware of
An attempt to take good care of
Those wounded souls, the jilted GI gents.
—*Trinidad, Sgt. Irving Caress*

CASUAL

If hopelessness had found a place
Of permanence upon his face
And dark despair all joys erase,
He's just a casual.

No outfit his to brag about;
No glow of pride, no welcome shout;
Only a spot to sweat it out;
Only a casual.

He's interviewed and classified;
Hope surges eagerly inside.
Alas, again the same old ride
And still a casual.

The skill that Army life has wrought,
The ribbons, records, all are naught;
A number now, unknown, unsought---
Unhappy casual.

He pays no heed to rumors rife
That dig in deep, then like a knife
Destroy all hope of movement, life---
Despondent casual.

Now if, in some distant year,
A plaintive voice should reach your ear
And plead, "Please get me out of here,"
It's just some casual.

These lines, so full of pain, express
Great agony; you'll never guess
How deep the hurt, that is, unless
You, too, are casual.
—*Camp Shelby, MS, S/Sgt. Irving Caress*

TIME

Time on a tropical island
Far from combat and strife,
Lush, equatorial stillness,
Unstirred by Army life.

Simmering heat of the tropics
Tempers, tests and anoints.
Monotony measured by patience
Pays off in discharge points.
—*Trinidad, S/Sgt. Irving Caress*

SWAN SONG

Newly commissioned officers
(At least it was reported)
Gave the first GI that they met
A buck when he saluted.

I'm being discharged any day,
I'm happy as a twister.
I'll gladly give a dollar to
The first guy who says "Mister."
—*Camp Shelby, MS, S/Sgt. Irving Caress*

VETERAN'S VOW

Never will I ever travel
On a boat again.
Give me asphalt cement, gravel---
I'll not float again.

I have had my share of sailing
On the stormy seas.
Still can feel my insides failing---
Just excuse me please.

All the luxuries you mention
Postwar brings about,
Leave me cold---and all dissension
Please include me out.

I won't even board a ferry,
Sailing sloop or yacht.
Just the thought of wavelets merry
Irks my soul a lot.

Trips in Europe, Egypt,
Burma May be luxuries.
This vet sticks to "terra firma,"
And stays home—at ease.
—*Camp Shelby, MS, Sgt. Irving Caress*

Elizabeth Itzen

OUR BATHROOM

Our bathroom's just like Broadway,
The kids go marching through;
If, you're sitting in the bathtub---
Well, that's too bad for you.

Privacy is something
That you only read about;
If you're bashful you'll go dirty
Until the lights go out.
      —ANC, Australia, 2nd Lt. Elizabeth Itzen

GREEN BANANAS

Oh, I picked some green bananas
And I pushed them down the hatch;
Now boys I think I'm dying
Cause my eyes don't even match.
I am sitting by the window
And my sight is getting dim.
Yes I know the end is nearing
"Cause the things about me swim.
So, boys, please lift me gently,
Put a pencil in my hand,
For, I'm gonna write my story,
How I died for Uncle Sam.
      —Australia, 2nd Lt. Elizabeth Itzen ANC

OFFICER OF THE DAY

So, I'm O.D.---Boy what a job. My duties are untold;
I shall related my troubles now, my tale of woe unfold.

First nonchalant and quite blasé a flyer makes the gate,
"You see," says he, "I'm all alone and looking for a date;

Fix me up---a little girl with eyes of blue.
Sometime when you're not O.D. I'll do the same for you."

Another man with peppy steps approaches from afar
The coast artilleries hit the deck and says he's up to par.

"I like 'em tall and dark and slim with teeth of pearly white.
Heaven help the army nurse Artilleries out to-night.

I fix each one up as they come in person or by phone
And out they go to dance or show but I must stay at home.

At twelve o'clock with light in hand I check each girlie in;
I chase the boys and stop the noise; The O.D. just can't win.
      —Australia, 2nd Lt. Elizabeth Itzen

A PRAYER

Dear God---Please give me peace of mind
And in my work please let me find
some kind of consolation.
I guess I've put up quite a bluff.
I really thought
I had the stuff to help them save our nation.
But now I find that I was blind
To all those things I left behind:
And fully understand
Without
Your help I cannot do
The many things they want me to---
I need your helping hand.
      —Australia, 2nd Lt. Elizabeth Itzen

THE WHOLE DARN INFANTRY

"Good bye," he said,
"And thank you nurse,
This has all been swell;
But now that I am well again
They'll send me back to hell."

He handed me an old grass skirt
That he had highly prized
"I know you had your eye on this.
It's a gift from all us guys."

"We're going back to mud knee deep
And cooties in our hair,
And any souvenir like that
Would never help us there.

"I hope you'll say a prayer or two
Not for only me,
But ask the Lord to look out for
The whole darn Infantry.

He turned and swiftly strode away
To join the other guys,
But not before I saw the tears
That welled up in his eyes.

I held the skirt in one limp hand
And watched him out of sight,
And thought of what a kid he was
And how that kid would fight.

So now each night I kneel to pray
And say "God just for me,
Please look out for my patient
And the whole darn Infantry."
—*Australia, 2nd Lt. Elizabeth Itzen*

TO SOME OF THE BOYS I KNEW

To you who flew so gallantly
We bow our head in memory
And know at last that you are free from earthly care.

And so we're copying your style,
Laughing at each weary mile
In hopes that you'll look down and smile from home up there.
—*Australia, 2nd Lt. Elizabeth Itzen*

PERSONAL REPORT

My life consists of bullie beef,
Soggy clothes and wiggly teeth,
Gun shot wounds and jungle rot
And days that are so bloomin' hot
That even hell compared to this
Would seem a simple life of bliss.
—*Australia, 2nd Lt. Elizabeth Itzen*

JUST THINKING

Parked alone on my army trunk
---the girls all have a date---
I shut my eyes and make believe
I'm in New Jersey State.
My trunk becomes a rocking chair, the lights are soft and low;
There's a fire in the fireplace with ashes all aglow.
Mother's baking a layer cake the fragrance fills the air,
And Dad is reading politics and of the county fair.
A roaring noise zooms overhead, I wake up with a start
And return to earth and war again with memories in my heart.
—*Australia, 2nd Lt. Elizabeth Itzen*

ONE DAY WITH A GOLD BRICK

I starch my cap and shine my shoes,
Then off to work I go,
Across the red dust cow lane
Where the hot wind always blows.

My tents are lined up in a row
With painted little signs
Telling what I'll find within
The heavy canvas blinds.

My patients lounge about the place
Cracking jokes and such,
And doing little odds and ends
But never very much.

The sun grows hotter than a fire,
We sweat and talk some more,
And cuss the guy right inside out
Who started up the war.

Five o'clock rolls slowly round
And so its time for chow;
The chow hounds get their mess kits out,
And exit with a bow.

And now the sun sinks slowly
Like a ball of angry red;
A cool breeze springs from nowhere
And so it's time for bed.

I go around and check each bed
With only half a will
To see how many angels
Took off---over the hill.

And so my day's completed,
And I will stroll once more
Back across the cow lane
Into the hen house door.
—*Australia, 2nd Lt. Elizabeth Itzen*

Harold Applebaum

THE LOVE OF ISLANDS

The love of islands is a recent one.
When spreading seas across the globe revealed
Their dots of land beneath the foreign suns,
The hearts turned seaward from the battlefields
And longed for haven shores and peaceful plains,
For homes protected by an ocean's breadth,
For solitude and shelter from war's rain,
For winds untainted by the smell of death.
But overhead are wings and motors' roar,
And nowhere are there peaceful fields to name
As safe from war, or any bloodless shore
Untouched by death, and from the tide of flame
Across the world, the retrogressing waves
Force back on Man his ancient love of caves.
   —*Camp Shanks, N.Y., Sgt. Harold Applebaum*

THE DRUMS

Some future year, while men still play at war,
And frightened moons float sickly through the skies,
All pale with flame and death—a Man will rise
Upon the earth, where He stood before,
And raise his voice. And men will stare at crags
And stumps and shattered city walls and say:
"What have we done? Some dynamite day
Will fling us, too, among the bloody rags
Of sky we've pulled down, fighting to be free!"
But loud the urgent drums renew the beat
To drown the gentle voice, and man's poor feet,
And waltz him to Armageddon's blast—
Not the first, nor the second, nor last!
   —*Camp Butner, NC, Sgt. Harold Applebaum*

THE DEATH OF PVT. JONES

Let's say that Pvt. Jones died quietly.
Let's say that when the first wave stormed the shore
A single shot went through his heart, and he
Slipped lifeless to the sand. Not one man saw
Him die, so busied they with lying hid
And crawling on, yet all men felt the breath
Of leaden wings come close, and when they did,
It made his passing seem a public death.
So much for Jones. He died as one of scores,
And on a distant beach. But when they bring
The news to those who count the cost of wars,
A private's death becomes a private thing.
How strange that war's arithmetic discounts
The spread of sorrow as the sorrow mounts!
   —*Camp Butner, NC, Sgt. Harold Applebaum*

MAN WITH A GUN

This clever piece, so firm against my cheek,
So finely wrought, so eager to be used,
Means immortality to me. I seek
No more protection from the fates than just
To aim its barrel at the foe and drop
My killers in the dust. To me this gun
Means I am God, in that my hands can stop
A life, or see a mortal justice done.
A pity then, when such a pow'r is mine
To force upon the world my godly will
And rout the alien creeds, that I can find
No man to say, "This God is good," or fill
Its bore with brain and soul so that it might
Judge once the difference between wrong and right.
   —*Camp Butner, NC, Sgt. Harold Applebaum*

THE NONCOMBATANTS

Mourn not, Madonna, that I do not smile,
Nor tease that my eyes are cold. There are days
For smiling, there are nights when the heart is old.
Here at our table there is wine and song.
Your beauty's a stunning fact.
Enchanted I sit within your glow, but I am racked
By short-wave dreams of battlegrounds
And isles where soldiers die, for on my head
Is blood, and on my heart my brothers lie.
I cannot drink the wine, nor look at you,
Nor hear the music's strain. I am ashamed.
Perhaps you understand. Out there in the rain
They wait for death, and you ask me to smile
And tease that my eyes are cold. There are days
For smiling, there are nights when the heart is old.
   —*Camp Butner, NC, Sgt. Harold Applebaum*

TO THE NEWLY DEAD

You came with nothing. Do you now have less?
Or does your dead mind still hold final pain
At steel or flame or having died in vain?
Or does the thought of home withhold your rest,
To know your loss will drop the weight of tears
On those you loved? Or at the last, the flash
Of memory, in panic at the crash,
Of girls unloved, of things undone, of years?
Remember now, you inadvertent dead.
Remember ere you bitter in your graves
And mock the framework of our creed.
He saves Your ghostly footsteps for future tread.
Go then. This time had seen your worthiness.
You came with nothing. Do you now have less?
—*SCSU, Lake Placid, NY, Sgt. Harold Applebaum*

THE INTROVERT

My mind and I are wary friends of all
Who happen by. In friendliness we might
Extend a hand in answer to a call
Or pass a word in jest, but let one sigh
Of fellowship appear, the merest trace
Of faith in what we are, or might soon be,
And we withdraw, throw masks upon the face,
And back toward isolate security.
For shame, you say, to trust no man and let
No friends approach? Know then that, once our door
Was wide to anyone, and once we did not forget
The best of men are rich, the worst are poor
In what we treasure most, and do not waste or buy.
—*SCSU, Lake Placid, NY, Sgt.
Harold Applebaum*

CPL. ROBERT HOLBROOK, SNIPER

You said you needed me; I did not doubt
That here was a need for men to fight your war.
I did not need the crass civilian shout
This would be dearer than the ones before.

I questioned not that I had never killed,
Nor hated well enough to thirst for blood.
I did not cry my heart was gently filled
With brother love or that I had a God.

I fought your war. I lay behind a tree
And aimed the fine, unerring gun at those
You pointed out to be my hated foes.
I'm sure your medal will look well on me.

But I must not kill again. I must not feel
The sweet precision of a newer gun,
The keener sight, the silver kiss of steel,
The love of weapons with which death is done.
The day I die, on some forsaken shoal,
Let me be decent and my conscience clean
With no barbaric frenzy on my soul---
No thrill of killing with a new machine.
—*Southwest Pacific, Sgt. Harold Applebaum*

MEMO FOR AVENGERS

Remember this sight, you strong.
Remember the children on the shore
Who reach to you as to the sun
In ghastly dawns. Look hard, look well
Upon their faces. See through the rags
To where the worms of every wasting curse
Have feasted long. Remember how
They run to you who are no gods at all
To kiss your feet and weep for joy.

Remember this when down your sights
Or in your courts the foeman makes his plea.
Remember, lest some future year
Another race will rise and "set men free"
The way the "liberators' blessed the Greeks.
Remember now against the day
When peace returns and all men say,
"The world is safe," and even then
Remember the one word, "Remember!"
—*SCSU, Lake Placid, NY, Sgt. Harold Applebaum*

THESE ARE THE YEARS

If you pause on the threshold of a year
And wonder, had you better not wait
Before you cross, the drag of doubt and fear
Will slyly check your step and let the date
Pass by. These are the changing years when faith
Means most, and blessed are the strong in heart.
These are the years when the hand of fate
Is locked with yours across a board to start,
And then the struggle till a hand goes down,
Forever then, a slave. these are the years
When surety's the ace and bluffs are thrown
And conquerors oblivious to tears.
Steel then your stride and meet it like a king---
Step forward, you can master anything!
—*SLSU, Lake Placid, NY, Sgt. Harold Applebaum*

LET THE PEOPLE COME

When this is done, let the people come
From all the lands of earth and walk around
The tattered world. Let them be awed, struck dumb
By what they see. Show them the battleground,
The shattered tanks, the buried guns, the stones
Of cities where the bombers passed. Point out
The graves of men or, where they fell, the bones
Of those who died too slow and id without.

Show them the worst of what there is to see;
Let them be sickened, horrified, aghast;
But let them look and feel and touch and be
Aware that future's signpost is the Past,
That these might happen soon again. Let these
Be War's last advertisement for Peace.
    —*SCSU, Lake Placid, NY, Sgt. Harold Applebaum*

COURAGE

Put the question to a man, or draw a line
And say that should he cross it he is brave---and dead.
Or on this side drink a paler wine.
Give him time to think, and inside his head
A pendulum will swing from flame to tear
And back to flame. For every second he can think,
For every moment reason reappear,
The bright quicksilver mind can writhe and shrink
Away from madness, back from death---alive.
Then, within the clock a cog will fall.
Find the pendulum at flame or fear, six or five---
And there will chime the second of the call.
So small the difference then, so set the rule;
Time and chance can make a man a hero or a fool.
    —*Camp Shanks, NY, Sgt. Harold Applebaum*

LINES ON IMPERMANENCE

Observe the wise philosopher at work---
A nerveless dynamo content to hum
And wreak his matchless strength on things that lurk
Like gravity beyond the earth, to find the sum
Of all man knows and does and is, to write
His truths like fire upon the human wall,
To chart the upward path, rejoice at sight
Of mortal climb beyond the mortal fall.
He goes to sleep, believing all is well,
But as he rests the night moves in to pry,
So that the morning's sums do not compare---
All due, no doubt, to nature's touch: a pair
Of spider webs, a rust where oil was dry.
Machines are tricky things. It's hard to tell.
    —*SCSU, Lake Placid, NY, Sgt. Harold Applebaum*

THE MASTERS

Now come the modern troglodytes to dig
Among the ruin of the cities, yank
The metal roots, collect the wire twigs,
Unearth the warped machines and scratch and clank
Their sides as if to bring the dead alive,
And then to gather every strange device
In one great cave and chant loud prayers, contrive
To bring the monsters proper sacrifice.

A feeble few among them call to mind
Some dim remembrance of the past, where once
The wise machines performed their will, but find
This greater shame---to try with wordless grunts
The magic of the old accustomed tone,
And find themselves unanswered and alone.
    —*SCSU, Lake Placid, NY, Sgt. Harold Applebaum*

Richard Armour

MENU FOR TOMORROW (AND THE NEXT DAY)

Fried eggs, farewell,
With your rasher of bacon;
You're shot all to hell
Unless I'm mistaken.

For eggs and ham
In a can, like a bomblet,
Means that eggs that are scram---
Bled or ham in an omelette.
       —*Fort Totten, NY, Lt. Richard Armour*

NAMING OF THE PARTS---G.I. BODY

This is a model '06 body,
Food fed, with now and then a toddy.
Its maximum effective range
Is subject to change,
This being chiefly on account
Of having seat and bipod mount.

This globe or spheroid is the head.
Remove it, and the body's dead.
Its function, as the experts recon,
Is principally to keep the neck on.
And though some teeth come out with gripping,
This is the limit of field stripping.

This cylinder or tube's the neck,
Which the head can nod and beck,
It also joins the head and trunk.
Without it, then, they'd both be sunk.
This cam that rises when I swallow
Is Adam's apple, if you follow.

This next group is the trunk or torso,
As full of parts or even more so,
The levers on the sides, my friends,
Are arms, with hands upon the ends,
While in the trunk are many organs,
Some working well, some not such bargains.

This is myself, this is my nature.
These are my parts, with nomenclature,
And I have told, without compunction,
The major facts about their function.
As gun-wise thus I disassemble
Look on me, fellow men, and tremble.
       —*Antiaircraft Artillery, Lt. Richard Armour*

AGE BEFORE BEAUTY

If chorus girls of forty-five
Cavort upon the platforms
Of every honky-tonk and dive
And flaunt their all-too-fat forms
While younger gals conceal their charms
In denim or khaki,
I tell you, gentlemen at arms,
Old Sherman wasn't wacky.
       —*Antiaircraft Artillery, Lt. Richard Armour*

WHAT'S IN A NAME?

What once was a meal,
In the Army's a mess,
But I'd be a heel
If I didn't confess
That a guy can grow fatter
From eating the latter.
       —*Lt. Richard Armour*

EARMARKS

That Engineers
Have hair in their ears
Is a saying I've never forgotten,
But, private to gen., Artillerymen,
Though not without hair, prefer cotton.
       —*Antiaircraft Artillery, Lt. Richard Armour*

OVER THE GUN BARREL

Of all the really dreadful sights
That I have ever seen,
The one that haunts me most at nights
Is guns in cosmolene.
       —*Ft. Totten, NY, Lt. Richard Armour*

ABOUT THE SIZE OF IT

Private Twirp is a lucky man,
Match his good fortune if you can.
Rare is his case, you must admit;
His G.I. pants are a perfect fit.
—*Fort Totten, NY, Lt. Richard Armour*

LET'S GO BUY NOW

They may not be beauties
Or neatly curved cuties,
But in the PX
The salesgirls are kind of
Good just to remind of
The opposite sex.
—*Antiaircraft Artillery, Lt. Richard Armour*

PRIVATE PROPERTY

Noncoms have their chevrons,
Lieutenants have their bars,
Colonels have their eagles,
Generals their stars.

What, then, has the private
Fastened to his arm,
Or resting on his shoulder
Of his uniform?

Only this (but tell me,
Who'd not like the same?);
On his arm or shoulder,
One delicious dame.
—*Antiaircraft Artillery, Lt. Richard Armour*

BEHIND THE UNDERWEAR EIGHTBALL

Heads you lose
And tails the same;
Whatever you choose
You lose the game.

Dice can be rolled
Or flip a nickel;
Cottons are cold
And woolies tickle.
—*Antiaircraft Artillery, Lt. Richard Armour*

A WORD TO THE WISE

No matter how spouted or bellowed or shouted
Or scowlingly, howlingly hissed,
Of all the words at the top kick's command
The sweetest, by far, is "Dismissed."
—*Antiaircraft Artillery, Lt. Richard Armour*

Josephine Pagliai

I MET HIM BY THE NONEDIBLE GARBAGE CAN

There will come a day, I pray there will,
When about me tiny grandchildren shall play.
No doubt, they'll ask me, "Where did you meet grandpop?"
And I will sweetly smile and proudly say:

"I met him by the nonedible garbage can,
Long ago when I was a Wac so strong and hale.
I was on KP that day, emptying the morning trash,
And he a yardbird goldbricking from some detail.

"He was extremely handsome in his dirty fatigue clothes
As our eyes did meet across the garbage can.
"Twas then I knew, grandchildren, that destiny had sent
Into my life my one and only man.

"All that day on KP I wondered, "Will he come again?"
And I just couldn't work worth a damn.
Oh, I will never forget the way your grandpop looked
As he stood beside the nonedible garbage can!

"Sure he showed up in our day room, and our courting nights began.
Such precious hours we spent before bed check!
Why, between KP and your grandpop, grandchildren, you can bet,
I was always an overworked, tired wreck.

"We were bush-whacking in the off-limit weeds the night
Your grandpop up and proposed to me.
I shouted out a 'yes!' before he'd change his mind,
So he made a married woman out of me.

"Yes that was long ago, when women were brave Wacs.
Your grandpop proved himself a rip-snorting man,
And to my dying day I shall remember how he looked when
I met him by the nonedible garbage can.
—*Camp Breckinridge, KY, T-4, Josephine Pagliai*

SPRING COMPLAINT

It is hard to be a soldier in the spring
When this harassed old world brandishes forth in beauty,
The tired faces glow with virile rapture,
The faded views sparkle with magnificent exuberance!

Then, instead of manning a gun with hate in your soul,
You want to stretch out eager arms to nature
And love with an intensity
That is terrifying, blessed.

Oh, it is hard to be a soldier in the spring—
To kill, when inside you the urge
To create cries out, vainly.
—*Fletcher Gen. Hosp, Cambridge, Ohio, T-4
Josephine Pagliai*

SPRINGTIME IN ODs

It is hard to be a soldier in the spring
When this harassed old world brandishes forth in beauty.
The tired faces glow with virile rapture,
The faded views sparkle with magnificent exuberance!

Then, instead of manning a gun with hate in your soul,
You want to stretch out eager arms to nature
And love with an intensity
That is terrifying, blessed.

Oh, it is hard to be a soldier in the spring---
To kill, when inside you the urge
To create cries out, vainly.
—*Fletcher Gen. Hosp., Cambridge, Ohio, T-4
Josephine Pagliai*

THE SOLDIER

In his hands he holds
The key of destiny,
His strength, his burdened back,
The plodding stubbornness of his feet
Are factors which determine how
The panting fires of humanity
Will be set ablaze.

To him all eyes are turned.
Dreamers, builders, yea, even the lowest and the mean
Watch breathlessly his march.
If he should fall, he takes with him
The glories of a priceless past,
Children's hopes, security of the old,

Mother's prayers, the beauty of all work,
Visions of a future throbbing
In every heart.

And because
In him lies everything,
With him goes all we have,
And all that we shall know.
He is the prince of peace who fights to build
Our paths into the treasured realms
Of earthly happiness.
   —*Fletcher General Hospital, Ohio, Sgt. Josephine Pagliai*

SPRING DAY

Heaven and earth are mating in
An endless blue delight.
Oh, I am young and will not know
This day of a man's grim plight!

The virgin grass is wooing me,
The air demands my heart.
Oh, shut out all life's cares; today
I am a dream apart!
   —*Fletcher General Hospital, Ohio, T-4 Josephine Pagliai*

MEMORY

There is no beauty like a memory.
There no one dies. The many I have met
Who laughed with me a while, revealed a thought,
Or touched with me the joy of sweet content---
Though in a night they quietly slipped away
Into a thousand fields I'll never see.
They are not gone so far that memory
Will not recall them back to me.
   —*Fletcher General Hospital, Ohio, Sgt. Josephine Pagliai*

MY BUDDIES

There were so many of them;
Women from farms; girls from cities,
Brawny, loud mouthed Westerners;
Fair, bashful Southerners
Who were afraid of the cold.
There were so many I met
And ate and worked and bunked with.
I took them all for granted.
But now I look back
And remember their faces
And suddenly feel lonely.
   —*Fletcher General Hospital, Ohio, T-4 Josephine Pagliai*

Margaret Jane Taggs

MILITARY COURTESY

When he and she, embracing, find
An officer on hand,
It's very hard to break away
And at attention stand.

Oh, how much better it would be
If either ma'am or sir,
Instead of saying just "At ease."
Would mention "As you were."
   —*Washington, D.C., Sgt. Margaret Jane Taggs*

LADIES OR SOLDIERS?

Here is a problem that is bound to tax
Minds of officers and of Wacs---
Shall the last come first or the first come last?
Shall he stand aside till the lady's passed
Or march, as an officer should do, well
In advance of enlisted personnel?
The second lieutenant goes ahead,
The colonel bows---she precedes instead;
Or both of them wait till it's now or never
And end in a knot that is hard to sever!
Confusion like this out there is none much completer;
It's plain that he doesn't know quite how to treat her.
He wonders, in spite of the bars on his blouse,
Is he officer, gentleman, just a mouse.
   —*Washington, D. C., Sgt. Margaret Jane Taggs*

HOST WANTED

The ladies of the U.S.A.
Have rallied round and found a way
To keep the soldier entertained
While for the wars he's being trained.
They shake his hand and pour his tea
And listen to his history.
They feed him cake and mend his pants,
Provide fair maids with whom to dance;
They see there's nothing he shall lack,
But what about the lonesome Wac?

Is there a man, do you suppose,
Who cares to listen to my woes?

Who'd waltz or jitter gallantly
Or sit and talk about just me?
Who'd take the time when day is done,
To show a Wac a little fun?
Remember (though I fear the worst),
If such there be, I saw him first!

Men of America arise!
Your duty before you lies.
Your wives and daughters, sisters, aunts
Aren't overlooking any chance
To do their good turn, be a pal,
And raise the fighting man's morale.
He will recall, when he departs,
Their gracious ways and friendly hearts.
They'll cherish him when he gets back.
But what about the lonesome Wac?
— *Washington, D.C., Sgt. Margaret Jane Taggs*

ARMY-NAVY COOPERATION

Our devotion we give to the Army
As a good Wac and soldier should do,
And yet we agree that our standard OD
Goes exceptionally well with dark blue.

He likes me. I know, for he told me.
His picture he willingly gave,
But I cannot deny there's a gleam in his eye
When he catches a glimpse of a Wave.

Now, no one can claim that I'm fickle.
Yet I have a peculiar feeling—
Be he tall, be he short, from starboard and port,
A sailor is plenty appealing!

So we should combine operations.
A joint-plans committee appoint,
To discuss our affairs and reflect upon theirs
When we find an appropriate joint.

There'll be a new zest to the battle.
We'll manage a quick victory,
When he's launched with his
Wave and the sailor I crave
Is plotting maneuvers with me!
— *Washington, D.C., Sgt. Margaret Jane Taggs*

GI GLAMOUR GIRL

She walked in beauty, if she walked at all.
And others gladly followed where she led;
She need not toil or spin, nor even call—
Some man was there to do the job instead.

She joined the Army, as a young girl will,
With thought of tailored uniform, her hair
A gleaming contrast to OD, the thrill
Of battle—they might send her anywhere!

The facts of life to her have now grown clear,
To sundry matters she must give attention—
For trash and garbage don't just disappear.
(The fate of flowing hair, we need not mention.)

She knows about KP, fatigue detail.
Exquisitely her fingers wring the mop.
Nowhere is there a kind, obliging male
To take it in his hands and bid her stop.

What wonder that her graceful figure droops?
This is the Army, babe! Let's end the scene
When lovely lady not to folly stoops,
But bends a knee to clean up the latrine.
— *Washington, D.C., Sgt. Margaret Jane Taggs*

GOOD SCENTS

They took away our pretty clothes,
Our silly hats, our nylon hose;
They made us cut our flowing hair
And gave us OD underwear.
We're soldiers now, of frills bereft,
But there's something we have left!
Redolent is the squad-room air,
As we uncork our bottles there.
There's Joy and Shocking and
Mais Oui, Desire, Risque, and Follow Me,
Tabu, Shanghai, Moment Supreme,
Old Spice, Heartbeat, Poetic Dream,
Evening in Paris and Allure,
Temptation, My Sin, Nuit d'Amour;
A thousand odors rise, as we
Express our femininity.

L'Envoi

Who thinks perfume gives charm its accents
Has never smelled assorted WAC scents!
— *Washington, D.C., Sgt. Margaret Jane Taggs*

THE RUBAIYAT OF MARGARET JANE TAGGS

Awake! The hosts of Dawn have put to rout
Night's misty legions; Brightness spreads about.
The strident Whistle sounding urgently
Conveys its Message "wake, arise, fall out!"

The Moving Finger writes, and we may read
The Future, so abidingly decreed;
For the Duration and for Six Months more
Our Piety and Wit is what we'll need.

Though some may moan and in Dejection sit,
While others, more rebellious, long to quit,
Inexorably comes the Answer back;
"This is the Army; you Girls asked for it."

Into the Corps we came, and why not knowing---
Except that we must serve, our Fervor showing;
And in it we shall serve, beyond a Doubt,
Although our qualms are willy-nilly growing.

Some on a Past of rare Refinement dwell,
While others of a rosy Future tell;
Yet many a Maiden, were the truth revealed,
Believes one Man, at hand, would do as well.

There's little Comfort in the thought that thou
Art far away beneath some Foreign Bough,
And if thou hast a Jug of Wine besides,
Thou art more fortunate than I am, now.

Then let us to the nearest Tavern fly,
Seek swift Forgetfulness in Gin and Rye;
Alas, for us no Solace from the Grape---
It is forbidden that a Wac get high.

Though roses bloom where buried Caesars bled
And I shall nourish Daisies when I'm dead,
The Dust I'll be concerns me not so much
As Dust the CO found beneath my bed.

The Past is dim, the Future far from clear,
But all we need to know is that we're here.
Our Part is to obey, to Forward March!
Then, turning, march as briskly to the Rear.

When Time brings to a Close this hectic Span,
When Destiny unfolds another Plan,
May One who goes this way, remembering,
Turn down for me an empty GI Can.
    —*Washington, D.C., Sgt. Margaret Jane Taggs*

A WAC COMES BACK

When she contemplates a soldier's life
And comes back home to be his wife,
Will all her Army training
Perfect her in those gentle arts
So well designed to soothe men's hearts,
Their self-esteem sustaining?

Will she arise when he comes in---
Down with abdomen, up with chin---
Stand till he says "At ease?"
Will she awake before the sun,
Will every household task be done
The way that he decrees?

Will he have dinner placed on trays,
In neat compartments, all his days?
And will she serve him well?
Will she no wish of his deny,
But "Yes, sir," be her prompt reply?
Ah, Mister, who can tell?
    —*Washington, D.C., Sgt. Margaret Jane Taggs*

SICK CALL

When one is feeling low and sickly
One wants her doctor summoned quickly;
She wants to lie at ease in bed,
Soft pillows underneath her head;
A dainty tray, a flower, a touch
Of tenderness would soothe her much.

Instead she must arise and dress,
Report her indisposedness;
Although she may with fever burn,
She must politely wait her turn,
While through her mind dark visions flit;
The casket and the flag on it.
Such harshness no one quite forgives,
Yet, every time, the patient lives!
    —*Washington, D.C., Sgt. Margaret Jane Taggs*

REPARTEE

I asked him if he liked the life, and wasn't soldiering fun? I said,
"This uniform we wear looks well on anyone!"
I told him I admired his style—from me his charm's not hidden,
But conversation died because he answered, "Are *you* kiddin'?"
So then I tried a different tack---I said the Army's tough.
He's overworked and underpaid, and hasn't stripes enough.
The things he really wants to do are by ARs forbidden.
We got exactly nowhere for he told me, "You ain't kiddin'!"
—*Washington, D. C., Sgt. Margaret Jane Taggs*

Bob Stuart McKnight

GOVERNMENT ISSUE

There are at least five hundred things
For which we stand in line
Though I can but remember
One hundred twenty-nine---

G.I. shoes to blister my feet,
G.I. comb to keep hair neat,
G.I. shad for the social elite,
Hep-Hep-Government Issue.

G.I. socks to warm my toes,
G.I. rag to blow my nose,
G.I. chaplains to share my woes,
Hep-Hep-Government Issue.

G.I. sunrise, rosy-pink,
G.I. shower, G.I. sink,
G.I. soap 'cause Gee, I stink.
Hep-Hep-Government Issue.

But all we want is a G.I. girl,
With a G.I. smile and a G.I. curl,
And a G.I. gleam in her G.I. eye,
Hep-Hep-Government Isssue.
—*Kessler Field, MS, Pvt. Bob Stuart McKnight*

I WAS GLAD TO KNOW YOU, SOLDIER

When I was a civilian, I had a lot of pals,
Good times every weekend, some pretty classy gals.
Then they took me in the Army and I had to start anew
So I think I'm pretty lucky to have met a guy like you.

I was glad to know you, soldier,
And I hate to see you go.
Just had time to get acquainted
Got me feelin' pretty low.

I'll be thinking of you, soldier,
And the hell we raised in town.
Fifty buck's still not enough
For a guy to get around.

If we should never meet again

Sure would be a shame.
But that's the way with soldiering,
So why should I complain?

Take it easy, keep that chin up
It won't be long, a year or so.
I was glad to know you, soldier.
Gee, I hate to see you go.
—*Keesler Field, MS, Pvt. Bob Stuart McKnight*

CORPORALS

Corporals, though opulent,
Are very seldom corpulent.
—*Scott Field, IL, Pvt. Bob Stuart McKnight*

RESTRICTED

Girls who live in a quiet block
Are often referred to as Private Stock.
—*Scott Field, IL, Pvt. Bob Stuart McKnight*

ARMY NURSES

Army nurses
Are unimpressed by curses.
—*Scott Field, IL, Pvt. Bob Stuart McKnight*

ADVICE TO YOUNG ROOKIES

Girls who are busty
Are apt to be lusty.

Mascaraed maidens with manners cute
Dwell in houses of ill repute.

Ladies with slant eyes
Aren't necessarily spies.

Ladies who the wrong way went
Sprinkle their bosom with hyascent.

When a girl says, "I love you like a brother,"
Find another.

The country girl
Is plenty virile.
Ladies who accost you on a well-lit street
Are indiscreet.
—*Scott Field, IL, Pvt. Bob Stuart McKnight*

RESOLUTION AT 3 A.M.

I would trade the biggest sloe-gin rickey
For a sloe-eyed look from Mariene Dietrichy.
—*Scott field, IL, Pvt. Bob Stuart McKnight*

LINES WRITTEN ON A LATRINE WALL

Some like guys with a sense of humor.
I like guys with a sense of rumor.
—*Scott field, IL, Pvt. Bob Stuart McKnight*

FIRST ARTICLE OF WAR

Don't trifle
With your rifle.
—*Scott Field IL, Pvt. Bob Stuart McKnight*

A LA CARTE

Wild-eyed unconservative rookies
Insist on tarts with their mama's cookies.
—*Scott Field, IL, Pvt. Bob Stuart McKnight*

ADVICE TO YOUNG LADIES

Sex is elemental,
So why be differential?
—*Scott Field, IL, Pvt. Bob Stuart McKnight*

SOLDIERS WITH A YEN FOR---

Soldiers with a yen for wenches
Usually are found on benches.

Soldiers with a yen for sin
Usually begin with gin.

Soldiers with a yen for vice
Find their week ends very nice.

Soldiers with a yen for trollops
Soon regret the usual follow-ups.
—*Scott Field, IL, Pfc. Bob Stuart McKnight*

MY GI HELMET

Like a soulful pregnant turtle
Is this helmet I am sporting,
So I think I'll call it Myrtle
And encourage her cavorting.
—*Scott Field, Ill, Pvt. Bob Stuart McKnight*

SUBJECT: FEMININE APPAREL

There's nothing that teases
Quite like black lace chemises.

Girls who long to be chased like mouses
Specialize in peek-a-boo blouses.

I've heard several salty rumors
Concerning lavender bloomers.

Can you blame a soldier if he should falter
When approached by a babe in a vict'ry halter?

A silky shirt with slinky slacks and nothing in between
Is quite as tantalizing as a Lana Turner dream.

Strapless gowns have their ups and downs,
And to a soldier, a girdle is just a minor hurdle.

It's all a matter of opinion:
As for me, you can have your chemises,
Your this and that;
I like a girl in a great big hat..
—*Maxton AAB, SC, Cpl. Bob Stuart McKnight*

A BROOKLYN SAGA

I'm Brooklyn's gift to the Army,
The cream of Flatbush row;
The gals there all adore me
No matter where I go.

I am muscled up like Atlas,
My biceps are delish;
And all the ladies tell me
I am their fav'rite dish.

Oh Brooklyn, Brooklyn, Brooklyn,
A Brooklyn bum am I;
I'll sing in praise of Brooklyn
Until the day I die.

I met a gal in England,
I asked her for a kiss;
She said, "Sir, I'm a lady,
But you I can't resist."

I met a gal in Iceland,
She was a maiden fair;
But when I turned the heat on
She said, "I just don't care."

Oh, Brooklyn, Brooklyn, Brooklyn,
That's where I want to be;
In bonnie, bonnie, Brooklyn,
My Brooklyn-by-the-sea.

I met a gal in Turkey,
Her father was a shiek;
He owned a Turkish harem,
I stayed there for a week.

Fatima dwelt in Egypt,
She had a lovely smile;
And, oh, the things that happened
While floating down the Nile.

Oh, Brooklyn, Brooklyn, Brooklyn,
A Brooklyn bum am I;
I'll sing the praise of Brooklyn
Until the day I die.
—*AAB, Maxton, SC, Cpl. Bob Stuart McKnight*

NOTE ON THE FOOD SITUATION

Dehydration
May be saving the nation,
But it's sure as hell killing me.

The K ration
Does not impassion
Me
(Nor does ration C),
And eggs when dehydrated
Are vastly overrated.

They say the soy
Contains oodles of gastronomic joy,
But to me it's still just one of the beans
(And you know what that means).

Yes sir, I am less than impressed
With this World-at-War and Army mess.
Give me back my ulcers and my three-inch steaks,

My super-acidity and chocolate layer cakes,
My shrimps a la Creole and lemon-cream pie.
Can you name a more beautiful way to die?

Frankly, things have come to such an unpretty pass that
I wouldn't be at all surprised to come up against some
delectable little dove
Who dishes out super-dehydrated love.

Dehydration
May be saving the nation,
But it's sure as hell killing me!
—*Maxton AAB, NC, Cpl. Bob Stuart McKnight*

MEMORANDUM

The world is full of gnats and chiggers
Who raise weird welts on our masculine figgers;
So may I suggest that we catch them in traps
And disperse them profusely on Nazis and Japs.
—*Maxton, AAB, NC, Cpl. Bob Stuart McKnight*

UNRELATED CONCLUSIONS

Any given part of Lana Turner
Is what is known as "cooking on the front burner."

A Flying Fort with a broken rudder
Is as useless as Elsie without her udder.
—*Maxton, AAB, SC, Cpl. Bob Stuart McKnight*

THE PROBLEM OF THE SOLDIER'S INTELLECT

Here we are fighting a war,
And what thanks do we get
When the Post Exchange insists on selling magazines that
insult a soldier's intellect?
For Example:
"Got an *Argosy*, babe?"
"Not a one, soldier, but how about------?"
"No I don't want a *Ladies Home Journal*
Or a *Woman's Home Companion* or *Vogue*.
I want a snappy story, One that's plenty gory,
With blood and thunder, and romance and gold.
I want a tale of Texas
That'll thrill my solar-plexus
With cattle rustlin' under the stars.
How about a gunman's gazette, chicken?
"Goodness, no! Now, why don't you try----?"
"No I don't want a *New Soldier's Handbook*
Or a *South Wall Street financial News*.
I want a dirty villain
A-shootin' and a-killin'
And a-fillin' up his belly with booze.
Say, hidin' right behind that
Better Babies is A *Superman*, I'll wager."
"Right you are, but no can sell.
That one's Reserved for the major."
—*APO 9396, Sgt. Bob Stuart McKnight*

A SAGA OF JUNE THE SIXTH

The C-47 was silent as a tomb
Except for the engines roarin' through the gloom,
Eighteen troopers not making a sound,
As flak lit the sky up for many miles around.
Then came the warning; then the D-Z bell;
And then I heard a trooper to his comrades yell:

"We're jumpin' into hell, boys; we're jumpin' into hell
"By the burst of the flak and the 'fifties' I can tell.
"Hang on to your chutes, boys; don't mind the battle-smell
"Till every bastard Jerry is on his way to hell!"

Oh, silent as the seagulls they floated down the sky,
Eighteen paratroopers, unafraid to die.
Some hit the flak bursts, some the 'fifties' leads
And some felt the ack-ack whistling past their heads.
Down on the Jerries, one by one they fell,
And then they heard a voice from out the darkness yell:

"We're landin' into hell, boys; we're landin' into hell!
"Kill the Huns by hundreds, like rats drowned in a well.
"Shout, "Geronimo!' boys. The stories we will tell
"When every bastard Jerry is at the gates of hell!"

When Normandy's sun rose, twelve of them were dead,
Hanging from the trees, their bellies full of lead.
Twelve brave troopers, slit from ear to ear,
With blood in their eyes but not a sign of fear.
Twelve men they buried in the flooded dell
When from a muddy grave they heard a trooper yell:

"We're waitin' here in hell, boys; We're waitin' here in hell.
"Don't despair of your fate, boys; the chow is goddam swell.
"Don't spare the knife, boys; don't spare the mortar shell
"Till every bastard Jerry is here with us in hell!"
—*Italy, S/Sgt. Bob Stuart McKnight*

A. L. Crouch

THE BLOODY MILD

Ho! you'd better 'ave the bitter
'Cause you'll 'ate the bloody mild,
'Tis fit for neither 'ealthy man
Nor constipated child.
But the bitter is a royal brew
On which King Henry smiled
So! you'd better 'ave the bitter
'Cause you'll 'ate the bloody mild!

My wife, she drinks the bitter
And her strength too well I've known;
She's dragged me 'cross the threshold
Like I weighed but 'alf a stone.
If she'd give up the bitter
For the mild, I tell you, chum,
I'd rule 'er like a 'usband should;
Right 'ere---beneath my thumb.

My daughter goes a-pubbin'
And she drinks the bitter straight
And 'as a beau each ev'ning,
Why, at least by 'alf-past eight.
She's not content with sippin'
Pints of mild or fancy wine.
My daughter is an eager lass
And not for wastin' time.

My great-great-great-aunt Katey,
Guv'ner, what a girl was she!
She took to drinkin' bitter
At the tender age of three,
But at the age of ninety
She took to mild and gin,
And, sure enough, at ninety-nine
The stuff had done 'er in.

Ho! you'd better 'ave the bitter
Cause you'll 'ate the bloody mild.
'Tis fit for neither 'ealthy man
Nor constipated child.
But the bitter is a royal brew
On which King Henry smiled.
So! you'd better 'ave the bitter
'Cause you'll 'ate the bloody mild!
  —France, S/Sgt. Bob Stuart McKnight

SIZES

One sadly realizes
That the supply-room sarge
Deals only in two sizes;
Too little and too large.
  —Camp Shelby, MS, S/Sgt. A. L. Crouch

TWO AMBITIONS

Two ambitions thrive in this
Army of millions
To come back alive and be civilians.
  —Camp Shelby, MS, S/Sgt. A. L. Crouch

CHOW HOUND

When every meal's a race
First in the line he stands,
With hunger in his face
And mess kit in his hands.
  —Camp Shelby, MS, S/Sgt. A.L. Crouch

CULINARY NOTES

Every slice of bread you see;
This policy sounds rash,
But it will keep your supper free
Of pudding and of hash.
  —Camp Shelby, MS, S/Sgt. A. L. Crouch

LIMERICK

There was once a GI in New Guinea
Whose cash never totaled a puinea;
For if some of the same
He would take to a game
He always came out without uinea.
  —Camp Shelby, MS, S/Sgt. A. L. Crouch

ALL ABOARD!

If you live in the East, they will send you West;
If you live in the North, they will send you South.
What the hell does it matter? The Army knows best.
So grab your luggage and shut your mouth.
  —*Camp Shelby, MS, S/Sgt. A. L. Crouch*

FIELD SOLDIER

In results that they say yield
We can make this comparison:
A bird in the field
Is worth two in the garrison.
  —*Camp Shelby, MS, S Sgt. A. L. Crouch*

PVT. BEN ADAMS

Pvt. Ben Adams (may his rank increase!)
Awoke one night from a deep dream of peace,
And saw within the moonlight in his tent---
Sullen and silent, as on mischief bent---
A sergeant writing in a little book.
Exceeding fear was in Ben Adams look,
When to the noncom in the tent he said,
"What's that you're writing?" The sarge raised his head
And, with a look made of all sweet accord,
Answered, "The names of those who go on guard."
"And is mine one?" gasped Adams. "Nay, not so,"
Replied the sergeant. Adams spoke more low,
But cheerily now, and said, "I beg you, then,
Go on away and let me sleep again."

The sergeant wrote and vanished.
The next night
He came again, with a great wakening light,
And showed the names of those with KP blessed;
And lo! Ben Adams' name led all the rest.
  —*Camp Shelby, MS, S/Sgt. A. L. Crouch*

THE PHANTOM SOLDIER

The government says he is missing
But the French all swear he is dead,
For several saw him go down
When Hememimat ridge ran red;
He fell in a bayonet charge
Where bullets were thick as hail---
They saw him go down with a curse and a frown
And the blood made his face look pale.
But dead men leave a body,
And his body was not there;
For after the battle was over
They looked for him everywhere;
So he was reported as missing
Though some of them swore he was dead
For they saw him go down with a curse and a frown
When Hememimat Ridge ran red.

Yet the Aussies al say he was with them
When they took a nameless hill,
And that it was two months later
(Could it be he was living still?)
He urged them on in battle
Till the enemy gave his ground
Then he died in the dust from a bayonet thrust—
But his body was never found.

Though many swept over the hilltop,
Many are lying there still.
And into the list of the missing
Went the names of those on the hill.
In the din and the dust of battle
He fell and they left him lie;
But the desert sand will understand—
There are men who refuse to die.

When the British out of Tarhuna
Took Tripoli by storm,
There was a stranger with them
In a British uniform;
He led the men into battle,
And several saw him fall;
But the light was too dim when they looked for him—
Or he wasn't there at all.

There are flames which burn in the spirit
Which nothing can ever quench,
Though the body be torn asunder
And left for dead in a trench,
For a soldier in his dying
Gives death itself a lie
When comrades inherit his flaming spirit---
There are men who refuse to die.
  —*Camp Shelby, MS, Sgt. A. L. Crouch*

TRIANGLE

Soldier, soldier. to whom do you write?
To my wife back home this pretty night.
You have new stationery, I see.
That girl in Portland bought it for me.
—*Camp Shelby, MS, S/Sgt. A. L. Crouch*

PAY-TROIT

He warbles patriotic platitudes
And waves his country's flag;
For when he strikes heroic attitudes
He fills the money bag.

At freedom's shrine his offering votive
(He won't miss it a lot)
Is prompted by the profit motive---
All hail the pay-troit!
—*Camp Shelby, MS, S/Sgt. A. L. Crouch*

WHAT PRICE GLORY?

The drug store cowboy, off to war,
Still flies at ceiling zero;
He walks into an Army store,
And swaggers out a hero.
—*Camp Shelby, MS, S/Sgt. A. L. Crouch*

SENTRY

I never knew a night could be so long,
Until I walked with a rifle on my shoulder
The hours when shadows deepen and grow colder;
The hours when darkness comes down swift and strong;
The hours when silence, like a leather thong,
Binds everything into a velvet folder,
While nothing moves, and only Time grows older---
Until a night bird stirs its throat with song.

I never knew a bight could be so lonely
Until I stayed awake for many men;
And, while hundreds were sleeping, challenged only
One who had been to town and back again.
Then, when I thought the night had come to stay,
The stars began to burn themselves away.
—*Aberdeen Proving Ground, MD O/C, A.L. Crouch*

SONNET

Shed no vain tears for us when we are gone,
Nor let the fangs of grief gnaw at your heart
Merely because we are a while apart
And may not come again.
Though we are drawn Into battlefields of war upon
A moments notice, let our leaving start
No sorrow train, nor yet impart
A trace of sadness which might linger on.
The soldiers business is death and flame,
And iron thunder rumbling through the night
While the Dark Angel writes the little names
In blood upon his book by the strange light
Of bursting shells. If you remember, only
Let it be with your prayers. Death is so lonely.
—*Aberdeen Proving Ground, MD, O/C A.L. Crouch*

VETERAN IN A CORNER BOOTH

"That shoulder loop?" he said, "A fourragere:
The First Division fought in Africa,
You know, and France (Free France) awarded us
Her highest battle honor. Now I'm home;
The fitful dream is over. Were we brave?
They called us brave and decorated us
For heroes, yet I say we left the brave
Behind in lonely places in the desert.

"Hill 609 was where the German strength
Gathered and coiled itself and then lashed out
Against us. They attacked with everything
They had; in thunderous haste, roaring with fire
And iron through our torn defensive lines,
While thirty-seven shells like rubber balls
Bounced off their armor plate. So we fell back
And back. Our gunfire scorched the earth for miles
Until at last we stopped them with our hands.

"Let's talk of something else. It hurts inside
For me to think of such things. For my part
I'm sick of war and I've come home to rest.
Don't ask me what the different ribbons mean.
Let me forget, for every campaign costs
A man the buddies who have shared their chow
And blankets with him. If these ribbons wore
Their battle stars, they'd have more than the flag
Itself; in every battle comrades fell.

"This is Tunisia; several mustered out
The hard way there, and I was almost with them.
An eighty-eight blast lifted me, a-whoomph!

And I was thrown for yards against a tree.
Two buddies grabbed me as I ran bat-blind
Straight for the front, for I was wild with pain
And shock. One of them said: 'It's Jim.
He's found Himself some *vino* and he's drunk again!'
Queer how I should remember what he said;
Later that day a Mark Four ran him down.

"The other's name was Kelly. That same night
Someone saw Kelly by the ghostly flare
Of bursting shells, asleep upon the sand,
Red with his own life's blood and strangely still;
And on his wrist a silver bracelet gleamed---
The one he had shown us, with his name
Above a heart, and underneath, these words---
'Lay off this guy; he's mine.' All that is just
One ribbon.

"Now I'm all tore up inside
And furloughed home, the curious crowd about
Poking their thoughts into the peace I prayed for
There on the battlefields. Leave me alone.
That's all I want, just to be left alone.
I'm sick of war and I've come home to rest."
  —*Aberdeen Proving Ground, MD O/C A. L. Crouch*

HOLIDAY THOUGHT

In the most distant places that you've ever read of,
On continent, island and isthmus,
Our soldiers are thinking of peace instead of
How many days until Christmas.
  —*Aberdeen Proving Ground, MD, O/C A. L. Crouch*

MECHANIC

If there's a truck that does not purr
And hit on every cylinder
He does. He works hard---now and then---
By rule of thumb (and he has ten).
  —*Aberdeen Proving Ground, MD, O/C A.L. Crouch*

WISHFUL THINKING

"The war's all over," some have said,
Vainly from hope commuting;
But they should get this through their head:
The war's all over but the shooting.
  —*OCS, Aberdeen Proving Ground, MD, O/C A.L.Crouch*

GI CASE HISTORIES

There was a GI from Tacoma
Who smelled a peculiar aroma;
He gasped, "It's old onions
Or somebody's bunions!"
And promptly dropped off in a coma.

There was a marine from N.Y.
Who ate with two knives and no F.
Till one night for a lark
He ate in the dark.
He now wears a hand made of C.
  —*Aberdeen Proving Ground, MD, O/C A.L. Crouch*

John Behm

HALF DREAMS

As a boy his half-dreams concerned themselves
with thoughts of the day he'd take over
the old man's bank and have enough dough to keep five
cigars in his breast pocket.

As a young man his half-dreams dwelled on Amy and
Louise.
Amy thought men stupid and died in sin,
so he married Louise.

As a businessman his half-dreams
crept around the day when the old man would die and he
and his family of five would move
into the big house on Latch Square.

He was beginning to grow plump and rosy and his eyes
were damp
when he was snatched away from the office and taught
the Articles of War.

But he was pale and lean when he lay in the mud with
blood on his face.

With gentle bewilderment
he sacrificed the half-dreams on the alter of
a place called Hill 19.

And in the big house on Latch Square sad Louise has
10 thousand dollars to build new
half-dreams.
    —*Camp Davis, NC, Pvt. John M. Behm*

FRANCE, 1944

Europe is a quiet land.
There is something dozing In the soil here
That all the noise and rattle of war
Will never awaken.

It is the sound sleep of the old philosopher
Resting in the shade,
The weary nod of the scholar
With the dusty book and the half-closed eye.

He has been everywhere,
Has seen it all,
And his taste for battle
Has long been satisfied.
Now he will not even turn his head
To watch these new warriors
Crawl through the hedge and
Die on his trampled breast.
He is not moved.

Listen to the earth call to us:
"Come back to your mother's womb
And rest awhile."

And the nervous poets look
At the tired dirt
While the jealous claw
That holds them fast to the great root
Of America
Slackens its grip,
As if the journey was over
And this at last
Was perhaps the spirit's final sanctuary.
    —*France, Pfc. John M. Behm*

THE SONGS OF ORPHEUS

I---Red Wine in a Cracked Glass

This is France.
This is the war.
This is three thousand miles away
From the dizzy Saturday nights,
From the grind of bells of Sunday morning,
From the coming into the dark house at dawn
When the air was gray,
From walking under the trees in the evening
From kissing you good night,
From the warm touch of lips In the summer.

Drinking sweet wine In a café.
The ruined city. The night.
A world of enemies and strangers.

This is the battle. This is the siege.
This is the weary warrior, Drunk with tears,
Watching the bright-lipped maidens
Dance and sing under the yellow light.

And the fat civilian with the beard like wire,
Wearing a tam and smoking a Lucky,
Sits in the corner, crooning a song in
Spanish And drinking,

Drinking, Drinking,
Red wine from a cracked glass.
—*France, Pfc. John M. Behm*

THE SONGS OF ORPHEUS

II---Purple Hyacinths in a Steel Helmet
This is France.
This is the war.
This is three thousand miles away
Form taxicabs slamming
Their brakes against the curb,
From the waves of heat quivering
Out of the pavements in August,
From drinking coffee in the all-night joint
Across from the station,
From buying bright neckties at the
Astor shirt shop
And guzzling cheap Scotch
In the dives down in the Village,
From the rain falling on the statues in the park
From the wind panting in the dark trees
At night.

Her name was Antoinette
After France's gayest, saddest queen..
Trembling, smiling
Antoinette;
Afraid, yet laughing,
Knowing not whether to trust or flee,
Only certain of mirth.

We stood on the hill
Watching the twilight
Fall like a closing eyelid
Over the valley,
Our faces cool now
After the scalding exit of the sun,
My helmet filled with the hyacinths we'd picked
And the night's breezes
Moving locks of dark hair
Over her cheek.

Like a tiny child at eh throne
Of an empress
I handed her a flower
And smiled into her dark eyes.

She is no longer gay.
She is no longer afraid.
—*France, Pfc. John M. Behm*

THE SONGS OF ORPHEUS

III---The Dropping of the Flares
This is France.
This is the war.
This is the three thousand miles away
From the long, bright and tree-protected streets
Flowing like laughing rivers
All over the city,
From the shadows moving in the mist
Over the shining, bellied bridge,
From the swan song of the ships
Pulling out of the harbor,
From the faraway voices of the children across the street.
Playing their games all day,
From the choirs chanting on the front porch
Of every good-looking girl in the neighborhood.
From all the sentimental songs they sang to each other,
Tone poems in the twilight:
"………*the stardust of a dream*…….."
"………*day and night, night and day*………"
From never saying good-by
And always knowing that the sun
Would surely shine in the morning.

Down at the airstrip,
Far in the green woods,
I watched the Havocs
Return one evening
From another run over the East.
Flak-heavy, they limped out of the grimy sky,
Dropping flares into the emerald branches of the trees,
And rolled, each one with a groan,
Against the soft earth.

The flares fell slowly,
Dazzling the broken, stormy heavens,
Making the thunder shine,
Lifting a sudden curtain
On a gaudy drama of wind and cloud---
O, a weird enchantment of night and day
Wherein the huge, smashed planes
Became striped fishes sinking
In a deep pool
And the little candles burning the sky
Chattered like a Greek chorus: "Lo, lo, lo!
We have the dead men on board."

And so there were
Five twisted bodies, cold and hard,
Five blank faces looking up at the cigarette lighters;
Ten stony eyes, unblinking under the torches.
Ten locked fists
(One holding a candy bar).

A quintet of stiff Americans
Lying side by side
On the lap of Mars.

And somewhere over here
At this very moment
There is a flare in the sky.

"Lo, we have dead men on board."
—*France, Cpl. John N. Behm*

THE SONGS OF ORPHEUS

IV---The Still City in the Moonlight
This is France.
This is the war.
This is the three thousand miles away
From the classic days of childhood,
From the dusty spring afternoons
Playing ball in the back lot,
From the whistling ball bouncing away
From the shinning bat and skipping toward third
Out of the pitchers reach,
From the long, futile slide into first
And the spiked defeat trying to make second,
From catching the high flies
And knocking one over the fence
On the last swing.

From going to the opera with the girl
Whose father played the second violin in the orchestra,
And the cold, sweet winter night in our faces,
Walking home after the last act:
From the ballets and the concerts,
The juke boxes and the jam sessions,
Carnegie Hall and the Paramount,
From the plays and films:
From youth's profoundly long-winded denunciations
Of this and that,
And the breathless child's worship
Of this and that;

From reading Thomas Wolfe until four in the morning:
From the teachers, the debates, the books,
The notes, the questions, the answers,
The questions that had no answers
And the answers that came before the questions,
From all the swift little question marks
Bouncing like blunt darts off the classroom walls
To lie unpolished on the floor
In the dust.

When the cloud passes,
The moon appears
And the ink of night
Runs off into the long shadows
Creeping down the alleys
Making the windows gleam,
So that the little squares
Are dotted with shifting eyes
And the park becomes a motionless drapery
Over the windows of the world.

But it is the silence
We'll never forget:
The silence that jerks the finger to the trigger
Keeping it there,
Trembling and wet,
The silence that comes after the bell in the smashed tower
Moans ten times
And says no more,
The silence of the vacuum burial of sound,
The epitaph of sweet noise,
When you know it will not ring again for an hour,
The silence that counts the ticking of your jumping heart.

Gently, foreigner,
Softly, O warrior from cities
That are never dark or still.
(Remember when you roamed the thoroughfares of home?
Remember the crescendo of the subway
And the blaze of midnight lights? The ecstasy of traffic?
Ah, Broadway in the rain!)

This is strange, is it not. O twitching hunter,
This crawling in the gutters,
Your little weapon tight
Against your pounding chest,
Your eight glittering bullets posed
As phantom sentinels
There in the empty night
Where the building lays its roof
Against the sky?

Make your prayer to the nothingness of sky.
Sing your hymn to the white darkness.
Oh Gods, squatting in the silent moonlight,
When it comes---
The whistle and the puff
That will shift the course of my blood
And lay me out in the puddles---
Let me see just long enough
To answer back: For I am a man
And cannot die, Not yet.
—*France, Cpl. John M. Behm*

THE SONGS OF ORPHEUS V

V---The Brother Who Fought In Spain

This is France.
This is the war,
This is the tree thousand miles away
From the ancient piano playing down in the parlor
And the naked bulb burning against
The flowered wallpaper upstairs;
From the sad Negro in the lobby
Of the little hotel on D Street,
Reading a detective magazine;
From the gunfire late at night
And the corpses in the gutter the next day,
The crowd watching;
From the rasp-voiced drunks sitting at the corner table
Waiting for someone to start a fight;
From the beer spilling on the bar
Staining the sleeve of your coat;
From the two big truck drivers going outside "To settle it";
From the painted women with twitching lips
And the dead-panned small-timers
With ice picks in their pockets;
From all the brawling, harsh and rich-blooded chaos
That is the sizzling-breathed, deep throated smoke-filled
Back room of America.

He was one of the first to see
The snub-winged Heinkel-112
Come racing over the mountains
To spray a shower of all-seeing lead
Over the little company of infantrymen
Lying in the ditches outside the town
They were to take.
This was Spain in the thirties,
When Berlin sent to Franco
A few new war toys to play with.

(I will never forget this
Saint-eyed warrior's tales.)

They kept him locked up In the cellar of a brothel
Somewhere near the border of Portugal,
Chained to a wall for almost a year,
Dieting on wads of wet bread that so swarmed with little crawling things
That his stomach became a heaving mush
And now he digits only tea and wine.
"*Garcon, une* bottle more, *s'il vous plait!*"

They dropped him one night
Into the hold of a freighter bound for Cyprus
And wished him *bon voyage,*
But he was there in Vienna
Fighting them again,
And he was one of the many
Who stood weeping under the loudspeakers
The night Kurt von Schuschnigg told the world
That Austria had died.

And he was in Paris Still trying to fight
When Hitler strolled under Napoleon's arch
And smiled.
When I asked him how he felt now
(This saint-eyed scholar of war),
Moving east again with the Americans,
He would not speak
He sniffed his bitter wine
And, I suppose, thought of
Those little planes gliding over the Pyrenees,
Dropping fire on his ragged army
Fighting in the shadows.
    —*France Cpl. John M.Behm*

A STRANGER AND ALONE

We are the insolent invaders with many unknowns.
We have come to England from far away
Bringing gifts of chewing gum and Chesterfields.

We are the harsh strangers---vain, hearty foreigners,
The aliens thoughtlessly trampling your calm vineyards.

The slim colored boys send our heavy trucks
Screaming along your narrow roads.
The big tanks rip up the pavings
Of your ancient towns.
The jeeps and weapons carriers
Do fifty-five around your z-shaped curves.
The half-tracks hold your traffic up for hours.

The countryside rings
With the blare and whirl of our machines.

We are loud and fast and wild and lusty.
We are drunken, proud, hard and potent.
We could drink your island dry if you would let us.
We are the terrible, mischievous warriors
From far away.

We are, I'm afraid,
Just a trifle bestial
For your highly tempered tastes.

But England,
Understand us:
Though we sneer and boast in the pubs,
Consume your beer and belittling your glory,
We tremble and are afraid in the streets
Before the blind audience of closed doors.
We are young men whose roots
Have been left far behind
In strange places called Brooklyn and Sacramento
       and Tucson and Thief River Falls and
          and Council Bluffs and Cincinnati and Coon Hol-
low.
We have been torn from the soil where we grew
And flung like exiles across an ocean
To a land we never dreamed of.

We are bewildered and weary,
Lonely to the point of madness.
And if we shout and curse
Through our quiet dreams,
Forgive us.

We are merely looking for a way to go home.
    —*Britain, Pfc. John Behm*

Section Ten
Featured Poem

LOVE WHISPERS TO THE WARRIORS

Love whispers to the warriors
Crowding the foreign shores.
Her tongue is hopeful promises
Of dreams to be restored.

And as low she stoops to whisper
Into their confused ear,
She marks them with the cross of death
And wipes away a tear.
—*Fletcher General Hospital, Ohio, Sgt. Josephine Pagliai*

Section Eleven
Reflections

Between the years 1942 and 1945, Yank magazine published several hundred poems written by soldiers serving in the United States military at locations around the world. The poets wrote poems about home, loved ones, and the war. They wrote serious, satirical, double entendre, and humorous poems.

In this anthology of those poems, Songs of the Warriors, several intriguing, important, and relevant social, historical, and existential themes emerged in the poems. On the other hand, a slight amount of caution should be exercised when reading these reflections

First, other readers might detect other themes in the anthology not detected or overlooked by the editor. Any bias, omission, or non-objectivity is the responsibility of the editor. Second, the censors may have played a role in the overall presentation of the poems which may have affected the detected and selected themes. Specifically, it is not known what the content of poems was that were rejected by the sensors. Furthermore, it is not known how many poems were rejected. So, a true sample representing the creative works of the poets remains unknown and unavailable. It is evident that the poets were aware of the power and control of the censors. It can only be imagined what the content of the poems would have been without censorship: caveat lector.

Third, an assumption has been made in presenting this anthology that there were not any hidden agendas or messages deliberately imbedded in the poems by the poets. They were ostensibly written for the enjoyment of the readers, but it is well known that soldiers used hidden codes in their letters home, so they could have done the same with the poems.

Finally, in the absence of any evidence in the poems, it can't be assumed that the editors of the magazine did or did not have an overall theme or agenda for the magazine. Other than the policies stated in the editorial section of each magazine, no detectable agendas or themes were discovered in the preparation of this anthology. The poems also did not seem to follow any specific order or sequence. It appears that the poems were published in a spontaneous and serendipitous fashion as they arrived in the mail and after censors intervened and screened the submissions.

With these thoughts in mind, the themes are identified, reflected, and presented for your consideration. The following discussion progresses in a quasi-chronological order.

Documentation

Early in 1942, security concerns were evident in the poems because there didn't appear to be any evidence of a clear and consistent format associated with the poems for identifying who wrote the poem and where the soldier-author was stationed. Either the magazine editors were overly cautious about revealing too much information that would be detrimental to the war effort, or the soldiers who wrote the poems were reluctant about revealing too much information about themselves. In any case, some of the documentation was vague, nonspecific, or missing. Some authors were identified as "anonymous" or "marine," from "overseas."

Transition

It was also evident early in 1942 that the magazine didn't receive enough poems to publish a designated section of poems. Or, many early poems were rejected until the poets who read the magazine saw what was being accepted for publication and made their submissions accordingly. Furthermore, early poems could have been rejected because the content of the poems was inappropriate or revealed too much sensitive military information. Whatever the case, poems appeared that had been previously published in local camp or air base publications. These previously published works provided a start-up and transition to a designated section of poems.

Orientation

Early dated poems reflected the shock, discomfort, and dissatisfaction of soldiers orienting, adjusting, and adapting to military life. Several poems appeared that expressed how uncomfortable the soldiers were with group sleeping arrangements, lack of privacy in bathrooms, KP (kitchen police) duty, and latrine duty. Other poems revealed the revulsions to army food like "Spam" and "Bully Beef." Overall, the poems reflected the timeless stress and strain of

leaving civilian life and adjusting to the regimentation of military life. The poems contained the same concerns that soldiers have experienced since ordinary citizens first became citizen soldiers.

Chain of Command

Early poems also revealed the major adjustment that soldiers faced with what they perceived as the arbitrary, unjustified, and illogical assignment of rank to superior officers. They also expressed dislike about receiving orders from commissioned and noncommissioned officers, especially sergeants and lieutenants. The poems reflected, not so subtly, that soldiers stewed and chafed under the burden, omnipotence, and constraint of the authoritarian chain of command.

Cross communication

By 1943, it became apparent that the magazine was receiving an adequate number of submissions to produce a specified and consistent section of poems. Poets were reading and responding to the poems written by other poets around the world. This cross communication was, no doubt, facilitated by the massive effort and complicated logistics of distributing the magazine around the world. The response by the soldiers, the quality of the poems, and the proliferation of poems testify to the success of this effort.

International

It also became apparent by 1943 that the poems were being submitted from bases in countries around the world. The duty assignments of the poets revealed how widely dispersed the soldiers were on bases in far-flung, isolated, non-combative and unfamiliar geographical places. Poems were published by poets stationed in the European war zone, including France, England, Italy, Germany, and North Africa. In addition, poems appeared in the magazine submitted by soldiers stationed in the Caribbean, including Trinidad, British Guiana, and Puerto Rico.

Many poems were written and published by war poets stationed in the Pacific war zone, including Hawaii, Marianas, Philippines, The Aleutians, Leyte, Saipan, Luzon, Guadalcanal, Iwo Jima, Okinawa, China, New Guinea, New Hebrides, New Caledonia, and Alaska. Finally, poems were written and published by soldiers stationed in Greenland, Iceland, Canada, Iran, and Australia.

These diverse locations truly revealed in the "Songs of the Warriors" not only an international flavor, but also a vast, complex, and encompassing war effort.

Women

The valuable contribution of women in both military services and industry during World War II, has been well documented. Nevertheless, it is worth noting that at least three of the twelve featured poets in this anthology are women. It is obvious women were a valuable part of the war effort, and it is equally obvious they were accomplished poets who wanted their creative works to be included as part of the poetry of the war poets. They not only succeeded, but also flourished.

Mortification

A striking and macabre transition in content appeared by 1944 when poems about war and death emerged in the submissions. Some of the poems were written by soldiers who observed pictures of dead enemy and American soldiers on pages of the magazine. Most of the poems reflected the reality of seeing dead American and enemy soldiers on the battlefield. Two of the most widely recognized, read, and reproduced poems by Don E. Rohrig, "The Ghost of Gona" and "Sunday at Sanananda," are intense, vivid, and visceral examples of the theme of mortification. His and other poems poignantly reflected and revealed the true agony, pain, horror, and mortification of the reality of death, inhumanity, nonexistence, carnage, randomness, and wanton destruction in the active, violent, and deadly war zones.

Contribution

By 1944, poems began to appear that revealed the realization by the poets that many soldiers were serving in non-combat roles. They were in assignments as clerks, personnel officers, weather observers, typists, and other stations that took them far from the combat zones. Their poems reflected deep personal questions and ambivalence about their individual contributions to the war effort and justifications for the wide differences between the sacrifices of front line and support troops.

An even deeper personal conflict reflected in the poems was the juxtaposition of two realities for many poets. They knew they were soldiers trained to fight, but they eventually realized they would never fire a shot at the enemy and probably sit out the war in a relatively safe but isolated outpost with few opportunities to achieve awards or commendations for bravery or personal sacrifice.

Alienation

Another trend that was reflected in the content of the war poems were the experiences of soldiers who were suddenly exposed to, awestruck by, and immersed in the different, opaque, and alien customs of cultures around the world. In 1942, very few soldiers had previously had the opportunity to travel around the world. The poems reflected their thoughts and feelings about living in other cultures, many in very primitive and unfamiliar conditions. They expressed alienation about living in countries with unfamiliar customs, religions, and social mores. For example, the poem, "Orders of the Day," by Y. Guy Owen, mentions that American soldiers must not speak to Moslem women. Furthermore, a poem by Jacob Richardson, "Bully Beef," mentions "…..frenchmen eating slimy snails and frogs," and "dusky natives frying crickets, roasting dogs." Finally, Edwin H. Roper wrote a poem, " 'Twas the Night before Mers-El-Salaam," which further expressed the alienation of soldiers.

Racism

Consistent with the zeitgeist and time period in which the poems were written, some subtle and not so subtle racist themes emerged in a few of the poems. For example, two poems, "Vice Versa," and "White Lies," express concern about American soldiers dating non-white ladies. The poems mentioned "yellow and brown" girls and that "every soldier from the states is growing color blind."

On the other hand, a poem, "Dim Out," was published from the Tuskegee Army Flying School, a famous black pilot training center. In addition, "The Fighting 24th," poem was published that referred to a regiment of famous black soldiers. Perhaps the most poignant poem concerning the theme of racial equality appeared that was written by a Marine, Pfc. Lewis Arthur, "Fellow Countrymen." The last nine lines of the poem are worth noting:

> A savage wrack-brain of my company
> Insinuates against the Negro's manhood.
> I quietly explain his error-----
> Or spit in his eye.
> Negros are not ashamed
> Naming me as one of their own.
> I am proud.
> I am whatever you are,
> You no less than I.

In the 1940's, the assertions in this poem would have been sensitive, if not very controversial. The military was segregated as was most of the southern United States. Furthermore, the dark horrific legacy of widespread lynchings of black citizens was fresh in the minds of Americans. The civil rights movement was twenty years in the future. It appears the magazine published both racist and anti-racist poems.

Origination

The geographical locations of where the soldiers who wrote the poems changed between 1942 and 1945.

Understandably, early in the publication of the magazine most of the poems originated from soldiers stationed in training camps in the continental United States. Later, poems began to be published that originated from soldiers stationed on distant bases after they had been transferred, transported, and relocated to duty stations around the world.

An interesting but unexplained reflection emerged that indicated that many poems originated from soldiers in the Pacific war theatre, but few from the European war theatre. One possible explanation for this imbalance was that after the invasion of Europe, the soldiers were moving so quickly across Europe that they were not in a position to submit poems, read the magazine, or be near a base where the magazine could be dropped and distributed. On the other hand, there were many air bases in the South Pacific, but few air bases on the continent of Europe where bundles of the magazine could be delivered or dropped from the air. Amazingly, the bundles of the prompt and irrepressible military periodicals were dropped on the French coast of Normandy shortly after the invasion. They, no doubt, originated from air bases in England. The magazine was distributed to bases in England, widely read, and yielded some poems that were submitted by soldiers stationed on bases in England.

Progression

One of the fascinating revelations to emerge from the poems was the documentation of progression in the rank and duty stations of a few of the featured poets. The most poignant, expressive, and creative example of this progression appeared in the poems written by Bob Stuart McKnight. Starting in 1942, he published two poems while he was stationed at Keesler Field, Mississippi with the rank of private. He then published nine poems from Scott Field, Illinois as a private. Next, he published two poems while he was stationed at Scott Field as a private first class.

He then published five poems while he was stationed at Maxon Army Air Base in South Carolina as a corporal. Next, he published a single poem from an APO (Army Post Office) as a sergeant. He then published a poem while he was stationed in Italy as a staff sergeant. Finally, he published his twenty first poem while he was stationed in France as a staff sergeant in 1945.

Not only does his record of publishing indicate what a prolific, talented, and empathic poet he was, publishing a poem every other month, but it also leaves a remarkable record of his military career. Was he writing and publishing poems as a clever way to let his family at home know he was alive and where he was stationed? Or, did he just love to write poetry? These questions may never be answered, but the result was an incredible literary documentation of his progression in rank and his duty stations during the war.

As could be expected in the poetry and songs of warriors, several political, social, and existential themes emerged in the anthology. These themes provide a rare historical look into the hearts and souls of soldiers at war. The passion, empathy, and creativity expressed in their songs has left us, both individually and aggregatively, with a national historical and literary treasure.